The Air Pilot's **Manual**

Volume 7

Contents

Editorial Team

Trevor Thom
A Boeing 757 and 767 Training Captain, Trevor has also flown the Airbus A320, Boeing 727, McDonnell Douglas DC-9 and Fokker F-27. He has been active in the International Federation of Airline Pilots' Associations (IFALPA), based in London, and was a member of the IFALPA Aeroplane Design and Operations Group. He also served as IFALPA representative to the Society of Automotive Engineers (SAE) S7 Flight-Deck Design Committee, a body which makes recommendations to the aviation industry, especially the manufacturers. Prior to his airline career Trevor was a Lecturer in Mathematics and Physics, and an Aviation Ground Instructor and Flying Instructor. He is a double degree graduate from the University of Melbourne and also holds a Diploma of Education.

Peter Godwin
Head of Training at Bonus Aviation, Cranfield (formerly Leavesden Flight Centre), Peter has amassed over 14,000 instructional flying hours as a fixed-wing and helicopter instructor. He has edited this series since 1995 and recently updated it to cover the JAR-FCL. As a member of the CAA Panel of Examiners, he is a CAA Authorised Examiner (AE), Instrument Rating and Class Rating Examiner, Fellow of the Royal Institute of Navigation (FRIN), and is currently training flying instructors and applicants for the Commercial Pilot's Licence and Instrument Rating. Previously he was Chief Pilot for an air charter company and Chief Instructor for the Cabair group of companies based at Denham and Elstree. Peter has been Vice Chairman and subsequently Chairman of the Flight Training Committee on behalf of the General Aviation Manufacturers' and Traders' Association (GAMTA) since 1992.

Graeme Carne
Graeme is a BAe 146 Captain with a dynamic and growing UK regional airline. He has been a Training Captain on the Shorts 360 and flew a King Air for a private company. He learned to fly in Australia and has an extensive background as a flying instructor in the UK. He has also been involved in the introduction of JAR OPS procedures to his airline.

Warren Yeates
Warren has been involved with editing, indexing, desktop publishing and printing Trevor Thom manuals since 1988 for UK, US and Australian markets. He currently runs a publishing services company in Ireland.

Acknowledgements
The Civil Aviation Authority; Ian Suren, Robert Johnson; Philip Ashworth, Stuart Bullock, Stuart Cheyne, Glyn Connick, Monica Farmer, Dave Montgomery, Captain R.W.K. Snell (CAA Flight Examiner [ret.]), Martin Sutton.

Introduction

Radio is your link to the rest of the world.

Using the radio professionally has become an essential requirement in the modern aviation environment. Radio provides the interface between you and others, especially the Air Traffic Service Unit (ATSU) whose frequency you are using. Normally you will communicate with the ATSU only, and not directly with other aircraft on that frequency. They will, however, be listening in and so will be aware of your movements.

Flight radio is easy to use

Press the transmit button, and speak clearly.

You will make life more comfortable for yourself (and others) if you can use the radio efficiently. You need to know:
- **how to use** the radio equipment; and
- **what to say.**

Our manual will help you to achieve this in an easy-to-follow manner. If you are a beginner, the first chapter will introduce you to cockpit radio equipment. For safety and efficiency, an aeronautical language has been developed with its own jargon. Many messages are best passed using this standard phraseology (such as "Cleared for take-off" and "Cleared to land"). The **Learning the Language** section will help you to do just that as your training progresses. There are several tables included which will provide a valuable reference for you in the future. Chapters 1 to 4 contain enough information for you to feel comfortable using the radio at your home aerodrome, and for flights to your training area.

Flying Further discusses procedures in the various classes of airspace you might fly in as you proceed cross-country. **When Things Go Wrong** considers the best means of communicating in emergency situations, and also what to do if your radio fails, thereby making voice communication no longer possible.

Putting it all Together takes you through some typical flights, and **How Radio Works** explains it all for those who do not like to use anything without knowing how it works.

The real test occurs in your day-to-day flying.

The *real* test. You should aim to pass the required test for your **Flight Radiotelephony Operator's Licence (FRTOL)** before completing your Private Pilot Licence training. But the *real* test occurs every day that you go flying in the future. Our aim is to help you pass the test, and then to be professional in the use of flight radio throughout the rest of your flying career.

Your use of the radio will improve with experience

If you are a student pilot, then you are probably a little wary of the radio. It is not very different to using a telephone, except that only one person can speak at a time – simultaneous transmission and reception is not possible.

Only one person can transmit at a time.

Most students have trouble understanding radio messages at first, but as you are exposed to it and build up your vocabulary of standard words and phrases, and as you get to know what messages to expect, your proficiency and confidence will grow.

Using the radio gets easier.

Ace radio operators are not born that way – they train themselves!

The people who staff the Air Traffic Service Units are highly trained and use the radio as part of their day-to-day lives. They are very professional. As a student pilot you are not expected to be an ace radio operator right at the start. You are a student battling to fly the aeroplane as well as trying to use the radio! The professional ATSU personnel will assist you in a friendly manner to improve your radio work.

Practice makes perfect.

Time spent listening to others is invaluable. Going flying with experienced pilots, making visits to control towers, radar rooms, flight service units and air/ground radio stations (all of which you are encouraged to do) is time well spent.

Learn from others.

Radio and Air Law

Because radio is the interface between you and the rest of the world, there is some commonality between this radio book and our book on air law. The aspects of air law relevant to using the radio are discussed here, and expanded on in Vol. 2 of *The Air Pilot's Manual*. A good understanding of the rules and regulations, as well as normal operating procedures, will help you to use the radio efficiently. You will display this by professional and confident radio work.

Follow the rules.

Your responsibilities

As an operator of flight radio, you are joining a select group of people. Various responsibilities go along with the privileges. You may only use flight radio for aeronautical use; you must use appropriate language; and you must not interfere in the transmission of messages from others, especially during emergencies.

Be responsible.

Using this book

While the material in this book was up-to-date at the time of printing, changes to radio and air traffic procedures occur from time-to-time. In addition to this book, you must refer to the UK Aeronautical Information Publication (AIP), aeronautical charts, Aeronautical Information Circulars (AICs), and the CAA's Radiotelephony Manual (CAP 413). Major changes to RT phraseology will be announced in AICs. Your instructor can introduce you to these publications.

The radio call examples in this book use the following conventions. Calls made by the pilot are enclosed in a grey box, with an aeroplane symbol at the beginning of the message. For calls made by an air traffic service unit, a symbol at the beginning of the message indicates the type of air traffic service unit making the call.

Pilot

Control Tower

Approach or Radar

Air/Ground radio station

Flight Information Service

Phonetic pronunciation

To help you learn phonetic pronunciation of words and numbers, we have written aircraft callsigns and numbers in the first few chapters as they should be pronounced, rather than as they are normally spelt. From the *Flying Further* section onward we use the normal spelling, as you should have got the hang of phonetic pronunciation by that stage.

Learning the Language
Cockpit Radios

Modern aircraft have several radios:
- ☐ **VHF-COM** for high-quality voice communication.
- ☐ **Navigation radios** (VHF-NAV forVOR and ILS/DME/ADF).
- ☐ **A transponder** for radar identification.

VHF-COM

VHF-COM provides high-quality voice communication.

Most aeroplanes are equipped with at least one high-quality radio for voice communications which operates in the *very high frequency* (VHF) radio band. Such a set is known as a VHF-COM (pronounced *vee aitch eff comm*) and is both a transmitter and a receiver. Most modern VHF-COMs have 720 channels, i.e. you can select it to one of 720 frequencies. At most aerodromes you will use only one or two frequencies. These are published in the Aeronautical Information Publication (AIP), mainly in the Aerodromes section (AIP AD), however, you will use them so often that they will quickly be committed to memory.

The VHF-COM set shown below is combined with a VHF-NAV (pronounced *vee aitch eff nav),* which is a second radio set used to receive signals from ground-based radio navigation aids. The VHF-NAV receives signals in a different frequency range to the VHF-COM and cannot be used to transmit messages.

■ *Figure 1-1* **A typical VHF-COM radio set (on left) tuned to frequency 124·95 megahertz, combined into one unit with a VHF-NAV receiver tuned to 114·10 MHz**

VHF-COM is easy to use.

The VHF-COM is easy to use. You only need to switch the set on, check that the correct frequency is selected, ensure that the microphone and/or headset is firmly plugged in, and turn the *receive-volume* up sufficiently.

Radio Set-Up in the Cockpit

In most training aircraft, the radio set-up consists of:

☐ **a microphone** for transmitting (hand-held or boom);

☐ **speaker and/or headset** (with attached boom-mike) for listening to the reception;

☐ **the electrical master switch,** possibly an avionics master switch (for *all* the radios), and *individual* ON/OFF switches for each radio, to connect the electrical power supply to the radios; and

☐ **an audio selector panel** to select where your voice goes, and what you can listen to.

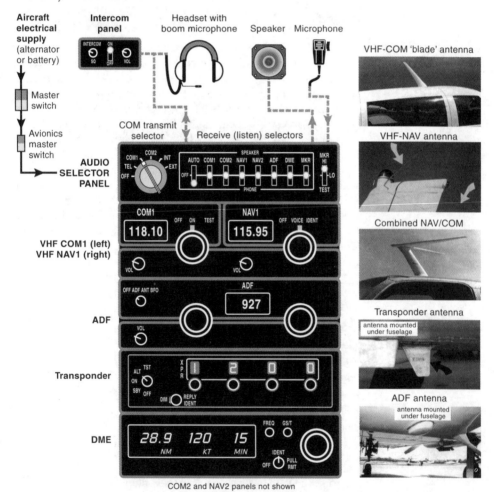

COM2 and NAV2 panels not shown

■ *Figure 1-2* **Typical cockpit radio set-up with corresponding antennas**

The Audio Selector Panel

The audio selector panel is like a simple telephone switchboard. It allows you to select just one direction for your voice to go (to *transmit* on VHF-COM-1 is usual), and one or more items of radio equipment to which you can *listen*.

There is one main switch, normally a rotary switch, which is used to select where the microphone audio signal generated by your voice is sent. It could, for instance, be sent to:

☐ **VHF-COM-1** for transmission;

☐ **VHF-COM-2** for transmission;

☐ **the intercom** that is connected to the earphones of the other pilot or person wearing a headset; or

☐ **the cabin speakers** for an address to the passengers (PA means *passenger address*).

*The transmit selector usually selects one radio to **both** transmit and receive.*

Often there is an *auto* switch that ensures that this selection of where your voice goes also selects *receive* automatically, so that if for instance you are transmitting on VHF-COM-1 you will automatically be *listening* on VHF-COM-1 as well (provided the volume is high enough).

*If desired, you can also select further radios to **listen-only**.*

As well as the *transmit* selector, there are *receive* selectors on the audio selector panel that enable you to *listen* to incoming signals from other radios either on the cockpit speaker or on the headphones. A typical situation could be to transmit and receive normal voice messages on VHF-COM-1, and to listen out on VHF-COM-2 when desired (for instance, to receive weather information such as the recorded ATIS or VOLMET aerodrome information, or to listen out on the emergency frequency 121·5 MHz). Early in your training, however, you will be busy enough listening out on just the one radio frequency that you are also using for transmitting messages.

The Intercom

The intercom improves internal communications.

The intercom itself does not involve the transmission of any radio signals. It merely enables better internal communications (intercom) within the cockpit between those wearing headsets (usually fitted with a boom-microphone). The headsets reduce unwanted noise from the engine, etc., and allows you to hear the voice messages more clearly.

Master Switches

Electrical power is supplied by either alternator or battery.

When the aeroplane's engine is running, and driving the alternator (as well as the propeller), the electrical power to the radios is supplied by the **alternator**. The alternator also recharges the battery, whose electrical energy will have been depleted by powering the engine starter motor during engine start.

When the alternator is not supplying power, for instance when the engine is stopped, then the **battery** will supply electrical power to the radios and any other electrical services that are switched on. Do not leave the radios or other electrical services (such as the landing lights) switched on for long periods when the engine is not running, since this will flatten the battery.

The electrical power reaches the radios via:
- ☐ the **electrical master switch;**
- ☐ the **avionics master switch;** and
- ☐ **individual radio** ON/OFF **switches.**

> *Avionics means*
> *aviation electronics.*

To avoid electrical shocks to sensitive radio equipment when starting the engine, which draws high electrical current from the battery and then allows the alternator to come on line, you should switch the radios off before engine start and engine shutdown. You can do this with the avionics master switch or the individual radio ON/OFF switches. Using just the avionics master switch has two benefits:

> *Switch the radios off for*
> *engine start-up and*
> *shutdown.*

- ☐ **all radios** are switched on or off with just one movement; and
- ☐ **volume and squelch settings** for individual radios are not changed.

The whole electrical system and each individual part of it, such as a radio, is protected from abnormally high current flow by fuses and/or circuit breakers (CBs). A blown fuse should only be replaced once and a popped circuit breaker reset once. If the fuse blows or the CB pops a second time, there is a genuine electrical problem.

> *Fuses and CBs protect*
> *electrical equipment.*

Individual Radio ON/OFF Switch and Volume Control

Each VHF-COM radio has an ON/OFF switch. This may be combined with the VOL control. Once the radio is switched on, the volume can be adjusted by rotation of the VOL control – clockwise to increase volume, anticlockwise to reduce volume. This adjusts the volume of what you receive; it does not affect the volume of your transmissions.

■ *Figure 1-3* **Separate ON/OFF switch and VOL control
(left), and a combined ON/OFF and VOL control (right)**

A suitable volume setting can be found by listening to other radio traffic, and adjusting the volume control to a comfortable level where you can clearly hear the messages. During the course of a flight you may have to re-adjust the volume. If there is no activity

> *Use the VOL control to*
> *adjust the volume of*
> *reception.*

on the radio for a period of time that makes you wonder if it is still working or not, say 5 or 10 minutes, you could "request a radio check" from a ground station to test your reception.

The Squelch Control

On the panel of many communications radios is a control labelled *squelch*. The function of squelch is to adjust the sensitivity of the receiver by eliminating unwanted weak signals that cause background noise (static, hash or hiss). This noise makes it difficult to hear the desired stronger signals. Some squelch controls are automatic and others are manual. Your flying instructor will advise you on your particular set.

Eliminate unwanted noise with squelch control.

TO ADJUST THE MANUAL SQUELCH CONTROL:

☐ **Turn the squelch up high** (clockwise), then turn the volume up until strong background noise is heard; then:

☐ **Rotate the squelch knob anticlockwise** until noise just disappears (or is at least at an acceptably low level). This means that *unwanted* noise from weak signals is electronically suppressed, allowing only the strong signals to be heard. Squelch is like a net or filter that catches all the noise, allowing only the strong, clear signals to pass through to the headset or speaker. Turning the squelch right down, however, may also cut out the signal that you want to hear as well as unwanted noise, if you are not careful.

☐ **If the desired signal is weak,** you may have to turn down the squelch. Despite the increased background noise the message may be better readable.

NOTE If your radio is receiving background noise, then it should also be capable of receiving voice messages. Another means of checking that your receiver is indeed functioning, apart from requesting a radio check, is to reduce squelch for a few seconds to check that the radio is receiving background noise

Frequency Selection

The frequencies allotted to aeronautical VHF-COM transmissions are from 118·0 MHz up to but not including 137·0 MHz (i.e. up to 136·975 MHz)

Adjacent frequencies are separated by 0·025 MHz (25 kHz). Typical adjacent frequencies are: 120·500, 120·525, 120·550, 120·575, 120·600. If you work it out, you will see that between 120·00 and 121·00 there are 40 possible frequencies. Therefore, in the VHF-COM range from 118·00 to 136·975, a total of (40 × 18) = 720 possible frequencies are available. Most modern VHF-COM radios are 720-channel.

Some VHF–COM sets show three digits after the decimal point (e.g. 120·500, and 120·525), whereas others show only two (e.g. 120·50 and 120·52 – even though 120·500 and 120·525 are the actual frequencies). In the case of 120·525, this is the only possible frequency containing the first five digits 120·52 – the frequencies either side of it are 120·500 and 120·550. Therefore it is safe to describe it as frequency 120·52.

This frequency, 120·52, is referred to as one two zero decimal five two, spoken phonetically as *"wun too ze-ro day-see-mal fife too."* Phonetic pronunciation shown here is used to make radio conversation very clear, and is covered in Chapter 2, *What to Say.*

The demand for radio frequencies will require further division of frequencies in future to 0.0083 MHz (8.33 kHz) spacings.

■ *Figure 1-4* **Two different presentations of frequency 120·525**

Most radios have an *outer* selection knob and an *inner* concentric selection knob. The outer, and larger, knob selects the 3 digits to the left of the decimal point (e.g. 120· or 121· or 133·, etc.); the inner, and smaller, knob selects the digits to the right of the decimal point (e.g. ·5 or ·525 or ·50, etc.).

NOTE Some radio sets require particular attention when selecting intermediate frequencies like "· something 25" or "· something 75". These sets may allow you only to select the first 2 digits after the decimal point using the inner selection knob, and then pull it out for a 0·025 increase. For instance, to select 123·525 you would first have to select 123·50, and then pull the inner selection knob out to get the 0·025 increase to 123·525. Similarly, to select 123·575, you would first select 123·55 then pull the knob out. Make sure that you know how to operate your particular radio set.

Preselecting frequencies

Newer radio sets may have a facility that enables you to preselect frequencies. You can have an *active* frequency, showing on the left side, with a preselected frequency on the right side waiting in *standby*. All frequency selection is done on the right side. Then, touching the transfer switch, also known as the *flip-flop* switch, transfers the standby frequency across to the active side and the previously active frequency over to the standby, and non–active, side. When you press the microphone switch you now transmit on the new active frequency.

A transfer switch enables you to preselect the next required frequency.

Flip-flop switch

■ *Figure 1-5* **A VHF-COM radio with a preselect facility**

Retain the old frequency in the standby window until you have established contact on the new frequency.

You could leave the old frequency in the standby window in case you want to return to it (for instance if no contact is made on the new frequency). Then, when you have contact on the new frequency, you can preselect the next likely frequency in the standby window.

Some VHF-COMs also have an electronic memory where you can store frequently used frequencies which can be retrieved quickly when you need them. This reduces your in-flight workload since you do not have to continually select and reselect the same frequencies each flight.

Published Frequencies

Radio frequencies for specific Air Traffic Service Units (ATSUs) are published in the Aeronautical Information Publication (AIP) Aerodromes (AD) and En Route (ENR) sections. Widely used frequencies may be shown on relevant aeronautical charts.

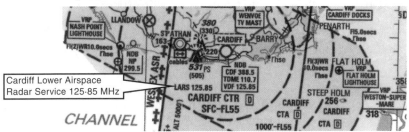

Cardiff Lower Airspace
Radar Service 125·85 MHz

■ *Figure 1-6* **Published frequencies on charts**

Frequencies at an Aerodrome

Very small aerodromes might have no ground-based radio station at all. Others might have a single Air/Ground (A/G) frequency. Busier aerodromes might have a Flight Information Service (FIS) which can supply information over the radio, and even busier aerodromes might have an Air Traffic Control tower (ATC) perhaps with several frequencies. You will quickly become familiar with the frequencies used at your home aerodrome. Your instructor might like to help you list them.

FREQUENCIES IN USE AT MY AERODROME		
A/G frequency	FIS frequency	ATC frequencies
✈ _____ MHz	A🏠 _____ MHz	🗼 Tower _____ MHz
		↘ Approach _____ MHz
		🗼 Ground _____ MHz

Airborne Frequency Changes

As your flight progresses, the ATSU that you are in contact with may often give you the next frequency to call. If, after selecting the new frequency, you do not get a response to your call, you should check your frequency selection (you may have selected 121·7 instead of 121·72, for instance). If still not successful, you could return to the previous frequency, identify yourself with your callsign and ask "Say again frequency". If absolutely necessary, you could transfer to the emergency frequency 121·5 (say if you have forgotten your previous frequency) and ask them for an appropriate frequency.

> When given a new frequency by an ATSU, write it down.
> Then select frequencies carefully and deliberately.

The Microphone

A microphone works in similar fashion to the ear. It converts sound waves into electrical signals. In the case of the ear, the electrical signals are sent to the brain via the auditory nerves; in the case of the microphone, the electrical signals are sent to a radio for transmission.

The basic component of most microphones is a diaphragm that is caused to vibrate by the sound waves created by your voice. The mechanical movement of the diaphragm is converted into an electrical signal which is superimposed onto a radio carrier wave and transmitted.

> The microphone converts your voice to electrical signals.

The old-fashioned **hand-held microphone** is still found in most aircraft, from small trainers to the largest airliners. There is usually a **cockpit speaker** that enables you to listen to messages. The hand-held microphone has an attached _press-to-transmit_ (PTT) button (also known as a _press-to-talk_ button), which must be pressed for your voice message to be transmitted.

> Transmit by pressing the PTT button.

A disadvantage of the hand–held microphone is that it occupies one of your hands, which sometimes is a bit of a juggling act if you have your left hand on the control column and need to adjust the throttle or write something down with your right hand.

A headset/boom-mike is more practical.

Modern aircraft also have provision for a **headset plus boom-microphone.** The headset sits on your head, and its attached boom can be adjusted so that the boom-mike sits just in front of your lips.

The transmit button for the boom-microphone is usually situated on the control column where you can press it without having to remove one of your hands from the control column. This leaves your other hand free to adjust the throttle or write something down. Communicating while actively controlling the aeroplane is therefore much easier. The switch for the boom-mike may move one way to transmit on the radio, and the other way for intercom.

A headset with attached boom-mike has three advantages:

- **A headset reduces** the noise level you experience from the engine and the airflow.
- **A headset enables** clearer inter-communication (intercom) within the cockpit.
- **A headset and boom-mike enables** you to keep both hands on the controls while transmitting, or use one hand to write messages.

Plug the headset and boom-mike in firmly and correctly.

Some headsets have separate volume controls for the left earphone and the right earphone. Often the headset and the boom-microphone leads are separate, and are designed so that they plug into sockets of different sizes, which prevents incorrect connections. If the headset/boom-mike combination does not function for one reason or another, then you can revert to the hand-held microphone and cockpit speaker.

Sidetone

Listen for the sidetone and your own voice when you transmit.

Radios are designed so that you can hear a **sidetone** and also **your own voice** when you transmit. Hearing your own voice helps you to make good clear transmissions with each word enunciated carefully. The sidetone is an indication that the radio is indeed transmitting, as is the fact that you cannot hear transmissions from other stations. If this is not the case, and you do *not* hear a sidetone and continue to hear transmissions from other stations, then your transmitter may have failed or your microphone may not be plugged in.

Using the VHF-COM

To obtain maximum benefit from using a VHF-COM system you
must understand:
- ☐ how to switch the set on;
- ☐ how to use the audio selector panel;
- ☐ correct microphone technique;
- ☐ correct radio phraseology, pronunciation, voice control; and
- ☐ fault-finding procedures to follow if the radio does not function properly.

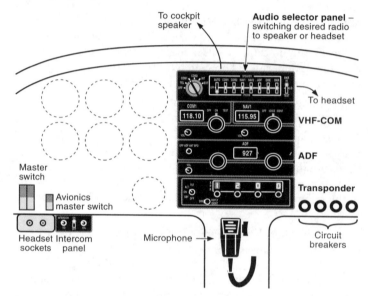

■ *Figure 1-7* **Typical radio set-up in the cockpit**

Switching on the VHF-COM

To prepare the VHF-COM for use:

GET ELECTRICAL POWER TO THE RADIO

- ☐ Switch on the electrical master switch.
- ☐ Switch on the avionics master switch.
- ☐ Check the individual radio is switched on.
- ☐ Check microphone and headset plugged in.

SET THE AUDIO SELECTOR PANEL

- ☐ Select transmitter to desired radio (usually VHF-COM-1),
  which in most aircraft will also select it to receive.
- ☐ Select the listen (receive) switch to speaker or phones (headset).

GET READY TO TRANSMIT

☐ **Select the desired frequency.**

☐ **Adjust the volume** to the desired level (this is receive-volume, it does not affect transmit volume).

☐ **Adjust the squelch** to cut out undesired background noise.

☐ **Request a radio check** (optional).

BEFORE TRANSMITTING

Listen out before transmitting.

☐ **Listen out** on the frequency to be used and do not transmit if someone else is transmitting. If two stations transmit simultaneously on the same frequency both transmissions may be blocked out. If a series of messages is being passed from the ATSU to an aircraft, especially if they are of high priority like a distress Mayday call, do not interrupt.

☐ **Before you transmit,** decide what you want to say. For most communications there is standard phraseology (easily learned) which simplifies things for both parties, i.e. for the person transmitting and for the person receiving.

☐ **Keep your messages short** and to the point. Having the wording of your intended transmission firmly in your mind (or even written down during the early stages of your training) prior to pressing the transmit button will help you avoid hesitation. Avoid long silences while transmitting, and avoid hesitation sounds like "ummm", "arrr", "errr", etc. You can achieve this if you prepare your message.

☐ **Be prepared to write down** any important messages that might be passed to you, such as an ATC route clearance or any messages too long to remember (in your initial training this could be runway in use, surface wind and altimeter setting; after a few flights, however, you will find it easy to remember them).

TO TRANSMIT

☐ **Actuate the press-to-transmit button** a second before you begin talking and keep it pressed until a second after your message is completed.

☐ **Speak with the microphone close to,** or just touching, your upper lip.

☐ **Do not significantly vary the distance** between your lips and the microphone.

☐ **Do not touch** the diaphragm area of the microphone when transmitting, otherwise scratching sounds caused by your fingers might also be transmitted.

☐ **Speak directly into** the microphone and not to one side of it.

☐ **Speak a little slower** than normal, but at normal volume; do not raise your voice or shout, and do not speak in a whisper – too soft and the transmission will be weak; too loud and the transmission may be distorted because the diaphragm is being driven from one extreme of its travel to the other.

☐ **When your message is completed,** release the transmit button (and make sure that it is not 'stuck' in the transmit position).

Your radio will continue to transmit as long as the press-to-transmit button is pressed or stuck in. Even if you are not speaking, the carrier wave will continue to be transmitted, blocking out other stations that are trying to call on that frequency. Therefore, at the end of each of your transmissions, ensure that the mike button is released and not stuck in the transmit position, known as a 'stuck mike' or 'open mike'. Some radio sets have a 'T' symbol which is illuminated when the radio is transmitting, which enables you to check whether it is transmitting or not. If your mike button is stuck, a couple of strong presses will probably release it to the non-transmit position.

Avoid a 'stuck' mike.

Pronunciation and Voice Control

Note the following important points.

☐ **Pronounce each word clearly** and ensure that you enunciate the end of the word clearly. Running words together, or slurring them, may make understanding difficult for the person receiving the message.

☐ **A slight pause** before and after transmission of numbers helps in their accurate transmission.

☐ **Maintain a constant speaking volume** – do not whisper (reception may be impossible) nor shout (which may distort the radio signal).

☐ **Do not lower your voice** at the end of the radio transmission.

☐ **Maintain an even rate of speech** slightly slower than normal conversation.

☐ **If parts of your transmission** have to be written down by the person receiving, then speak a little slower.

Listen Out

You should always listen out on the frequency in use, particularly for any calls that are directed to you. The mention of your callsign should grab your attention. Always be ready to write down any important messages.

Listen out for your callsign.

You should also listen in to other calls that are being made so that you remain aware of what is going on in the airspace around you. Many professional pilots listen out and transmit on their primary radio VHF-COM-1, and also listen out on their second communications radio VHF-COM-2, perhaps selected to the emergency frequency 121·5 or to an ATIS frequency where tape-recorded aerodrome information is continually being broadcast. These pilots must ensure that the second radio does not distract them from listening out on the main frequency. In your early training you will be busy enough coping with just the one radio.

What If the Radio Does Not Work?

Very occasionally the radio may not work. Usually the reason is a human factor – wrong frequency selected, volume turned right down, squelch turned right up, microphone and headset not plugged in, and so on. On rare occasions, it is a genuine radio failure. Radio failure is discussed in detail later in the book; however, the main points are discussed here just in case it happens early in your training. (Most unlikely!)

Fly the aeroplane accurately. The aeroplane does not need a radio to fly safely, and as pilot this is your main responsibility. Then you could:

☐ check the frequency;
☐ check the switching (ON/OFF, audio selector panel, VOL, squelch);
☐ check headset and microphone firmly plugged in;
☐ check circuit breakers and fuses (reset once only).

If the radio still does not function, squawk 7600 on your transponder to alert radar controllers, transmit blind, and stay in visual conditions and land at the nearest suitable airport.

You may make a radio check with an air traffic service unit (ATSU) at your aerodrome before taxiing, or at any time you want to in flight.

Navigation Radios

During the early stages of your training you will most likely not be using the navigation radios; however, the following simple explanation may be of interest to you.

Most aircraft are fitted with several radios which can be selected to the frequency of ground-based radio transmitters designed to aid in navigation, i.e. radio-navigation aids, also known as navaids. Typical radio navigation sets are:

VHF-NAV. Can be selected to ground-based VOR (VHF omnidirectional radio range) stations to assist in tracking, or to ILS (instrument landing system) ground stations aligned with a runway to assist in precision approaches to land (the use of which requires advanced training).

DME. Distance measuring equipment, which measures the slant range from the aircraft to the ground-based DME transmitter, often co-located with a paired VOR (i.e. the VOR and the DME are paired).

ADF. Automatic direction finder, with a needle that points at the selected ground-based **non-directional beacon (NDB).**

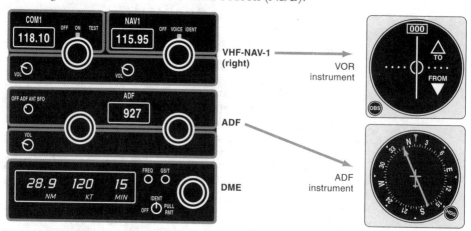

■ *Figure 1-8* **Typical navigation radios**

You cannot *transmit* messages on navigation radios, but you may be able to *receive* voice messages on VOR and NDB frequencies. Aerodrome weather information (such as ATIS – automatic terminal information service) is often transmitted on a VOR frequency. The VHF-NAV can be used to select frequencies from 108·00 MHz up to, but not including, 118·00 MHz (which is a lower frequency band than that used for VHF-COM: 118·00 MHz up to, but not including, 137·00 MHz).

ATIS is often available on a VOR frequency.

Aircraft may also have aids such as GPS (global positioning system), which can fix your position very accurately using signals from satellites.

Transponders

Primary ground radar used by air traffic control (ATC) picks up all aircraft within radar range and displays the position of each on a radar screen as a single blip. It also sometimes picks up unwanted radar reflections from high ground, and occasionally from road vehicles, which causes unwanted indications on the radar screen.

Your transponder improves radar identification.

Associated with most primary radars is a **secondary surveillance radar (SSR)** which can trigger strong responses from your onboard transponder. This will intensify the strength of your blip on the air traffic controller's screen, and can add information such as your flight level and possibly your callsign. The transponder enables strong and unique radar returns. On many transponder panels a small reply-monitor light flashes to indicate that the transponder is being interrogated by a ground SSR station.

■ *Figure 1-9* **Primary radar antenna used by ATC; the small bar mounted on top is the SSR equipment for transponder interrogation**

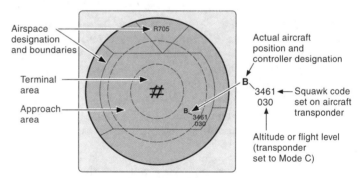

■ *Figure 1-10* **Typical ATC radar screen**

There is no voice communication via the transponder, though you may talk to the radar controller on the VHF-COM.

Mode selection

The transponder function switch has a number of positions: OFF; SBY (standby); ON; ALT (altitude); TST (test).

OFF: transponder is totally off.

STANDBY: the transponder is warmed up ready for use, but not actually transponding.

ON: the transponder will reply to any interrogating signals from the ground, using the four-letter code set in the transponder control panel, enabling identification by the radar controller but not transmitting altitude information. This is known as Mode A (pronounced *Mode Alpha*).

ALTITUDE: As for ON (and Mode A) plus an additional feature whereby your flight level is displayed on the radar controller's screen in hundreds of feet. This capability is known as Mode C (pronounced *Mode Charlie*) or altitude-reporting.

■ *Figure 1-11* **Typical transponder panel**

Code selection

The transponder code is a four-digit number which can be selected using four knobs, each digit being from 0 to 7 (i. e. one of eight possibilities 0, 1, 2, 3, 4, 5, 6, 7). This means there are $(8 \times 8 \times 8 \times 8) = 4,096$ possible codes, and so this type of transponder is often called a 4096 transponder.

Transponder codes are always expressed digit by digit, e.g. squawk 5000 is pronounced "Squawk five zero zero zero".

A typical code to squawk on your transponder is 7000 (conspicuity code). The radar controller may assign you a specific code, such as 3472 ("squawk three four seven two"), which you would then select. There are also certain codes which you would select in specific abnormal situations such as 7700 (emergency), 7600 (radio failure), 7500 (unlawful interference or hijack).

> **Special transponder codes**
> **2000** *crossing international boundary*
> **7000** *conspicuity*
> **7500** *unlawful interference or hijack*
> **7600** *radio failure*
> **7700** *emergency*

Ident

If a controller asks you to "Squawk ident," you should press the **ident button** on your transponder for about 1 second. The ident signal results in your return on the radar screen being accentuated.

> *Squawking ident accentuates your radar blip.*

SSR Language

The radar controller may use some specific transponder language when communicating with you on VHF-COM. Although this is covered in Chapter 2, *What to Say*, we reproduce it here to make it easier for you later on when using this manual as a reference book. There is no need for you to learn these phrases just yet.

PHRASE	MEANING
Squawk (code)	Set the mode and code as instructed
Confirm squawk	Confirm the mode and code set on the transponder
Recycle (mode) (code)	Reselect assigned mode and code
Squawk Ident	Press the ident button for about 1 second
Squawk Mayday	Select emergency code 7700
Squawk Standby	Select STBY
Squawk Mode Charlie	Select altitude reporting ALT
Check altimeter setting and report your level	Check pressure setting and report your level
Stop squawk Mode Charlie	Deselect altitude reporting (change from ALT to ON)
Stop squawk Mode Charlie, wrong indication	Stop altitude report (change from ALT to ON), incorrect level read-out
Verify your level	Check and confirm your level

New Transponder Developments: TCAS

There have been developments in the last few years that have increased the value of transponders with regard to air safety. One such advance is the *traffic-alert and collision-avoidance system*, known as TCAS (pronounced *tee-cass*) or ACAS (pronounced *ay-cass*). TCAS is fitted to advanced aircraft, enabling them to read the transponder signals from other nearby aircraft (relative position and level) and determine if a collision is likely. If the TCAS computer calculates that a collision risk exists, then a warning is automatically given to the pilot by the equipment, with guidance provided (for instance to climb or to descend) to avoid the potential collision. This is of great value in non–visual conditions such as in cloud or at night.

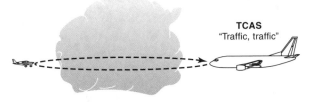

■ *Figure 1-12* **TCAS in action**

Even though your aircraft is *not* likely to be fitted with TCAS, your transponder can be read by other aircraft that do have TCAS, such as airliners. This is one reason why transponders are left on in non-radar environments well away from ground radar stations.

Remember that transponders should not be selected ON until you are about to take off. STANDBY or OFF should be selected again immediately after landing and vacating the runway.

Switch your transponder on, even in a non-radar environment.

Now complete: **Exercises 1 – Cockpit Radios.**

(Exercises and Answers at back of book.)

Learning the Language
What to Say

This chapter introduces standard radio language. Read it through once to get the general idea, then periodically return to it as your training progresses. The most important thing in radio communication is that the message gets across efficiently so that the frequency is not blocked unnecessarily and made unavailable for use by others.

English is the language of aviation.

In aviation, English is the generally accepted language for radio communications and whenever possible standard phraseology should be used. Some extremely important items, such as the call-signs of aircraft, are often spelled out letter by letter. In summary, when communicating by radio, you should:

- **use only the English language;**
- **use standard phraseology** whenever possible;
- **be concise and unambiguous;**
- **avoid inflections** of the voice, especially when asking a question; instead, use an interrogative (questioning) word or phrase (e.g. "Confirm climb to altitude three thousand feet);
- **not be over-polite** (*please* and *thanks* are unnecessary).

Letters (Phonetic Alphabet)

In transmitting individual letters the following standard words, which make up the phonetic alphabet, should be used. Stress the syllables that are printed in **bold.** Thus, in the word *November,* the second syllable *vem* is emphasized so that it is pronounced *No-vem-ber.*

THE PHONETIC ALPHABET					
Letter	*Word*	*Transmitted as*	*Letter*	*Word*	*Transmitted as*
A	Alpha	**Al**-*fah*	N	November	No-**vem**-ber
B	Bravo	**Brah-voh**	O	Oscar	**Oss**-*cah*
C	Charlie	**Char**-*lee*	P	Papa	Pah-**pah**
D	Delta	**Dell**-*tah*	Q	Quebec	Keh-**beck**
E	Echo	**Eck**-*oh*	R	Romeo	**Row**-*me-oh*
F	Foxtrot	**Foks**-*trot*	S	Sierra	See-**air**-*rah*
G	Golf	Golf	T	Tango	**Tang**-*go*
H	Hotel	Hoh-**tell**	U	Uniform	**You**-*nee-form*
I	India	**In**-*dee-ah*	V	Victor	**Vik**-*tah*
J	Juliett	**Jew**-*lee*-**ett**	W	Whiskey	**Wiss**-*key*
K	Kilo	**Key**-*loh*	X	X-ray	**Ecks**-*ray*
L	Lima	**Lee**-*mah*	Y	Yankee	**Yang**-*key*
M	Mike	Mike	Z	Zulu	**Zoo**-*loo*

The most common use of the phonetic alphabet is in the transmission of aircraft **callsigns**. Aircraft registered in the UK have a registration name that consists of "G-" followed by four letters. For instance, the callsign that we will use predominantly in this manual is G-BATC. This is pronounced phonetically as, *"Golf Brah-voh Al-fah Tang-go Char-lee."* Having established two-way communications, the ATSU might initiate an abbreviated callsign G-TC, i.e. 'G' or aircraft type followed by the last two letters of the callsign. This would be pronounced as *"Golf Tang-go Char-lee."*

The phonetic alphabet is also used whenever it is thought necessary to spell a word to ensure correct understanding of a message (such as the names of towns in position reports) if radio reception is poor or if any confusion arises. For instance, an ATSU might say *"Report at ELKAS, Eck-oh Lee-mah Key-loh Al-fah See-air-ah."*

There are some common aviation abbreviations, however, that are usually pronounced directly without using the phonetic alphabet, such as QNH (an altimeter subscale setting), and the various radio navigation aids – ILS (instrument landing system), NDB (non-directional beacon), VOR (VHF omni range), DME (distance measuring equipment); also the meteorological term CAVOK (pronounced *kav-oh-kay*, which means ceiling and visibility OK). Many of these terms will be new expressions to you but will become very familiar with experience. See the abbreviations list on page 183.

Numbers

When you are transmitting single digits you should use the following words, stressing the syllables in **bold**:

NUMBER OR NUMERAL ELEMENT	PRONUNCIATION
0	**ze-ro**
1	**wun**
2	**too**
3	**tree** (or **three**)
4	**fow**-er
5	**fife**
6	**six**
7	**sev**-en
8	**ait**
9	**nin**-er
decimal	**day-see-mal**
hundred	**hun-dred**
thousand	**tousand** (or **thousand**)

It is especially important to differentiate between 5 (pronounced *fife*) and 9 (pronounced *nin-er*) because, when spoken normally, they are often confused. If there is a decimal point in the number then it is indicated by the word *day-see-mal*. For example, an instruction to G-BATC to change frequency to 118·4 MHz (megahertz) would be transmitted as:

> Golf **Brah-voh Al**-fah **Tang**-go **Char**-lee
> Contact Blackpool Tower on **wun wun ait day-see-mal fow**-er

NOTE An easy way to learn the phonetic alphabet and number pronunciation is to practice using car registration numbers as you drive. YRN195P would be pronounced:

> **Yang**-key **Row**-me-oh No-**vem**-ber **wun nin**-er **fife** Pah-**pah**

The Transmission of Numbers

All numbers shall be transmitted by pronouncing each digit separately (e.g. 10 is *wun ze-ro*, 236 is *too three six*), except for:

- whole hundreds (e.g. 500 is *fife hun-dred*);
- whole thousands (e.g. 7,000 is *sev-en tousand*); and
- combinations of thousands and whole hundreds (7,500 is *sev-en tousand fife hun-dred*).

For example:

> G-TC maintaining flight level **wun hun-dred.**

The words "one hundred" and "one thousand" are pronounced in full, rather than "one zero zero" or "one zero zero zero." This is particularly important when referring to flight levels. For instance, you would say "flight level one hundred" for FL100, but "flight level one one zero" for FL110.

NUMBER	TRANSMITTED AS
50	*fife ze-ro*
85	*ait fife*
612	*six wun too*
900	*nin-er* **hun-dred**
3,000	*tree tousand*
3,500	*tree tousand fife hun-dred*
12,000	*wun too tousand*
12,700	*wun too tousand sev-en hun-dred*
12,755	*wun too sev-en fife fife*

There are some exceptions to this "hundreds and thousands" rule, where the whole number is expressed digit by digit even if it ends in a hundred or a thousand. For instance:

☐ **Time** is expressed digit by digit, e.g. time 1800 UTC is pronounced *"wun ait ze-ro ze-ro."*

☐ **Altimeter pressure settings** are pronounced digit by digit, e.g. QNH 1000 is pronounced *"kew enn aitch wun ze-ro ze-ro ze-ro."*

☐ **Transponder codes** are pronounced digit by digit, e.g. squawk 5200 is pronounced *"squawk fife too ze-ro ze-ro."*

☐ **Headings** are pronounced digit by digit, e.g. heading 200 is pronounced *"heading too ze-ro ze-ro."*

☐ **Numbers in aircraft callsigns** are pronounced digit by digit, e.g. Aer Lingus Flight 300 is pronounced *"Shamrock tree ze-ro ze-ro."*

☐ **Radio frequencies** are pronounced digit by digit, e.g. 126·72 is pronounced *"wun too six day-see-mal sev-en too."*

☐ **Wind direction and speed** is pronounced digit by digit, e.g. W/V 100/25 is pronounced *"wun ze-ro ze-ro, at too fife knots."*

☐ **Runway directions** are pronounced digit-by-digit (to the nearest 10 degrees), e.g. a runway heading 132 degrees magnetic would be called Runway *wun tree;* Runway 09 is called Runway *zero nin-er.*

☐ **Flight levels** other than FL100 are pronounced in full, e.g. FL200 is pronounced as *"flight level two ze-ro ze-ro."*

When using the **clock code** to identify the position of other aircraft, whole numbers may be used. For instance, an aeroplane ahead of you to the left, and at a higher level, could be described as being "eleven o'clock high." An aircraft straight ahead of you but slightly lower would be "twelve o'clock low."

Occasionally cloud cover is expressed as eighths of the sky covered. *Eighths* in radio transmissions is expressed as oktas. A little over half the sky covered, say ⅝, would be expressed as *fife* oktas.

Time

Because aeroplanes are continually moving from one time zone to another, it is the internationally accepted practice in aviation to use a specific time reference known as **coordinated universal time (UTC)** for all expressions of time in radio transmissions and on flight plans, etc. UTC is based on longitude 0° which passes through Greenwich, near London. UTC is the local standard time in Britain which is used on clocks and watches.

Aviation uses the 24-hour clock and UTC.

NOTE Until recently this time reference was known as Greenwich Mean Time (GMT). While UTC has a more academic definition and is more precise than GMT, the only practical effect in aviation is the name change from GMT to UTC. Sometimes UTC is referred to as *Zulu time,* symbolised by the letter 'Z', e.g. 0812Z.

Usually say minutes only. When transmitting time it is usual only to say the minutes of the hour. However, if there is any possibility of a misunderstanding, then the hour in UTC should also be included.

TIME	TRANSMITTED AS
0815	**wun fife** (or **ze-ro ait wun fife**)
1720	**too ze-ro** (or **wun sev**-en **too ze-ro**)
2300	**too tree ze-ro ze-ro**
0400	**ze-ro fow**-er **ze-ro ze-ro**

The subject of *time* is treated in more detail in Volume 3 of *The Air Pilot's Manual,* and in the CAA-published AIP (Aeronautical Information Manual). A brief summary is all that we require here.

In aviation we use the 24-hour clock – the day beginning at 0000 and ending 24 hours later at 2400 (which is of course 0000 for the next day). For example:

- ☐ 8:30 in the morning is 0830.
- ☐ Midday (12 noon) is 1200.
- ☐ One hour later, 1 pm, is 1300 (i.e. 1200 plus 1 hour).
- ☐ 4:30 in the afternoon is 1630 (i.e. 1200 plus 0430).
- ☐ 8 pm is 2000 (i.e. 1200 plus 0800).
- ☐ 8:17 pm is 2017.

Summer Time

In the UK, the local time is moved forward by 1 hour at the end of March and becomes known as British Summer Time (BST). This enables us to make better use of the longer daylight hours resulting from the earlier sunrise and later sunset. The UK local time reverts back to UTC at the end of October when summer is over and the days are closing in.

For example, 1200 UTC in summer is 1300 BST, and 1300 is what would be set on clocks and watches. Whereas in winter, when UTC is British local standard time, 1200 would be set on clocks and watches.

Central European Time

The local time in Continental Europe is normally 1 hour ahead of UTC and is known as Central European Time (CET). For example, 1300 CET = 1200 UTC.

Standard Procedural Words and Phrases

The most important thing in flight radio is for your message to be unambiguous and clearly understood. For this reason you should use plain English and simple phrases. To make radio communications uniform, standard words and phrases have been devised. Their meanings are clear; they are brief and occupy less air time. Whenever possible you should use this standard phraseology.

The Air Traffic Services personnel of the CAA, your partners in the use of radio, will use this standard phraseology whenever they can. If you cannot recall the appropriate standard phraseology for your particular situation, or if there is no standard phrase for the information that you wish to convey, then just go ahead and use plain, concise English.

The meaning of most standard words or phrases is usually self-explanatory, and a list of some of common phraseology follows. These should be gradually memorized, and this will occur as you gain experience. The most important phrases are shaded, and you should start to learn them now.

Use standard phraseology whenever possible.

WORD OR PHRASE	MEANING
......*AT YOUR DISCRETION*	ATC clearing, or Flight Information Service advising, pilot to commence manoeuvre when pilot wants to.
ACKNOWLEDGE	Let me know that you have received and understood this message.
AFFIRM	Yes. Note: "Affirm" is used instead of "affirmative" to further differentiate from and avoid confusion with its opposite "negative".
ALL STATIONS	All stations (aircraft and ground) on this frequency.
APPROVED	Permission for proposed action granted.
BASE	Turning onto the base leg of the circuit pattern.
BACKTRACK	Proceed in direction opposite to that of runway in use when on the ground.
BREAK	Indicates the separation between messages.
CANCEL	Annul the previously transmitted clearance.
CANCEL DISTRESS	Cancel Distress (and pass details, e.g. crew of sinking yacht now safely on shore).
CANCEL MAYDAY	Cancel Mayday emergency (and pass details, e.g. engine restarted).
CHANGING TO ......[1]	I intend to call .... (station) on .... (frequency) Note: The word "to" is only used if followed by the station name. Using "to" before a frequency could create confusion with the number "2".
CHECK	Examine a system or procedure (no answer is normally expected).
CLEARED	Authorized to proceed under the conditions specified.
CLEARED FOR TAKE-OFF	Only used when the aircraft is cleared for take-off. At all other times "departure" is used.
CLEARED FOR IMMEDIATE TAKE-OFF	Clearance to take off without delay.
CLEARED TO LAND	You are cleared to land on the nominated runway.

Learn the shaded terms first.

WORD OR PHRASE	MEANING
CLIMB FLIGHT LEVEL ...... **CLIMB TO ALTITUDE** ......[1] **CLIMB TO HEIGHT** ......[1]	Climb to and maintain stated flight level... Note that the word "to" is omitted from messages relating to flight levels, e.g. "Climb flight level four five. When "to" is used, the words "altitude" or "height" follow, then the figures, e.g. "Climb to altitude four thousand feet."
CONFIRM	Have I correctly received the following ....? or Did you correctly receive this message?
CONTACT	Establish radio contact with .... (your flight details have been passed).
CONTINUE	Continue with manoeuvre (e.g. approach/heading).
CORRECT	That is correct.
CORRECTION	An error has been made in this transmission (or message indicated). The correct version is ....
CROSS RUNWAY	Taxi instructions to cross an active runway.
DESCEND FLIGHT LEVEL ...... **DESCEND TO ALTITUDE** ......[1] **DESCEND TO HEIGHT** ......[1]	Descend to and maintain stated flight level. Note that the word "to" is omitted from messages relating to flight levels, e.g. "Descend flight level four five. When "to" is used, the words "altitude" or "height" follow, then the figures, e.g. "Descend to altitude four thousand feet."
DISREGARD	Consider that transmission as not sent.
DOWNWIND	In the circuit pattern abeam the upwind end of the runway in use.
EXPECT	Expect the stated item (e.g. landing runway, onward clearance, delays, etc.). This is to allow you to plan ahead, but is not a clearance.
EXPEDITE	Perform manoeuvre as quickly as safely possible (hurry up).
FINAL	After turning from base leg of the circuit pattern onto final approach.
FOLLOW	Adjust your taxi path or flightpath and/or speed to follow the specified aircraft.
FREECALL	Call .... (unit) (your details have not been passed – mainly used by military ATC).
GO AHEAD	Proceed with your message, in reply to "Ready to copy?" clearance.
GO AROUND	Discontinue the approach and go-around into the visual circuit, or carry out the missed approach procedure, as appropriate.
...... **HEAVY**	Large aircraft in the **heavy** wake turbulence category, e.g. "Delta 145 heavy."

WORD OR PHRASE	MEANING
HOLD POSITION	ATC requesting taxiing aircraft to stop in present position.
HOW DO YOU READ?	What is the readability of my transmission?
IMMEDIATELY	Indicates an exceptional circumstance requiring immediate action by the pilot.
I SAY AGAIN	I repeat for clarity or emphasis.
KNOWN TRAFFIC IS	Traffic, whose current flight details and intentions are known to the controller.
LATE DOWNWIND	Somewhere on the downwind leg of the circuit pattern, past the normal point for calling "Downwind".
LINE UP or LINE UP AND WAIT	Taxi onto the runway, and into position ready for take-off, but do not take off.
LONG FINAL	Between 4 and 8 miles on a long straight-in approach to land.
MAINTAIN	Hold current altitude.
MAYDAY MAYDAY MAYDAY	Distress call from a pilot with details following.
MAYDAY TRAFFIC ENDED	Cancellation of emergency communications and radio silence.
MONITOR	Listen out on (frequency).
NEGATIVE	No; or, Permission not granted; or, That is not correct.
NO KNOWN TRAFFIC	ATC reporting no known traffic that will conflict with you.
ORBIT LEFT/RIGHT	Make a 360° turn left/right.
OUT[2]	This exchange of transmission is ended and no response is expected.
OVER[2]	My transmission is ended and I expect a response from you.
PAN-PAN PAN-PAN PAN-PAN	Urgency call from a pilot with details following.
PASS YOUR MESSAGE	Proceed with your message. You may sometimes hear the phrase "Go ahead". This is still an ICAO-approved term, though the UK CAA has dropped it.
PRACTICE-PAN PRACTICE-PAN PRACTICE-PAN	Pilot making a practice PAN-PAN call on emergency frequency 121·5 MHz.
RADIO CHECK	Request for radio serviceability check. See table opposite.
READ BACK	Repeat all, or the specified part, of this message back to me exactly as received.

READABILITY SCALE

1	Unreadable
2	Readable now and then
3	Readable but with difficulty
4	Readable
5	Perfectly readable

WORD OR PHRASE	MEANING
READY FOR DEPARTURE	*Pilot reporting all checks complete and ready for take-off and departure.*
READY TO COPY?	*(Are you) ready to copy? (details such as an ATC route clearance or weather) etc.*
RECEIVED . . . . **(information code letter)**	*Advice to ATC that the pilot has received and understood the specific automatic terminal information (ATIS) for that particular aerodrome. Note that if you receive an altimeter pressure setting from the ATIS prior to departure, and it is not given again by the ATC unit, you must read back that pressure setting, e.g. "Received information Bravo, QNH 1012."*
RECYCLE CODE	*Set your transponder to standby, then reselect the assigned code and mode.*
REPORT	*Pass requested information.*
REPORT ESTABLISHED	*Report when you are established on the stated flightpath or track.*
REPORT FINAL	*Report when you are within 4 nm of runway on final approach.*
REPORT LONG FINAL	*Report when you are between 4 nm and 8 nm from runway on final approach.*
REQUEST	*I should like to know . . . . or I wish to obtain . . . .*
ROGER	*I have received all of your last transmission. Note: Under no circumstances to be used in reply to a question requiring a direct answer in the positive sense ("affirm") or negative sense ("negative").*
RUNWAY VACATED	*Pilot reporting that aircraft has now vacated active runway (crossed holding point and is completely on taxiway).*
SELCAL	*Selective calling on HF radio.*
SAY AGAIN	*Repeat all, or the following part of your last transmission.*
SPEAK SLOWER	*Reduce your rate of speech.*
SQUAWK	*Set this squawk code and mode on your transponder.*
SQUAWK MODE CHARLIE	*Set Mode C (altitude reporting) on your transponder.*
SQUAWK IDENT	*Press the ident button on your transponder.*
SQUAWK MAYDAY	*Select code 7700 on your transponder.*
SQUAWK STANDBY	*Set Standby mode on your transponder.*
STANDBY	*Wait and I will call you. Note: No onward clearance to be assumed.*
STOP CLIMB (DESCENT)[3]	*Revised clearance to a new flight level or altitude which will be reached prior to the originally cleared (and now cancelled) flight level or altitude.*

WORD OR PHRASE	MEANING
STOP IMMEDIATELY	*Aircraft specified taxiing or taking off to stop immediately.*
STOP TRANSMITTING. MAYDAY	*All stations, other than the one transmitting the Mayday call, to temporarily cease transmissions.*
TAXI TO . . . . . . VIA	*Taxi instructions to taxi as specified.*
TRANSMITTING BLIND ON (FREQUENCY)	*Pilot transmitting with a suspected receiver failure (i.e. possibly can transmit, but cannot receive messages).*
TURN (LEFT/RIGHT) HEADING . . . . . .[1]	*Turn in the direction indicated onto the stated magnetic heading.*
VACATE RUNWAY	*Taxi clear of active runway.*
VECTORING FOR	*Radar vectors (heading) for final approach or stated procedure.*
VERIFY	*Check and confirm.*
WHEN READY	*Clearance to climb to or descend to the stated flight level or altitude at the pilot's discretion.*
WILCO	*I understand your message and will comply with it (abbreviation for will comply).*
WORDS TWICE	*As a request: Communication is difficult. Please send every word twice.* *As information: Since communication is difficult, every word in this message will be sent twice.*

1. *The words 'to' and 'for' should be avoided when preceding numbers such as altitudes, headings or frequencies, unless separated by another word. This avoids confusion with the numbers '2' and '4'.*

2. *'Over' and 'out' may be omitted after initial contact has been firmly established provided no possibility of confusion or ambiguity will result. These words are not often used in VHF transmissions which are usually very clear, but may be used in HF (high frequency) transmissions in remote areas which are often difficult to hear clearly.*

3. *In relation to level instructions, the phrase 're-cleared' should **not** be used.*

Conclusion

Fluency in using the radio and thinking of the right phraseology will come with practice. Practice will make you proficient. If you find that you are unsure of what to say, or are having difficulty understanding what is being said to you, tell the controllers that you are a trainee pilot so that they can assist you by perhaps speaking slower and choosing simpler phraseology, etc.

Visit an ATSU. The staff will be pleased to see you and you will learn a lot from them.

Now complete: **Exercises 2 – What to Say.**

Learning the Language
Aerodrome Operations

In this chapter we look at some of the general principles of radiotelephony (R/T) around aerodromes so that you can get started.

Some standard phrases and phonetic pronunciation are introduced – these were covered in detail in Chapter 2, *What to Say*, which you might like to refer to from time to time as you go through this chapter.

Then we look at the main types of aerodromes one by one. At this stage in your training you need only look at the category into which your home aerodrome falls. Later, when you start flying further on cross-country flights, you can then refer to the category of aerodromes which you will be visiting.

The 5 Key R/T Positions
There are 5 key radiotelephony (R/T) positions for taxi and circuit operations at an aerodrome. If you get these fixed in your mind right from the beginning of your training you will have no trouble operating at any aerodrome in the UK, or elsewhere, for the rest of your career. The 5 key R/T positions are illustrated below, with the points you need to consider at each of them.

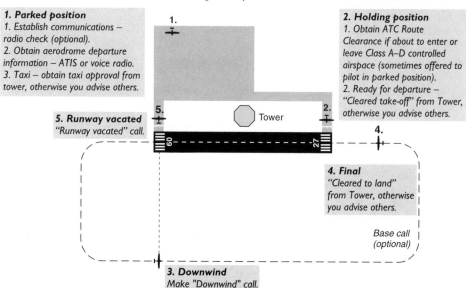

1. Parked position
1. Establish communications – radio check (optional).
2. Obtain aerodrome departure information – ATIS or voice radio.
3. Taxi – obtain taxi approval from tower, otherwise you advise others.

5. Runway vacated
"Runway vacated" call.

2. Holding position
1. Obtain ATC Route Clearance if about to enter or leave Class A–D controlled airspace (sometimes offered to pilot in parked position).
2. Ready for departure – "Cleared take-off" from Tower, otherwise you advise others.

4. Final
"Cleared to land" from Tower, otherwise you advise others.

Base call (optional)

3. Downwind
Make "Downwind" call.

Tower

■ *Figure 3-1* **The 5 key R/T positions**

Types of Aerodromes

Aerodromes fall into one of two types:

☐ **aerodromes with ATC** (Air Traffic Control), where ATC *clearances* are required to operate on the aerodrome (i.e. to take off, and land); and

☐ **aerodromes with either FIS** (Flight Information Service) or **A/G** (Air/Ground radio) to provide information and advice. There may of course be **no radio** at all. At FIS, A/G or no-radio aerodromes, *you* are completely responsible for aerodrome operations and ATC clearances are not required (nor available), but you should *advise* others of your movements.

Types of Air Traffic Service Units (ATSU)

There are three main types of air traffic service units (ATSU) that may be active at an aerodrome:

📡 **Air Traffic Control (ATC)** provides a control and information service; issues ATC clearances to enter Class A–D controlled airspace; or clearances within the air traffic controlled ATZ.

📡 **Flight Information Service (FIS)** provides an information service.

📡 **Air/Ground radio (A/G)** provides a very basic information service.

The nature of an ATSU (ATC, FIS or A/G) and its designated name is published in the Aeronautical Information Publication (AIP AD and ENR), but is also obvious from its designator, which is used in communications with aircraft.

The nature of an ATSU is indicated by its name.

📡 **An ATC unit** is indicated by its place name followed by its function, such as *Ground, Tower, Approach, Director, Radar, Delivery* (i.e. clearance delivery).

📡 **An FIS unit** is indicated by its place name followed by the word *Information.*

📡 **An Air/Ground** unit is indicated by its place name followed by the word *Radio.*

As you are passed from frequency to frequency during a flight, you can determine the nature of the new ATSU from its name.

The nature of an ATSU service at an aerodrome may vary at different times. An aerodrome that is very active for most of the day may be ATC during the busy hours, and then downgrade to an FIS service at night or for weekends.

Check what level of ATSU is currently operating at your aerodrome.

Your Home Aerodrome

Most of your training flights will begin and end at your home aerodrome. The aim of this chapter is to help you become familiar with its R/T requirements, and also the R/T calls you need to make as you proceed from the aerodrome to your training area, which might be some miles away, and back again.

You should determine which type of ATSU operates at your aerodrome and then concentrate on its procedures. The questions you need to ask are:

☐ **Does my aerodrome** have an air traffic control service?
☐ **Yes.** See page 45.
☐ **No.** If not, then what radio facilities does it have?
  – FIS (Flight Information Service): see page 41.
  – A/G (Air/Ground radio): see page 43.
  – None (i.e. no-radio): see page 45.

Some General Principles

You will assimilate a lot of radio language by hearing others and by practising. Since this is an introductory chapter to get you going, we will now summarise some of the main points to look out for, and then cover them in detail later in the book.

Booking Out

"Book out" each flight.

A pilot intending to make a flight should contact the ATSU or other authority at the aerodrome of departure to inform them of the proposed flight. This is known as booking out, and is separate from filing a flight plan. The booking out can be made in person, by telephone, or (at certain aerodromes) by radio. If you have filed a flight plan, there is no need to book out.

Aircraft Callsigns

Callsigns are expressed phonetically.

Aircraft callsigns are spoken using the phonetic alphabet. Our aeroplane G-BATC is referred to as Golf Bravo Alpha Tango Charlie, which is spoken phonetically as "Golf **Brah-voh** Al-fah **Tang**-go **Char**-lee", where the bold letters indicate emphasis. The callsigns of aircraft registered in the UK begin with 'G' for Great Britain, followed by a four-letter callsign.

An ATSU may initiate an abbreviated callsign.

To avoid being long-winded, the person you are speaking with at an Air Traffic Service Unit (ATSU) may initiate an abbreviation to G-TC, i.e. 'G' and then the last two letters 'TC'. "Golf **Tang**-go **Char**-lee" is not as long-winded as "Golf **Brah-voh** Al-fah **Tang**-go **Char**-lee." Once the ATSU initiates the abbreviation, you may then continue to use it on that frequency.

You would revert to your full callsign when transferring to a new frequency, and any ATC route clearance to enter controlled airspace will also use your full callsign.

You might care to write down the registration of your aircraft and how is it spoken phonetically in full and also in abbreviated form. (Refer to your instructor, or see Chapter 2.)

My aircraft is registered as G-................................, which is spoken phonetically as:

☐ in full:..
☐ in abbreviated form:...

To help you to become familiar with the phonetic alphabet we illustrate how the words should be pronounced. For instance, November is the phonetic letter for N and is pronounced *No-vem-ber,* with the spoken emphasis on *vem.* The phonetic alphabet was discussed in detail in Chapter 2.

Practise the phonetic alphabet.

Placement of Callsigns

The general rules are:

1. INITIAL CALL. When first contacting an ATSU, address the ATSU station you are calling followed by your callsign, e.g. "Blackpool Tower, Golf Bravo Alpha Tango Charlie".

2. PASSING A NEW MESSAGE TO THE ATSU. After a response from the ATSU to confirm that it is receiving you, such as "Golf Bravo Alpha Tango Charlie, Blackpool Tower", or "Golf Bravo Alpha Tango Charlie, Blackpool Tower, pass your message", you should continue with your callsign followed by your message: e.g. "Golf Bravo Alpha Tango Charlie, request taxi instructions". Then each time you initiate a new conversation you should follow this pattern: your callsign, your message.

3. IN RESPONSE. When responding to a message from the ATSU, you should answer the message followed by your callsign. For instance, you would answer the following message from the tower, "Golf Bravo Alpha Tango Charlie, cleared for take-off", with "Cleared for take-off, Golf Bravo Alpha Tango Charlie".

EXAMPLE 1 IN THE PARKED POSITION

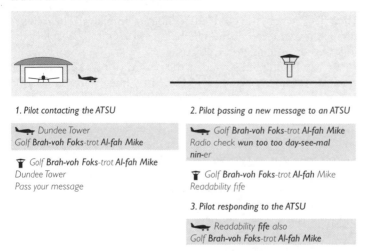

1. Pilot contacting the ATSU

Dundee Tower
Golf **Brah-voh Foks**-trot **Al-fah** Mike

Golf **Brah-voh Foks**-trot **Al-fah** Mike
Dundee Tower
Pass your message

2. Pilot passing a new message to an ATSU

Golf **Brah-voh Foks**-trot **Al-fah** Mike
Radio check **wun too too day-see-mal nin**-er

Golf **Brah-voh Foks**-trot **Al-fah** Mike
Readability **fife**

3. Pilot responding to the ATSU

Readability **fife** also
Golf **Brah-voh Foks**-trot **Al-fah** Mike

■ *Figure 3-2* **Establishing contact on the ground**

EXAMPLE 2 RETURNING TO THE AERODROME

1. Pilot contacting the ATSU

Wycombe Tower
Golf **Al-fah Key**-loh **You**-nee-form Mike

Golf **Al-fah Key**-loh **You**-nee-form Mike
Wycombe Tower
Pass your message

2. Pilot initiating an exchange with ATSU

Golf **Al-fah Key**-loh **You**-nee-form Mike
Fife miles north
Heading wun ait ze-ro
Altitude **tree tousand**
VFR
Estimating Wycombe at **ze-ro ait**
Request joining instructions

Golf **Al-fah Key**-loh **You**-nee-form Mike
Join left-hand downwind
Runway **too nin**-er
Height **wun tousand** feet
QFE **wun ze-ro ze-ro fife**

3. Pilot replying to ATSU

Join left-hand downwind
Runway **too nin**-er
Height **wun tousand** feet
QFE **wun ze-ro ze-ro fife**
Golf **Al-fah Key**-loh **You**-nee-form Mike

■ *Figure 3-3* **Returning to the aerodrome**

Read Back

Vital items of any message from an ATSU must be read back.
Some important read back items for you at this early stage in your
career are:

- ☐ **Runway clearances** from ATC (e.g. cleared for take-off,
  cleared to land, holding point, line up, backtrack, cross active
  runway etc.).
- ☐ **Runway in use.**
- ☐ **Altimeter settings** QNH or QFE so that your altimeter indi-
  cates correctly – see Chapter 4, *Aerodrome Information.*
- ☐ **Frequency changes** to ensure that you change to the desired
  frequency and not an incorrect one.
- ☐ **ATC route clearances.**
- ☐ **Heading changes** requested by the ATSU.
- ☐ **Level or altitude instructions.**
- ☐ **Speed instructions.**
- ☐ **Transponder squawk instructions.**
- ☐ **Type of radar service:** Radar Advisory Service or Radar
  Information Service – Chapter 6, *R/T in Uncontrolled Airspace.*
- ☐ **VDF direction finding information** (QDM – see page 85).

It is not required that you read back taxi instructions; however, it shows good airmanship to do so. Taxiing the wrong way at Manchester, for instance, could be embarrassing if you accidently found yourself, due to taking a wrong turn, face-to-face with a large jet also on the taxiway.

You only have to read back the items listed above, followed by your callsign. Any other messages (e.g. surface wind) are simply acknowledged with your callsign.

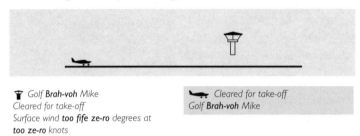

Golf **Brah-voh** Mike
Cleared for take-off
Surface wind **too fife ze-ro** degrees at
too ze-ro knots

Cleared for take-off
Golf **Brah-voh** Mike

■ Figure 3-4 **Read back the required items followed by your callsign**

Uncertain of Message

Radio talk is often difficult to understand for a beginner. The messages passed may be vital to flight safety so, if you do not understand the message or any part of it, ask the ATSU to "Say again", or "Say again all after .....", or "Say again all before ....". If you advise the ATSU that you are a student pilot, then they will be particularly understanding. Remember that flight safety is a partnership between pilots and ATSUs.

If you read back any item of the clearance that is incorrect, the controller will say "negative", and then repeat the correct information, and then wait for or ask for a read back.

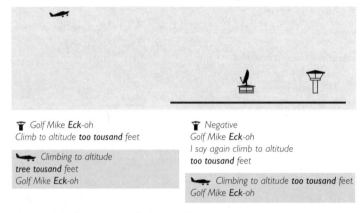

Golf Mike **Eck**-oh
Climb to altitude **too tousand** feet

Climbing to altitude
tree tousand feet
Golf Mike **Eck**-oh

Negative
Golf Mike **Eck**-oh
I say again climb to altitude
too tousand feet

Climbing to altitude **too tousand** feet
Golf Mike **Eck**-oh

■ Figure 3-5 **Correcting a faulty read back**

Unable to Comply

If you receive an instruction with which you cannot comply, you should advise ATC "unable to comply" and give the reason. A possible reason may be the limitations of your licence.

The example in Figure 3-6 assumes a PPL holder with no instrument qualifications of any kind. Following the controller's instruction would put the pilot into cloud or Instrument Meteorological Conditions (IMC), though the pilot is only qualified to fly in Visual Meteorological Conditions (VMC).

The controller will not know in advance the limitations of your licence, so it is up to you to recognise what you can and cannot do and respond accordingly.

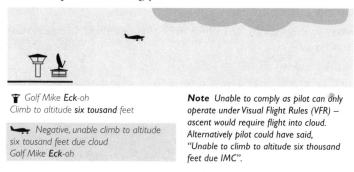

🛉 *Golf Mike Eck-oh*
Climb to altitude six tousand feet

🛩 *Negative, unable climb to altitude six tousand feet due cloud*
Golf Mike Eck-oh

Note *Unable to comply as pilot can only operate under Visual Flight Rules (VFR) – ascent would require flight into cloud. Alternatively pilot could have said, "Unable to climb to altitude six thousand feet due IMC".*

■ *Figure 3-6* **Unable to comply with an ATC instruction**

Acknowledgement

You can acknowledge a radio message that requires no read back with your callsign only, or with an appropriate word followed by your callsign.

- ☐ **"Roger"** means "I have received all of your last transmission."
- ☐ **"Wilco"** means "I understand your message and will comply with it."

🛉 *Golf Tang-go Char-lee*
Surface wind is **too fife ze-ro** *degrees at* **tree ze-ro** *knots*

🛩 *Roger*
Golf Tang-go Char-lee

🛉 *Golf Tang-go Char-lee*
You are number **too**
Report downwind

🛩 *Wilco*
Golf Tang-go Char-lee

■ *Figure 3-7* **Acknowledging messages not requiring a read back**

Aerodrome Information

An ATC unit may have the ability to tape-record the aerodrome information (such as runway in use, surface wind, QNH and QFE, temperature, cloud coverage and base) and make it available on a separate VHF-COM or VHF-NAV frequency. This lets you copy the aerodrome information without having to speak to ATC. This tape-recorded *automatic terminal information service* is known as the ATIS (pronounced *ay-tiss*).

Listening to the ATIS is efficient.

The recorded ATIS information is updated regularly and each updated version is designated by a different code letter: Alpha, Bravo, Charlie, etc. When contacting ATC you should inform them that you have "Information Alpha" or Information Bravo, Charlie or Delta as the case may be.

NOTE If you obtain a pressure from the ATIS prior to departure that is not given again by the ATC unit, then you must read back that pressure setting.

If there is no ATIS, then you can "Request departure information" from the ATSU before taxiing. Typical departure information passed by the ATSU officer will include runway in use, surface wind, QNH and/or QFE.

Aerodrome information is also available from the ATSU.

Radio Check and Readability Scale

You may check the radio when in the parked position and making first contact with the ATSU. If you do request a radio check then you should specify the frequency you are using, because the ATSU officer might be listening out on more than one frequency. The purpose of a radio check is to confirm satisfactory two-way communication. You may request a radio check at any time. Similarly, an ATSU might ask you for a radio check at any time there is doubt about satisfactory two-way communications. The readability scale is listed below.

READABILITY SCALE	MEANING
1 "wun"	Unreadable
2 "too"	Readable now and then
3 "tree"	Readable but with difficulty
4 "fow-er"	Readable
5 "fife"	Perfectly readable

The **radio check** may be made as a separate communication with the ATSU, or combined with other requests such as for **departure information** (runway, surface wind, QNH and QFE) and/or **taxi instructions.** If you call for taxi instructions and do not indicate that you have received the ATIS, the ATSU will assume that you do not have the departure information and most likely will pass it to you without further request.

Conversation 1 of 3

🛬 Sywell Information
Golf **Brah-voh Al-***fah* **Tang**-go **Char**-lee
Request radio check on **wun too too day-see-mal sev**-en

🛫 Golf **Brah-voh Al**-*fah* **Tang**-go **Char**-lee
Sywell Information
Readability **fife**

🛬 Your readability fife also
Golf **Brah-voh Al**-*fah* **Tang**-go **Char**-lee

Conversation 2 of 3

🛬 Golf **Brah-voh Al**-*fah* **Tang**-go **Char**-lee
Request departure information

🛫 Golf **Brah-voh Al**-*fah* **Tang**-go **Char**-lee
Runway **ze-ro tree**
Surface wind **ze-ro too ze-ro** degrees at **wun fife** knots
QNH **wun ze-ro wun too** millibars
QFE Runway **ze-ro tree,** **nin**-er **nin**-er **ait** millibars

🛬 Runway **ze-ro tree**
QNH **wun ze-ro wun too** millibars
QFE Runway **ze-ro tree, nin**-er **nin**-er **ait** millibars
Golf **Brah-voh Al**-*fah* **Tang**-go **Char**-lee

Conversation 3 of 3

🛬 Golf **Brah-voh Al**-*fah* **Tang**-go **Char**-lee
Taxiing for runway ze-ro tree
VFR flight to the northeast

🛫 Roger
Golf **Brah-voh Al**-*fah* **Tang**-go **Char**-lee

Conversations 1, 2, 3 combined

🛬 Sywell Information
Golf **Brah-voh Al**-*fah* **Tang**-go **Char**-lee
Request radio check on **wun too too day-see-mal sev**-en, and taxi instructions
VFR flight to the northeast

🛫 Golf **Brah-voh Al**-*fah* **Tang**-go **Char**-lee
Sywell Information
Readability **fife**
Runway **ze-ro tree**
Surface wind **ze-ro too ze-ro** degrees at **wun fife** knots
QNH **wun ze-ro wun too** millibars
QFE Runway **ze-ro tree, nin**-er **nin**-er **ait** millibars

🛬 Readability five also
Taxiing for runway **ze-ro tree**
QNH **wun ze-ro wun too** millibars
QFE Runway **ze-ro tree, nin**-er **nin**-er **ait** millibars
Golf **Brah-voh Al**-*fah* **Tang**-go **Char**-lee

🛫 Roger
Golf **Brah-voh Al**-*fah* **Tang**-go **Char**-lee

■ Figure 3-8 **Separate calls in the parked position (left); and a combined call (right). Combined calls are obviously more efficient.**

If at any time you are having trouble reading ATSU messages, then the readability scale can be used to describe the degree of difficulty.

mumble mumble too tousand squeal squeal take-off

Blackpool Tower
Golf **Brah-voh Al**-*fah* **Tang**-go **Char**-lee
Readability **wun**
Say again

Golf Brah-voh Al-*fah* **Tang**-go **Char**-lee
Blackpool Tower
Now on the standby transmitter
I say again
Climb to altitude **too tousand**
Cleared for take-off

Climb to altitude **too tousand**
Cleared for take-off
Golf **Brah-voh Al**-*fah* **Tang**-go **Char**-lee

■ *Figure 3-9* **Re-establishing good two-way communications**

Listening Out

Having made contact on a particular frequency, you should listen out on that frequency for any messages directed at you. When listening out, take note of any messages to or from other nearby aircraft so that you can build up a picture of the overall situation, known as situational awareness. If there are no transmissions on your frequency for a considerable time, say 5 or 10 minutes, you can always request a radio check to confirm adequate two-way communications still exist.

> *Always keep an ear cocked for your callsign.*

Transferring Frequencies

☐ **Normally you will be advised** when to change to a new ATSU and given its frequency. Acknowledge this by repeating the frequency followed by your callsign, and then make the transfer.

☐ **Initiate contact** on the new frequency by using the ATSU's name, followed by your callsign.

> ***"Contact ..."*** *means change to the next station, who has been given your flight details.*

Golf **Tang**-go **Ecks**-ray **See**-air-rah **Foks**-trot
Contact Manchester Approach on
wun wun nin-er **day-see-mal fow**-er

Manchester Approach on
wun wun nin-er **day-see-mal fow**-er
Golf **Tang**-go **Ecks**-ray **See**-air-rah **Foks**-trot

changes frequency

Manchester Approach
Golf **Tang**-go **Ecks**-ray **See**-air-rah **Foks**-trot

Golf **Tang**-go **Ecks**-ray **See**-air-rah **Foks**-trot
Manchester Approach, I have your details
Pass your message

Approach   ATC

■ *Figure 3-10* **Knowing you are transferring to an ATC frequency**

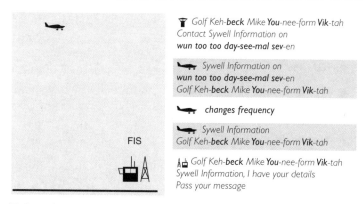

■ *Figure 3-11* **Knowing you are transferring to an FIS frequency**

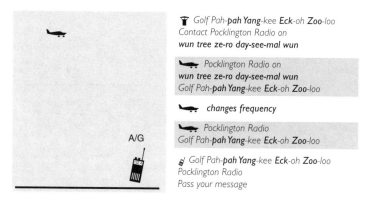

■ *Figure 3-12* **Knowing you are transferring to an A/G frequency**

Passing Your Flight Details

Sometimes an ATSU transferring you to a new frequency will have already passed your flight details to the new ATSU. This can happen out of your hearing by telephone, or by paper or voice if the officers are both sitting in one room. The Approach and Tower and Ground controllers in a control tower are often within earshot, as are two officers in the one room at London Centre which looks after a large part of the southern UK. In such cases, the new frequency will know all about you even before you come on to that frequency.

> *"Freecall ..." means change frequency to the next station, and your details have **not** been passed on.*

On other occasions, the new ATSU may *not* have received your flight details. In such cases, you should **freecall** the ATSU. A freecall is basically a 'cold' call, i.e. a call not expected by the ATSU. In a freecall to a new ATSU you would state the name of the ATSU followed by your callsign. Most likely the ATSU will then ask you to "Pass your message" or "Pass your details".

Pass your flight details in the following order: callsign, aircraft type, then **PHACER**.

☐ **Callsign**

☐ **Aircraft type**

☐ **P** **Position** (where appropriate, you can include departure point and destination, e.g. "PA-28 from Exeter to Eaglescott").

☐ **H** **Heading**

☐ **A** **Altitude** (or flight level).

☐ **C** **Conditions** (VFR or IFR).

☐ **E** **Estimate** (estimated time over your next en route position or at the destination aerodrome).

☐ **R** **Request** (if any, or state your destination or intentions).

Prestwick Approach
Golf Al-fah Brah-voh Char-lee Dell-tah

↘ *Golf Al-fah Brah-voh Char-lee Dell-tah*
Prestwick Approach
Pass your details

Golf Al-fah Brah-voh Char-lee Dell-tah
Warrior
P *wun ze-ro miles south of Turnberry*
H *Heading ze-ro tree ze-ro*
A *Too tousand feet on Regional QNH wun ze-ro too fife*
C *VFR*
E *Estimate Prestwick at fow-er ait*
R *Request overfly Prestwick at too tousand, destination Strathaven*

↘ *Golf Al-fah Brah-voh Char-lee Dell-tah*
Report the zone boundary at Ayr lighthouse
Aerodrome QNH wun ze-ro too fow-er

Cleared to Strathaven at too tousand
Wilco
Regional QNH wun ze-ro too fow-er
Golf Al-fah Brah-voh Char-lee Dell-tah

■ *Figure 3-13* **Passing flight details**

Priority of Messages

Some messages are more important than others. For instance, a distress Mayday call from an aircraft experiencing a fire and making an emergency landing must take precedence over a normal operations radio call from another aircraft. The order of priority in which an ATSU will handle radio calls is as follows.

1. DISTRESS MESSAGES: Mayday, Mayday, Mayday.

2. URGENCY MESSAGES: Pan-Pan, Pan-Pan, Pan-Pan.

3. DIRECTION-FINDING MESSAGES: QDM (homing), QDR, QTE.

4. **FLIGHT SAFETY MESSAGES:** Operator messages or meteorological messages of *immediate* concern to an aircraft in flight, e.g. flight plan changes, reports of windshear or thunderstorms.

5. **METEOROLOGICAL MESSAGES:** Aerodrome or en route weather information to an aircraft *not* of immediate safety concern.

6. **FLIGHT REGULATORY MESSAGES:** Operator messages *not* of an immediate safety nature, e.g. maintenance messages, scheduling changes for passengers or crew, aircraft movement changes.

Some of these terms may be unfamiliar to you at the moment, but most will be explained in the course of this book.

Aerodromes with FIS

A FIS is an information service, and identified by the word "Information".

A **Flight Information Service (FIS)** is an information ATSU staffed by licensed FISOs (FIS officers). FISOs are licensed and regulated by the CAA, though not to the same extent as air traffic controllers. A Flight Information Service is designated in radio calls by its name followed by the word *Information*. For instance, the FIS at Northampton (Sywell), operating on frequency 122·70 MHz, is referred to as "Sywell Information". An FIS is available at Blackbushe aerodrome and is referred to as "Blackbushe Information". FIS typically operates from a well-equipped room at an aerodrome. Take time out to visit one.

The main purpose of an FIS is to *assist* pilots to operate safely and efficiently, especially in busy areas like the Aerodrome Traffic Zone (ATZ) surrounding an aerodrome. If you are operating in the ATZ you should be in contact with the relevant Air Traffic Service Unit (ATSU), which in this case is the FIS. An FIS is *not* authorised to issue ATC clearances, but can provide:

☐ **a flight information service (FIS),** such as weather, unserviceabilities at aerodromes, etc;

☐ **a traffic service** reporting known traffic to you; and

☐ **an alerting service** ready to alert *search and rescue* (SAR) services if necessary.

No ATC Clearances are Required

At an aerodrome with an FIS you do *not* require ATC clearances to operate on the aerodrome, nor is there anyone authorised to issue clearances. With an FIS, the pilot makes the final decisions, such as when to taxi, line up, take off, and land. You should, however, show good airmanship and:

☐ **take advantage** of the information the FIS can provide; and

☐ **advise the FIS** of your planned movements.

A FIS cannot issue ATC clearances.

FISOs cannot issue ATC clearances, but they may pass clearances on behalf of other agencies, e.g. London Control. FISOs may say "Take off at your discretion", or "Land at your discretion".

Circuit Calls at FIS Aerodromes

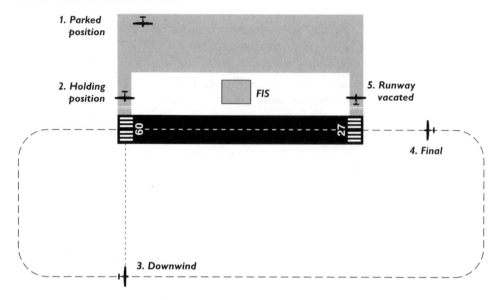

1. Parked Position

🚗 *Halfpenny Green Information*
Golf Bravo Alpha Tango Charlie
Request radio check frequency one
two three decimal zero

📅 *Golf Tango Charlie*
Halfpenny Green Information
Readability five

🚗 *Readability five also*
Golf Tango Charlie

🚗 *Golf Tango Charlie*
Ready to taxi

📅 *Golf Tango Charlie*
Runway two seven, left-hand circuit
Surface wind two seven zero at
one zero knots
QFE one zero zero three

🚗 *Golf Tango Charlie*
Taxiing to the holding point of Runway
two seven
QFE one zero zero three

2. Holding Point

An ATC Route Clearance is not
required for this flight, since we are
remaining in the circuit area, and are
surrounded by Class G airspace.

🚗 *Golf Tango Charlie*
Ready for departure

📅 *Golf Tango Charlie*
Take off at your discretion
Surface wind one two zero at
one five knots

🚗 *Taking off*
Golf Tango Charlie

3. Downwind

🚗 *Golf Tango Charlie*
Downwind to land

📅 *Golf Tango Charlie*

4. Final

🚗 *Golf Tango Charlie*
Final

📅 *Golf Tango Charlie*
Land at your discretion
Surface wind one one zero at
five knots

🚗 *Landing*
Golf Tango Charlie

5. Runway Vacated

🚗 *Golf Tango Charlie*
Runway vacated

📅 *Golf Tango Charlie*

■ *Figure 3-14* **Operating at an aerodrome with an FIS**

Aerodromes with A/G Radio

An **Air/Ground radio station (A/G)** is an information ATSU staffed by a radio operator who has qualified for a CAA certificate of competency to operate on aviation frequencies. An A/G radio station is designated in radio calls by its name followed the word *Radio*.

For instance, the A/G operating at Pocklington, operating on frequency 130·1 MHz, is referred to as "Pocklington Radio". The Air/Ground service provided at Elstree aerodrome is called "Elstree Radio".

The radio operators are not licensed, nor are they closely supervised by the CAA. This is not to say that they are not good, but that the minimum requirements for an Air/Ground radio operator are not as high as for air traffic controllers or flight information service officers. The level of radio competency could be about that of an average pilot, and the level of service provided will not be as high as that from an FIS, since there may not be any sophisticated equipment available. An A/G may be able to provide only a very basic information service. Typically, A/G radio operates from a small room at an aerodrome, but it could also just be from a mobile radio.

An A/G radio operator can provide:
- **a basic information service,** such as weather, unserviceabilities at the aerodrome, etc;
- **a basic traffic service** (reporting known traffic to you); and
- **an alerting service** (ready to alert *search and rescue* (SAR) services if necessary).

No ATC Clearances are Required

At an aerodrome with an A/G radio station you do *not* require ATC clearances to operate, nor is there anyone authorised to issue clearances. You should, however:
- **take advantage** of the information that the A/G radio station operator can provide; and
- **advise** the A/G of your planned movements.

An A/G radio station operator is not authorised to issue ATC clearances, nor will an A/G radio operator go as far as to say "Take off at your discretion", as would a flight information service officer (FISO). However, like FISOs, A/G operators may pass clearances on behalf of other agencies.

Circuit Calls at A/G Aerodromes

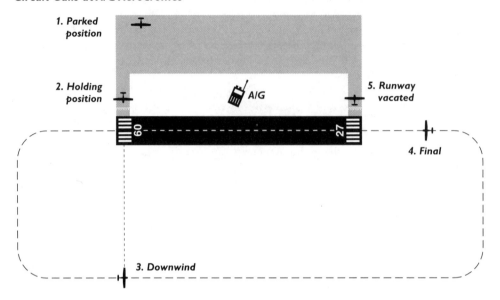

1. Parked Position

 Huddersfield Radio
Golf Bravo Alpha Tango Charlie
Request radio check on frequency one
two two decimal two

🛩️ Golf Tango Charlie
Huddersfield Radio
Readability five

 Readability five also
Golf Tango Charlie

 Golf Tango Charlie
Request departure information

🛩️ Golf Tango Charlie
Runway zero seven in use
QNH one zero two zero
QFE nine nine two millibars

 Runway zero seven
QNH one zero two zero
QFE nine nine two millibars
Golf Tango Charlie

 Golf Tango Charlie
Taxiing to Runway zero seven

🛩️ Roger
Golf Tango Charlie

Note You could combine the above
calls by saying "Golf Tango Charlie,
ready to taxi."

2. Holding Point

An ATC Route Clearance is not
required, since we are remaining in
the circuit area, and are surrounded
by Class G airspace.

 Golf Tango Charlie
Ready for departure

🛩️ Golf Tango Charlie
I have no known traffic
Surface wind zero five zero at
one zero knots

 Golf Tango Charlie
Rolling

3. Downwind

 Golf Tango Charlie
Downwind to land

🛩️ Golf Tango Charlie

4. Final

 Golf Tango Charlie
Final

🛩️ Golf Tango Charlie
Surface wind zero eight zero at
one five knots

 Golf Tango Charlie

5. Runway Vacated

 Golf Tango Charlie
Runway vacated

🛩️ Golf Tango Charlie

■ Figure 3-15 **Operating at an aerodrome with an A/G radio**

Aerodromes with No Radio Facilities

At an aerodrome where there is no radio station, you are responsible for everything and have to gather your own information, such as wind direction, suitable runway, and other traffic in the area.

Since there is no radio station to address your radio calls to, it is appropriate to make an *"... radio"* call to all traffic in the area using a suitable frequency, say that of the nearest ATSU or London Information or Scottish Information.

Old Warden (Biggleswade) has an Air/Ground radio station, but it not always manned. At such times when it is not operating, it would be appropriate to make your advisory calls addressed to "Old Warden Radio". This informs other aircraft in the area of your intentions.

No ATC Clearances are Required

At an aerodrome with no radio station you do *not* require ATC clearances to operate, nor is there anyone authorised to issue clearances or to provide you with any information. You should, however, *advise* all traffic in the area of your planned movements.

Aerodromes with an ATC Service

An ATC aerodrome is just that. It has an active control tower staffed by highly qualified air traffic controllers, and provides an **Air Traffic Control (ATC)** service. ATC is, of course, authorised to issue ATC clearances.

ATC can issue ATC clearances.

Each air traffic controller has completed a demanding CAA course, is licensed, and is closely supervised by the CAA. They may have sophisticated equipment, such as radar, available for their use.

An ATC unit can provide:
- **a control service** (at applicable aerodromes and in controlled airspace);
- **a flight information service** (FIS), providing information such as weather, any unserviceabilities at aerodromes, etc;
- **a traffic service** (reporting known traffic to you); and
- **an alerting service** (ready to alert *search and rescue* (SAR) services if necessary).

*ATC is a **control** and an **information** service, and identified by a functional word such as "Tower".*

An ATC unit is designated in radio calls by its place name followed by its function. For instance, there are several ATC frequencies at Manchester airport, such as Manchester *Ground,* Manchester *Tower* and Manchester *Approach*. Other ATC units are *Director,* and *Radar*.

Circuit Calls at ATC Aerodromes

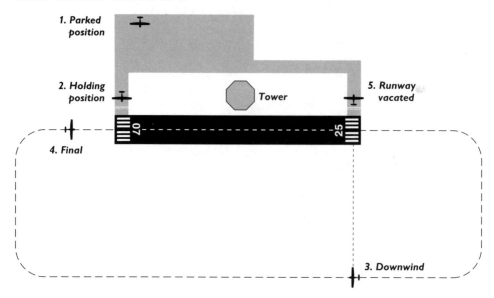

1. Parked Position

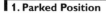 Blackpool Tower
Golf Bravo Alpha Tango Charlie
Request radio check on frequency one
one eight decimal four and departure
information

🕱 Golf Tango Charlie
Readability five
Runway zero seven
Surface wind zero eight zero at
one zero knots
QNH one zero one zero
Thunderstorms one zero miles to the
northeast
Taxi to the hold of zero seven via
taxiways Bravo and Alpha

🛩 Runway zero seven
QNH one zero one zero
Taxi to hold of zero seven via Bravo
and Alpha
Golf Tango Charlie

2. Holding Point

An ATC Route Clearance is not
required for this flight, since we are
remaining in the circuit area.

🛩 Golf Tango Charlie
Ready for departure

🕱 Golf Tango Charlie
Cleared for take-off

🛩 Cleared for take-off
Golf Tango Charlie

3. Downwind

🛩 Golf Tango Charlie
Downwind

🕱 Golf Tango Charlie
Report final

🛩 Wilco
Golf Tango Charlie

4. Final

🛩 Golf Tango Charlie
Final

🕱 Golf Tango Charlie
Cleared to land

🛩 Cleared to land
Golf Tango Charlie

5. Runway Vacated

🛩 Golf Tango Charlie
Runway vacated

🕱 Golf Tango Charlie

■ Figure 3-16 **Operating at an aerodrome with an ATC service**

Aerodrome Traffic Zones (ATZs)

The airspace surrounding an aerodrome is known as an **Aerodrome Traffic Zone (ATZ)**. ATZs are designed to protect air traffic around aerodromes, and commonly have the following dimensions.

ATZs operate at most UK civil and military aerodromes. ATZs are not allocated a specific airspace classification, but adopt the class of the airspace within which they are located.

The standard dimensions of an ATZ are:
- **from ground level to 2,000 feet** above aerodrome level (aal);
- **within the area** bounded by a circle of radius:
  - (i) **2 nm,** where length of longest runway is 1,850 m or less; or
  - (ii) **2.5 nm,** where longest runway is greater than 1,850 m;
  - the centre of the circle is the mid-point of the longest runway.

NOTE Some 2 nm ATZs are expanded to 2.5 nm radius to provide at least 1.5 nm clearance from the end of all runways. Such exceptions are listed in AIP ENR.

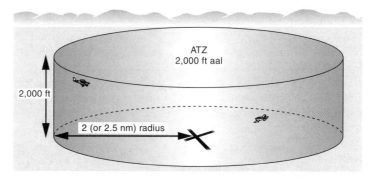

■ *Figure 3-17* **Dimensions of an Aerodrome Traffic Zone (ATZ)**

Rules to Enable Safe Flight in an ATZ (Rule 39)

Refer to Rule 39 of The Rules of the Air in the Air Navigation Order (ANO) about flight in ATZs. An aircraft must not fly within an Aerodrome Traffic Zone unless the pilot-in-command:
- **has the permission** of the appropriate Air Traffic Control (ATC) unit; or
- **where there is no ATC unit,** has obtained sufficient information from the Flight Information Service (FIS) unit to enable flight within the zone to be made safely; or
- **where there is no ATC or FIS unit,** has obtained information from the Air/Ground (A/G) radio station at the aerodrome to enable the flight to be made safely.

Aircraft flying in an ATZ must:
- ☐ **maintain a continuous watch** on the appropriate radio frequency notified for communications at the aerodrome or, if this is not possible, keep a watch for visual instructions;
- ☐ **where the aircraft has radio,** give position and height to the aerodrome ATC or FIS unit or A/G radio station, as the case may be, on entering and leaving the zone; and
- ☐ **make any other standard calls** or requested calls.

These requirements apply at:
- ☐ **a Government aerodrome** at such times as are notified (usually H24, i.e. continuous);
- ☐ **an aerodrome having an ATC or FIS unit,** during the hours of watch;
- ☐ **a licensed aerodrome having A/G radio communication** with aircraft, during the hours of watch, and whose hours of availability are detailed in AIP AD.

NOTE When an ATZ is established in a class of airspace having more stringent rules than those of an ATZ (e.g. Class D airspace), then the more stringent rules take precedence.

Depiction of Aerodrome Traffic Zones

ATZ locations and details (radius, hours of watch and radio frequency) are listed in AIP ENR and any amendments notified by NOTAM (Notice to Airmen). They are also shown on new UK 1:500,000 and CAA 1:250,000 aeronautical charts; however, ATZs located wholly in controlled airspace are not shown on 1:500,000 charts to avoid congestion on the chart. *Pooley's Flight Guide* lists aerodrome operating hours; in the main these coincide with ATZ hours.

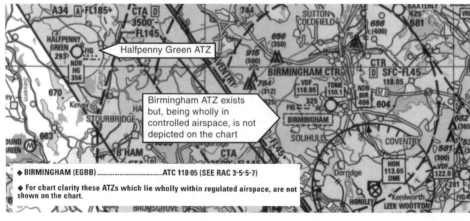

■ *Figure 3-18* ***ATZs outside controlled airspace are shown on***
the 1:500,000 chart

CAA 1:500,000 charts have a list of Aerodrome Traffic Zones printed on the left-hand side, along with the Air/Ground frequency of the responsible radio unit at the aerodrome.

UK AERODROME TRAFFIC ZONES (ATZs)
SERVICES/RT FREQUENCIES (MHz). UK AIP RAC 3-9-2

AERODROME TRAFFIC ZONE (ATZ), is regulated airspace from the surface to 2000ft AAL within a circle centred on the notified mid-point of the longest runway, radius 2·0NM (RW≤ 1850m) or 2·5NM (RW≥1850m), where Mandatory Rules apply.
Most Government Aerodrome ATZs are H24.

```
ABERPORTH (EGUC)....................................AFIS 122·15
ANDREWSFIELD(EGSL)...............................A/G 130·55(SEE RAC 3-5-21-17)
BARKSTON HEATH (EGYE) .........................INITIAL CALL ATC CRANWELL 119·0
BEMBRIDGE (EGHJ) ...................................AFIS & A/G 123·25
BENSON (EGUB)...........................................ATC 120·9
* BIGGIN HILL (EGKB)...................................ATC 129·4
◆ BIRMINGHAM (EGBB)................................ATC 118·05 (SEE RAC 3-5-5-7)
BLACKBUSHE (EGLK)...................................INITIAL CALL FARNBOROUGH/ODIHAM APP
                                                    125·25, AFIS & A/G 122·3 (SEE AGA 3-1)
BODMIN (EGLA) ...........................................A/G 122·7
BOSCOMBE DOWN (EGDM)........................ATC 126·7 (SEE RAC 3-9-2-4)
BOURN (EGSN) .............................................A/G 129·8
◆ BOURNEMOUTH/Hurn (EGHH)..................ATC 119·625 (SEE RAC 3-5-29-1)
◆ BRISTOL (EGGD)........................................ATC128·55 (SEE RAC 3-5-7-1)
◆ BRIZE NORTON (EGVN) ............................ATC 119·0 (SEE RAC 3-5-8-1)
CAERNARFON (EGCK)..................................ATC VALLEY 134·35, A/G 122·25
                                                    (SEE UK AIP AGA 3-1-17)
```

■ *Figure 3-19* **Example list of ATZs from a CAA 1:500,000 chart**

Departing an Aerodrome and its ATZ

At an aerodrome with ATC, you will be given departure instructions, which you should follow. If unable, then advise ATC.

At a aerodrome with FIS or A/G, you may be given advice on how to depart the circuit. *You* decide, however, on the best departure path to take.

Normally you depart by:
- **extending the upwind leg** immediately after take-off to circuit pattern altitude, then departing in the direction you want, avoiding conflict with any aircraft in the circuit pattern; or
- **continue climb in the circuit pattern** until over the top of the aerodrome at 2,000 feet aal (i.e. 1,000 feet above the pattern altitude), and then depart in any direction.

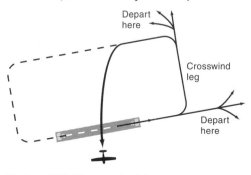

■ *Figure 3-20* **The standard departure**

Arriving at an Aerodrome and its ATZ

Before entering an ATZ, you should:

- ☐ **Listen to the ATIS** if available.
- ☐ **Obtain an ATC route clearance** if you have to enter controlled airspace Class A–D (which may exist some distance before you get to the ATZ).
- ☐ **Call at 15 nm or 5 minutes flying time** (whichever is greater) from the ATZ boundary with callsign, aircraft type, then **PHACER**: P: position; H: heading; A: altitude; C: conditions (VFR or IFR); E: estimated time at the aerodrome; and R: request.
- ☐ **Plan an entry** into the circuit pattern.

At a aerodrome with ATC, the first frequency you would contact is "Approach" (otherwise "Tower"). ATC will give you joining **instructions,** which you should follow. If unable, advise ATC. Once in the circuit, make the normal R/T calls plus any others requested. Do not land at an ATC aerodrome without having heard "Cleared to land" directed at you from the tower.

At an aerodrome with FIS or A/G, you should call the FIS ("Information") or A/G ("Radio") at 15 nm or 5 minutes before reaching the ATZ boundary. The FIS or A/G may give you **information** on which runway is in use and how to enter the circuit pattern. You should carry out a **standard join,** which is to overfly the field at 1,000 feet above the circuit altitude (i.e. 2,000 feet above aerodrome level), and then descend on the dead side of the circuit to the normal pattern altitude. Make a call when "descending dead side", and then at the usual points in the circuit.

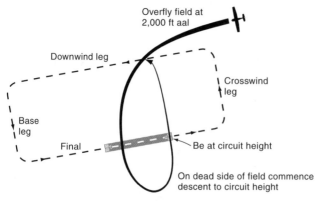

■ Figure 3-21 **The standard overhead join**

FIS may give you advice to "Land at your discretion", and give you the current surface wind. A/G may just give you the current surface wind. At a no-radio aerodrome you will get nothing.

Military Aerodromes

Military aerodromes are surrounded by a normal ATZ the same as civil aerodromes; however, there is also a **Military Aerodrome Traffic Zone (MATZ)** larger than the ATZ to allow more room for fast aircraft to manoeuvre, and to make instrument approaches. Each MATZ contains a smaller ATZ, and the normal ATZ rules apply within this ATZ, i.e. you should be in radio contact with the aerodrome ATSU. The ATZ rules must be obeyed at all times, even when the MATZ and ATSU is *not* active.

NOTE Requests to transit a MATZ should be made at least 15 nm or 5 minutes flying time before reaching the zone boundary, whichever is sooner.

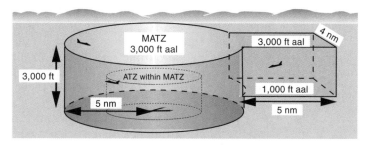

■ *Figure 3-22* **A Military Aerodrome Traffic Zone (MATZ)**

Military aeroplanes may fly a circuit pattern different from the normal civil circuit pattern.

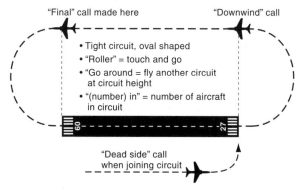

■ *Figure 3-23* **The military circuit pattern**

After the initial climbout, a military aircraft may fly a steady banked turn onto the downwind leg (instead of a straight cross-wind leg). After a straight downwind leg to abeam or past the touchdown end of the runway, the military aeroplane may commence a steady banked turn onto a very short final leg (instead of flying a straight base leg). The "downwind" radio call is made in the usual position abeam the upwind end of the runway, but the "final" call is made at the end of the downwind leg just before commencing the steady turn all the way around on to final. In a civil circuit, the "final" call is made after you have turned onto final.

Military terminology is also a little different from civil terminology. "Go around" from a military controller means "fly another circuit." "Three in" means that there are three aircraft in the circuit pattern. "To roll" or a "roller" means to fly a touch-and-go landing (i.e. to keep rolling).

An Example Flight to the Training Area

During your early flying training your flight instructor will be showing you how to taxi from the parked position into a take-off position on the runway. Then you will take off, depart the circuit pattern, and fly away to the training area. After the air exercise is completed, you will return inbound to the aerodrome, join the circuit pattern for an approach and landing, and then vacate the runway. You can commence learning the correct radio calls during these flights.

The purpose of this section is to show you a typical example of a flight to and from the training area upon which you can build. The aerodrome illustrated has an air traffic control service. This means that you need approval to taxi, and ATC clearances to enter and operate on the runway.

> *Handling the radio correctly and knowing what to say will enable your flight training to progress more quickly.*

You may not be familiar with all of the terminology that you come across in this chapter; however, it will be introduced and explained later in the book.

In the Parked Position

With the aeroplane in the parked position, you can listen to the current aerodrome information on the ATIS (automatic terminal information service) frequency if one is available, otherwise the tower will pass you the departure information when you taxi. You can, if desired, request a radio check from the tower. At some major aerodromes you may have to ask for approval to start your engine. When your engine is running, you can request approval to taxi.

> *Remember to listen out before transmitting to avoid cutting across other transmissions.*

When you receive approval to taxi, you should acknowledge the instructions, followed by your callsign. Although a read back of taxi instructions is not strictly required, it is good airmanship to do so at ATC aerodromes. In this example, you are at Blackpool airport and flying an aeroplane registered G-BATC with the callsign *Golf Bravo Alpha Tango Charlie.*

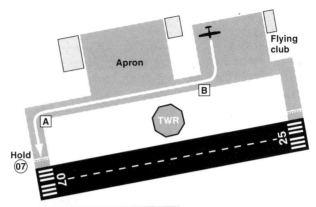

✈ Blackpool Tower
*Golf Brah-voh Al-fah Tang-go Char-lee
Request radio check and taxi instructions
from the flying club*

🎙 *Golf Tang-go Char-lee
Readability fife
Taxi to the hold of Runway ze-ro sev-en
via taxiway Brah-voh and Al-fah
QNH wun ze-ro too ze-ro*

✈ *Taxi to the hold of ze-ro sev-en
via Brah-voh and Al-fah
QNH wun ze-ro too ze-ro*

Note *At your airfield there may be a
requirement to add the flight details, e.g.
"VFR training flight to the north-east, two
people on board, for one hour, endurance
two hours."*

*You may have passed these details
when booking out by phone or by filing a
flight plan. Consult your instructor for your
particular airfield requirements.*

■ Figure 3-24 **Taxi call**

Taxiing

Unless otherwise specified, taxi instructions from the tower will
have a clearance limit, which is normally the holding point for the
runway in use. You may be given taxi instructions like:

- ☐ **"Taxi to the holding point two seven"** (approval to taxi to
  the holding area of the runway, *not* onto the runway itself);
- ☐ **"Cross runway three six"** (approval to cross an active runway);
- ☐ **"Enter runway zero seven"** (approval to enter an active runway);
- ☐ **"Line-up"** (enter the runway and taxi into the line-up position);
- ☐ **"Backtrack"** (enter the runway and taxi along it to the beginning of the take-off run); or
- ☐ **"Vacate"** (taxi off the runway).

You must read back these instructions, followed by your callsign.

At the Holding Point

You would normally stop your taxiing at the holding point for the runway or in the holding bay where you can perform your engine run-up checks and the pre-take-off checklist. If possible, you would do these checks parked facing into the wind.

If you will immediately be entering controlled airspace Class A–D, then you should request an **ATC route clearance** (also called a departure clearance) to do so. (This is *not* a take-off clearance!)

When ready for departure turn and face the final approach path so that you have a good view of other aircraft about to land on the runway. Call the tower and inform them "Golf Bravo Alpha Tango Charlie, ready for departure". Note that the term *take-off* is not used at this stage, but only when the tower finally says "(callsign) cleared for take-off".

Check final approach for traffic before making your holding point call.

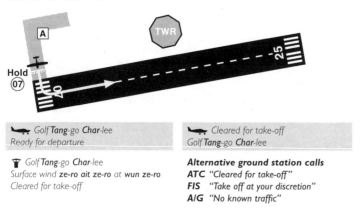

Golf *Tang-go* **Char**-lee
Ready for departure

Cleared for take-off
Golf *Tang-go* **Char**-lee

Golf *Tang-go* **Char**-lee
Surface wind **ze-ro ait ze-ro** *at* **wun ze-ro**
Cleared for take-off

Alternative ground station calls
ATC "Cleared for take-off"
FIS "Take off at your discretion"
A/G "No known traffic"

■ *Figure 3-25* **Ready for departure and take-off calls**

After making your call, "Golf Bravo Alpha Tango Charlie, ready for departure", you may get one of a number of responses from the tower, such as:

- ☐ **"Golf Tango Charlie, hold position"** (do not move).
- ☐ **"Golf Tango Charlie, line-up"** (enter the runway and line-up ready for take-off – but do not start the take-off).
- ☐ **"Golf Tango Charlie, line-up and wait"** (same meaning as above).
- ☐ **"Golf Tango Charlie, backtrack"** (enter the runway and taxi back along it to the start of the runway to where you want to start your take-off run, then turn into the line-up position and stop).
- ☐ **"Golf Tango Charlie, vacate"** (taxi off the runway).

You may be given a **conditional line-up clearance**, for instance to line-up after an aircraft currently on final approach has landed. A conditional clearance is given in the order:

- ☐ **Callsign.**
- ☐ **Condition.**
- ☐ **Identification of conditional subject.**
- ☐ **Instruction.**

For example: "Golf Tango Charlie, after the landing PA-28 on final approach has landed, enter, backtrack, line-up, and wait." Conditional clearances must be read back.

Departing the Aerodrome Traffic Zone (ATZ)

A certain amount of airspace surrounding most aerodromes in the UK is designated as an Aerodrome Traffic Zone (ATZ, pronounced *ay-tee-zed*). This is to provide some order for the intense aerial activity that can occur at or near aerodromes on occasions.

After you take off, you will manoeuvre to depart the ATZ, which may or may not be busy, and proceed to the training area for your air exercise.

Departing the Circuit

Follow any ATC instructions given. If ATC is not active at your field, plan a circuit departure that will not conflict with other aircraft in the circuit or with any aircraft joining it. Also, follow any special procedures applicable to your field.

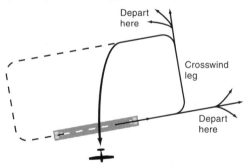

■ *Figure 3-26* **Departing the circuit**

Departure is normally from the crosswind leg unless otherwise specified.

Another way to depart an ATZ is to extend the upwind leg as you climb out after take-off and then, when clear of other circuit traffic, set heading for the local training area or the first leg of your cross-country flight. Another method is to continue the climb in the circuit direction to the overhead, 1,000 feet *above* circuit height, which at most aerodromes is at 2,000 feet aal or above.

Once outbound to the local training area, ensure that QNH is set in the subscale so that the altimeter will read altitude above mean sea level (amsl). Heights of mountains, radio masts, etc. are shown on charts as heights amsl.

Figure 3-27 shows the radio calls used when departing an ATZ.

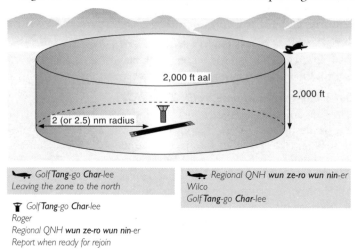

Golf Tang-go Char-lee
Leaving the zone to the north

Golf Tang-go Char-lee
Roger
Regional QNH wun ze-ro wun nin-er
Report when ready for rejoin

Regional QNH wun ze-ro wun nin-er
Wilco
Golf Tang-go Char-lee

■ *Figure 3-27* **Calls for departing the ATZ for the training area**

Having left the ATZ, it is good airmanship when in the training area to keep a listening watch on the local frequency, or call for a Lower Airspace Radar Service (see page 80).

Returning to the Aerodrome from the Training Area

You have finished your air exercise in the training area and want to return the airfield. Firstly, orientate yourself as to where you are in relation to the airfield (you should always know where you are!), and then plan your return. Listen to the ATIS or request the aerodrome information.

Joining the Circuit

You should always know the elevation of the aerodrome you intend to use. Approaching the circuit, set the altimeter subscale to the aerodrome QNH or QFE. With QNH set, the altimeter will read altitude *above mean sea level* (elevation of the runway above mean sea level at touchdown); with QFE set, it will read height above runway level (zero feet at touchdown). See Figure 3-28.

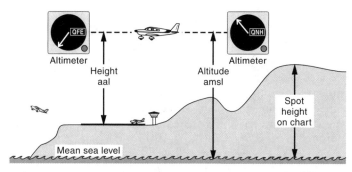

■ *Figure 3-28* **The altimeter reads altitude above mean sea level (amsl) with QNH set; height above aerodrome level (aal) with QFE set**

When arriving at the aerodrome, follow any Air Traffic Control instructions given. If ATC is not active at your field, plan an arrival that will not conflict with other aircraft in the circuit (preferably a standard join) and follow any special procedures applicable to that field.

If your aerodrome has a Flight Information Service (FIS) or an Air/Ground radio station (A/G), they may be able to inform you of weather conditions at the aerodrome and any known traffic.

The radio calls used are as follows.

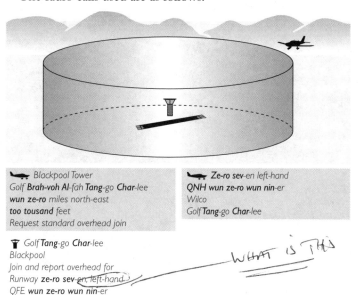

Blackpool Tower
Golf **Brah-voh Al-fah Tang**-go **Char**-lee
wun ze-ro *miles north-east*
too tousand *feet*
Request standard overhead join

Ze-ro sev-en *left-hand*
QNH **wun ze-ro wun nin**-er
Wilco
Golf **Tang**-go **Char**-lee

Golf **Tang**-go **Char**-lee
Blackpool
Join and report overhead for
Runway **ze-ro sev**-en, *left-hand*
QFE **wun ze-ro wun nin**-er

WHAT IS THIS

■ *Figure 3-29* **Requesting a standard overhead join**

If there is no control tower, FIS or A/G at your aerodrome then carry out a standard join, see Figure 3-30.

The Standard Overhead Join

The standard overhead join is a very good way to join a circuit, especially in a non-radio environment. As you fly overhead the airfield at 1,000 feet above the circuit height, which is usually 2,000 feet above aerodrome level, you can check:

> Some airfields have different circuit heights. Check AIP AD or Pooley's Flight Guide.

- ☐ **the windsock** to determine which runway to use;
- ☐ **other traffic** in and around the circuit; and
- ☐ **the circuit direction,** designated in a signals area at some airports.

The standard overhead join is a safe and convenient way to get a picture of what is happening at the airfield and to prepare for joining the circuit pattern for an approach and landing.

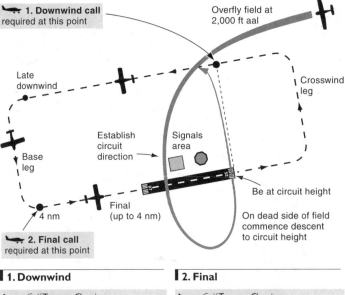

> Exercise caution when you cross the upwind leg at aerodromes with long runways. Aircraft taking off may reach circuit height by the end of the runway.

1. Downwind call required at this point

Overfly field at 2,000 ft aal

Late downwind

Crosswind leg

Establish circuit direction →

Signals area

Base leg

4 nm

Final (up to 4 nm)

Be at circuit height

On dead side of field commence descent to circuit height

2. Final call required at this point

1. Downwind	**2. Final**
🛩 *Golf Tang-go **Char-lee*** *Downwind to land*	🛩 *Golf Tang-go **Char-lee*** *Final*
🗼 *Golf Tang-go **Char-lee*** *Report final*	🗼 *Golf Tang-go **Char-lee*** *Wind **ze-ro ait ze-ro** at **wun ze-ro*** *Cleared to land*
🛩 *Wilco* *Golf Tang-go **Char-lee***	🛩 *Cleared to land* *Golf Tang-go **Char-lee***

■ *Figure 3-30* **Standard overhead join – calls for downwind and final**

Other Approach and Join Methods

The air traffic controller (ATC) or the flight information service officer (FISO) may give you a more direct approach: ATC by controlling traffic in the zone and slotting you in; or FISO by passing you information on traffic and the runway in use, making a direct join without an overfly more convenient.

Bearing this in mind, you could be asked to join downwind, on base leg, or even straight-in. Remember to always keep a good lookout, particularly in the circuit direction. For example, other traffic may appear on base leg as you join straight-in. Aircraft already in the circuit have priority over those joining.

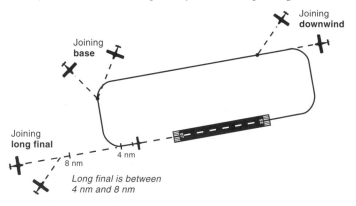

■ *Figure 3-31* **Joining the circuit**

Taxiing in from the Runway

Once you have landed, a taxi call may be required. For instance, you may want to refuel the aircraft before taxiing back to the club. It is also good airmanship to advise "runway vacated".

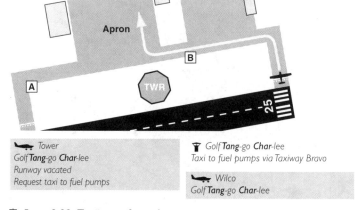

■ *Figure 3-32* **Taxiing in from the runway**

After reading the radio call summaries on the following pages,
complete: **Exercises 3 – Aerodrome Operations.**

Circuit Radio Calls

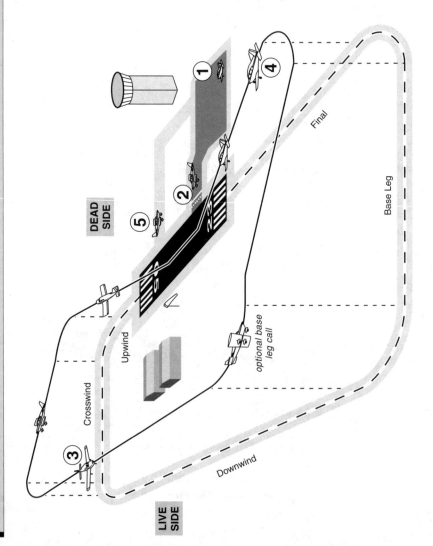

Wake Turbulence

If large aircraft are operating at your aerodrome, you must beware of wake turbulence. ATC will separate light aircraft from heavy jets by up to five minutes to avoid wake turbulence.

Refer to your flying instructor for guidance.

CAA separation requirements are detailed in a pink AIC and in a CAA safety sense leaflet.

See also Vol. 4 of The Air Pilot's Manual.

Circuit Radio Calls

1. On the Apron

🗣 Coventry Tower
Golf Bravo Alpha Tango Charlie
On the apron
Request taxi

📻 Golf Bravo Alpha Tango Charlie
Coventry Tower
Taxi to the holding point of
Runway two three
QFE one zero one eight

🗣 Taxi to the hold of two three
QFE one zero one eight
Golf Bravo Alpha Tango Charlie

At the holding point carry out power
checks and pre-flight checks then turn to
face the approach.

2. Holding Point

🗣 Golf Bravo Alpha Tango Charlie
Ready for departure

📻 Golf Tango Charlie
Back-track and line-up Runway 23

🗣 Back-track and line-up Runway 23
Golf Tango Charlie

Enter the runway, back-track to the 23
numbers, turn around and line-up in the
take-off direction on the centreline and
wait.

Look out for other traffic.

📻 Golf Tango Charlie
Surface wind two four zero degrees at one
zero knots
Cleared for take-off

🗣 Cleared for take-off
Golf Tango Charlie

3. Downwind

Abeam the upwind end of the landing
runway, make the downwind call with your
intentions, e.g. "Downwind for touch-and-
go,""Downwind for land," or "Downwind
for go-around."

🗣 Golf Tango Charlie
Downwind for touch-and-go

📻 Golf Tango Charlie
Report turning base
You are number two to a PA-28 on
base leg

🗣 Wilco
Visual number one
Golf Tango Charlie

Do not worry if you cannot make your
downwind call in the exact position abeam
the upwind end of the runway. You can
always make it a 'mid-downwind' or a 'late-
downwind' call.

Base Leg (if requested)

As you are about to turn base, make a
'turning base leg' call if a base call was
requested by ATC.

🗣 Golf Tango Charlie
Turning base leg

📻 Golf Tango Charlie
Continue approach
One on the runway

🗣 Wilco
Golf Tango Charlie

4. Final

🗣 Golf Tango Charlie
Final

📻 Golf Tango Charlie
Surface wind three four zero degrees at
eight knots
Cleared touch-and-go

🗣 Cleared touch-and-go
Golf Tango Charlie

5. Runway Vacated

A runway vacated call is not required
in this case since you are flying a
touch-and-go.

"Land After" Instructions

Under certain conditions* the controller may
give a "land after" instruction when a
preceding aircraft has already landed but
has not yet vacated the runway.

If the pilot has the subject aircraft in sight
and can maintain safe separation he may
land at his discretion.

Your response to the controller on deciding
to follow a "land after" instruction would be
"G-TC landing after the [Cessna etc]".

A "land after" instruction is not a clearance
so do not respond "G-TC cleared to land
after".

This procedure does not apply if the
preceding aircraft is making a departure or
touch-and-go.

* Conditions for "land after" procedure:
• Daylight hours only.
• Runway state such that braking ability not
  compromised.
• Following pilot has the preceding aircraft in
  sight and can maintain adequate
  separation.
• Procedure can only be used at aerodromes
  with an Air Traffic Control service.

Go-Around Calls

Should you for some reason be unable to land, say because a vehicle enters the runway, you would have to carry out a missed approach. You or the tower may initiate a go-around. At an airfield without ATC, it is entirely up to you.

6a. Pilot-Initiated Go-Around

🛩 *Golf Tango Charlie*
Going around

📡 *Golf Tango Charlie*
Roger, report downwind

6b. Tower-Initiated Go-Around

📡 *Golf Tango Charlie*
Go-around
I say again, go-around
Acknowledge

Safely establish the aircraft in the go-around, then acknowledge Air Traffic.

Aviate, Navigate, Communicate.

🛩 *Going around*
Golf Tango Charlie

1. Missed Approach

Make a climbing turn to the dead side (to the right in this case).

Then join the circuit at the appropriate point.

For the go-around, manoeuvre your aircraft to the dead side of the circuit for the climb-out, then join the crosswind leg, then downwind. **Look out for traffic joining crosswind.**

Crosswind

Upwind

DEAD SIDE

Final

Base Leg

Downwind

LIVE SIDE

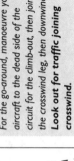

Going around

Dead side

Live side

Learning the Language
Aerodrome Information

The **weather conditions** at an aerodrome, either the *actual* weather for immediate operations or the *forecast* weather for later operations, are of vital importance to every pilot. Strong crosswinds may make a runway difficult or even impossible to use. Low cloud might make a visual circuit at a safe altitude impossible. Poor visibility might make visual flight difficult or impossible. Good weather with light winds might be nice to know about.

If you are a pilot on the ground at an aerodrome, you can of course observe the local weather and aerodrome conditions by looking at the sky, checking the windsock, noticing if it is raining or snowing or windy or foggy, noting if the runway surface is damp, wet or flooded, and so on. If you are in flight en route to a distant aerodrome, however, then you may not be able to judge the weather conditions for your approach and landing.

In general, Air Traffic Service Units (ATSUs) are equipped with measuring equipment and are able to provide you with *accurate* weather information upon which you can base your operational judgements. Whilst weather is of vital importance, other aerodrome factors (such as closed runways or taxiways) are also of importance, and this information can be made available to you by the ATSU (as well as in published NOTAMs, etc.).

Information from an ATSU

An ATSU can provide aerodrome information directly by normal **voice radio** to each pilot that requires it but, as you can imagine, this would involve a lot of repetition at busy aerodromes, a higher workload for the ATSU officer, and would block the frequency for long periods. To avoid this, two systems of **tape-recorded messages** which are periodically updated have been devised:

- ☐ **ATIS** – an automatic terminal information service for one particular aerodrome (referred to consecutively as *Information Alpha, Information Bravo, Information Charlie,* etc. as updates occur; and
- ☐ **VOLMET** – a *voice weather broadcast* for a *series* of major aerodromes in one area.

Automatic Terminal Information Service (ATIS)

The recorded ATIS (pronounced *"ay-tiss"*) is usually continuously available on a dedicated VHF-COM frequency and/or on the frequency of a nearby VOR which you can select on your VHF-NAV radio. Any recent changes in conditions can be modified on the ATIS recording or passed directly to the pilots concerned by normal voice radio. ATIS frequencies and the hours of operation are listed in AIP AD and other publications such as *Pooley's Flight Guide*. To save you time in the future, you should commit to memory the ATIS frequency for your home aerodrome. As can be seen from the illustration below, listening to the ATIS prior to taxiing or approaching an Aerodrome Traffic Zone (ATZ) significantly reduces radio time.

▌Scenario 1

Conversation 1 of 2

> 🛬 Prestwick Tower
> Golf Bravo Alpha Tango Charlie
> Request departure information

> 📡 Golf Bravo Alpha Tango Charlie
> Prestwick Tower
> Runway one three
> Surface wind one five zero degrees, one eight knots
> Visibility six kilometres
> Cloud few at one thousand two hundred feet, scattered at three thousand feet, broken at seven thousand feet
> Temperature one eight, dewpoint one five
> QNH one zero zero four millibars
> Runway one three QFE one zero zero two millibars
> Runway zero-three/two-one closed due to works in progress

> 🛬 Runway one three
> QNH one zero zero four
> Golf Bravo Alpha Tango Charlie

Conversation 2 of 2

> 🛬 Golf Bravo Alpha Tango Charlie
> Flying school apron
> Request taxi for VFR flight to Newcastle

> 📡 Golf Bravo Alpha Tango Charlie
> Taxi to Runway one three

> 🛬 Taxi to Runway one three
> Golf Bravo Alpha Tango Charlie

▌Scenario 2

Pilot has already listened to ATIS.

> 🛬 Prestwick Tower
> Golf Bravo Alpha Tango Charlie
> Flying school apron
> Information Bravo
> Request taxi for VFR flight to Newcastle

> 📡 Golf Bravo Alpha Tango Charlie
> Prestwick Tower
> Taxi to the holding point of
> Runway one three

> 🛬 Taxi to holding point of
> Runway one three
> Golf Bravo Alpha Tango Charlie

■ *Figure 4-1* **The advantage of listening to the ATIS – it saves you and the tower time**

The Format of an ATIS

The weather information contained in the ATIS is usually updated every 30 minutes following the routine weather observations taken at 20 minutes past the hour and 50 minutes past the hour at many aerodromes, and the ATIS is then given a later phonetic name, changing say from *Information Uniform* to *Information Victor* to *Information Whiskey*.

So that the aerodrome ATSU knows that you have received the latest ATIS for that aerodrome, you should specify its code identifier (e.g. *Information Whiskey*) when making first contact. If the information has changed, the ATSU will advise you of significant changes.

ATIS broadcasts are typically less than 30 seconds in duration and include:

☐ **Aerodrome name.**
☐ **ATIS identification.**
☐ **Time of origin of weather report.**

☐ **Runway(s) in use.**
☐ **Surface wind.**

☐ **Visibility.**
☐ **Instrument RVRs** if applicable *(instrumented runway visual range when visibility is very poor).*

☐ **Weather** (e.g. precipitation).
☐ **Cloud** (only cloud with a base 10,000 feet aal or lower).
☐ **Temperature and dewpoint** (if the temperature drops to the dewpoint a fog may form).

☐ **QNH.**
☐ **QFE** for the runway in use.

☐ **Trend** if applicable (e.g. NOSIG means no significant changes expected in the 2-hour period following the time of the weather observation; TEMPO means that the stated conditions might exist for temporary periods of up to 60 minutes between the stated times; BECOMING indicates that the forecast change in weather will be permanent).

☐ **Short-term information** regarding unserviceable navaids, taxiways, a displaced threshold, etc.
☐ **Any other routine information** useful to pilots using the aerodrome.

☐ **A repeat of the information identifier.**

NOTE The term CAVOK (meaning ceiling and visibility OK and pronounced *"kav-okay"*) may be used in place of visibility, weather and cloud, provided:
  – visibility is 10 kilometres or more;
  – there is no cloud below 5,000 feet aal, or below the minimum sector altitude, whichever is higher, and no cumulonimbus clouds (i.e. thunderstorms);
  – no precipitation reaching the ground, no thunderstorms, no shallow fog or low drifting snow.

A typical ATIS could be:

Belfast Information Foxtrot at time one seven two zero.
Runway in use two five.
Surface wind two six zero degrees, one four knots gusting two two knots.
Visibility one five kilometres.
Cloud – scattered at two thousand feet, broken at five thousand feet.
Temperature plus one seven, dewpoint plus one one.
QNH one zero zero zero millibars.
Runway two five QFE nine nine one millibars.
NOSIG.
Taxiway Alpha north of Taxiway Bravo closed.
Birds reported in the vicinity of threshold runway two five.
Report Information Foxtrot received on first contact with Belfast.

F 1720Z
25
260/14–22
15
S020, B050
+17/+11
1000 QNH
25 QFE 991

■ *Figure 4-2*
A shorthand summary of the Belfast ATIS

You can develop a shorthand for writing this information down, since no person is capable of retaining so much information in their short-term memory for very long. You need only write down what you feel is vital, e.g. information identifier, runway in use, wind, and QNH.

Omission of Some Words, and Non-Standard Phraseology
When there is no possibility of confusion arising, some obvious words or phrases may be omitted, such as: surface wind, degrees and knots; visibility and metres; cloud and feet; millibars.

For instance, a wind of 270/20 may be reported as "Surface wind two seven zero degrees, two zero knots"; or "Wind two seven zero degrees, two zero knots"; or "Wind two seven zero, two zero"; or simply as "Two seven zero, two zero".

Also, you may find some air traffic controllers and flight information service officers who, when recording the ATIS, use slightly nonstandard phrases. You should use your common sense to interpret these messages and, if you do not understand them, ask for clarification from the ATSU on the normal frequency.

Here is an example of an actual ATIS where slightly nonstandard phraseology with respect to time and visibility has been used.

M 1150Z
  27
  200/9
  12
  B022
  15/11
  1016 QNH
  27 QFE 995
  Portland 1013
  Cotswold 1011

■ Figure 4-3
Summary of the Bristol ATIS

> This is Bristol Information Mike.
>
> Time eleven fifty.
>
> IFR arrivals can expect radar vectors to the ILS.
>
> Runway two seven.
>
> Two zero zero magnetic, nine knots.
>
> Twelve kilometres.
>
> Broken cloud two thousand two hundred.
>
> Temperature plus fifteen, dewpoint plus eleven.
>
> QNH one zero one six.
>
> QFE Runway two seven, nine nine five millibars.
>
> Regional QNH at time thirteen hundred: Portland one zero one three; Cotswold one zero one one.
>
> Report Information Mike on first contact with Bristol Approach.

Notifying Receipt of ATIS

To avoid ATC repeating aerodrome information which you already have obtained from the tape-recorded ATIS, you should advise them that you have received "Information (code)" on first contact with the aerodrome ATSU, e.g. *Information Delta:*

☐ on the ground – before taxiing; and

☐ in the air – on your first contact with the ATSU before entering the ATZ.

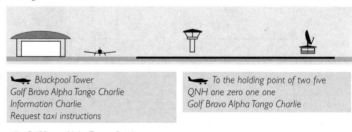

> ✈ Blackpool Tower
> Golf Bravo Alpha Tango Charlie
> Information Charlie
> Request taxi instructions

> ✈ To the holding point of two five
> QNH one zero one one
> Golf Bravo Alpha Tango Charlie

> ☗ Golf Bravo Alpha Tango Charlie
> Blackpool Tower
> Taxi to the holding point of Runway two five

■ Figure 4-4 **Informing the ATSU that you have the ATIS**

The Importance of QNH or QFE

Always ensure that your altimeter is set correctly.

One of the most vital pieces of information included in weather reports is the pressure setting to set in your altimeter pressure window (also known as the altimeter subscale).

QNH is the atmospheric pressure which, when set in the pressure window of the altimeter, causes it to read altitude, the vertical distance above mean sea level. With QNH set, the altimeter will read aerodrome elevation above mean sea level when the aircraft is on the ground at the aerodrome.

> With QNH set, the altimeter reads altitude (above mean sea level).

For example, at Land's End aerodrome with QNH set, the altimeter would read approximately 401 feet amsl (above mean sea level). To fly a circuit pattern at 1,000 feet above the aerodrome elevation, you would fly so that the altimeter (with aerodrome QNH set) indicates 'elevation + 1,000 feet', which at Land's End would be an *altitude* of 1,401 feet amsl – in practical terms 1,400 feet amsl.

QNH is the most commonly used pressure setting for aerodrome operations around the world. QNH at an aerodrome varies from hour to hour as pressure systems move across the country, and so has to be periodically updated. Regional QNH is the lowest forecast pressure for a designated area. See Vol. 2 of *The Air Pilot's Manual* or AIP ENR for more information.

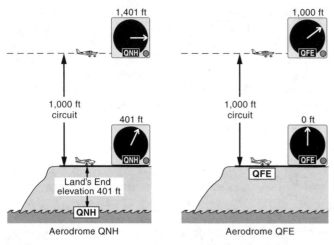

■ Figure 4-5 **Set aerodrome QNH or aerodrome QFE for circuit operations**

QFE is the pressure at runway level. With QFE set in the pressure window of your altimeter, it will read zero when you are on the runway, i.e. 0 feet aal (above aerodrome level).

> With QFE set, the altimeter reads height above the runway.

To fly at 1,000 feet above the aerodrome, you would fly so that the altimeter (with runway QFE set) indicates 1,000 feet aal.

QFE is often used in the UK by civil pilots and by military pilots to indicate *height* above the runway. Be very clear what you are setting in the pressure window of your altimeter. QFE, like QNH, also has to be updated periodically.

NOTE Air pressure drops about 1 millibar for each 30 feet gained. Therefore, for an aerodrome of elevation 1,200 feet amsl and a QNH of 1020 millibars, you would expect the QFE to be approximately $(1,200 \div 30) = 40$ millibars less at QFE 980. It always pays to check!

UNITS OF PRESSURE. The traditional unit of pressure in the UK is *millibars* (mb), but the SI unit for pressure, *hectopascals* (hPa), is being introduced in some CAA publications. As 1 mb = 1 hPa the change has no significance other than the name change. Most European countries use hectopascals (hPa). The USA uses *inches of mercury* (″Hg) instead.

STANDARD PRESSURE which is set in the altimeter pressure window when you climb above the *transition altitude* (typically 3,000 feet amsl in the UK) is 1013.2 mb or hPa, or the inches of mercury equivalent, 29.92″Hg.

Leaving a Frequency

Advise the ATSU when you leave a frequency, and then again when you return to it.

If you are flying in an aircraft that has only one VHF-COM radio, and the ATIS at your destination aerodrome is only available on a VHF-COM frequency, then you can advise the Air Traffic Service Unit (ATSU) that you will be leaving the frequency for a few minutes. Since most ATIS broadcasts last for less than 30 seconds, this should be long enough for you to copy the aerodrome information (even if you have to listen to it several times), and then return to the communications frequency. The same applies if you want to copy a VOLMET, except that the VOLMET broadcast could go on for several minutes. Advise the ATSU when you are back on frequency.

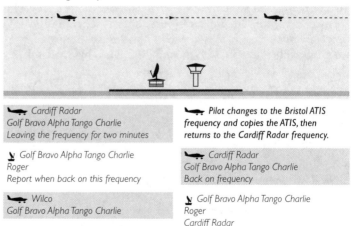

Cardiff Radar
Golf Bravo Alpha Tango Charlie
Leaving the frequency for two minutes

Golf Bravo Alpha Tango Charlie
Roger
Report when back on this frequency

Wilco
Golf Bravo Alpha Tango Charlie

Pilot changes to the Bristol ATIS frequency and copies the ATIS, then returns to the Cardiff Radar frequency.

Cardiff Radar
Golf Bravo Alpha Tango Charlie
Back on frequency

Golf Bravo Alpha Tango Charlie
Roger
Cardiff Radar

■ *Figure 4-6* **Leaving the frequency**

Voice Weather Broadcast (VOLMET)

Whereas an ATIS is for a specific aerodrome, the VOLMET broadcast usually covers a *group* of major aerodromes in the same vicinity. VOLMET is generally used by aircraft en route to one of these aerodromes, or using one or more of them as a potential alternate aerodrome.

> A VOLMET broadcast contains the weather for each of a group of aerodromes.

The VOLMET broadcast contains similar (but not identical) information to the ATIS of each of the aerodromes – for instance, the runway-in-use is not mentioned in the VOLMET broadcast (you would obtain this when you are a bit closer to the aerodrome under consideration and listen to its latest ATIS).

The specific frequencies on which VOLMET is broadcast, the hours of operation, and the aerodromes included in the particular VOLMET broadcast are published in AIP GEN and publications such as *Pooley's Flight Guide*. A full VOLMET broadcast, because it covers a number of aerodromes, may last for several minutes.

London (South)   128.60   H24   Continuous

Actual weather and forecast trend for:
Birmingham, Bournemouth, Bristol, Cardiff, Jersey, Luton, Norwich, Southampton, Southend.

London (North)   126.60   H24   Continuous

Actual weather and forecast trend for:
Blackpool, East Midlands, Leeds/Bradford, Liverpool, London/Gatwick, Manchester, Newcastle, Isle of Man/Ronaldsway, Teesside.

■ *Figure 4-7* **Some of the main VOLMET broadcasts**

The domestic UK VOLMETs are broadcast on VHF frequencies. Aircraft flying well away from the coast and out of VHF range, for instance over the Atlantic, can use international VOLMETs which are broadcast on long range HF by the Royal Air Force, by Shanwick (Shannon in Ireland and Prestwick in Scotland), by New York, by Gander in Newfoundland, etc.

The VOLMET content for each of the aerodromes includes:
- ☐ **Aerodrome name.**
- ☐ **Time of origin** of weather report.
- ☐ **Surface wind.**
- ☐ **Visibility.**
- ☐ **RVR** if applicable *(runway visual range* when visibility is very poor).
- ☐ **Weather** (e.g. precipitation).
- ☐ **Cloud.**

- ☐ **Temperature and dewpoint** (if the temperature drops to the dewpoint a fog may form).
- ☐ **QNH.**
- ☐ **Trend** (if applicable, e.g. NOSIG means no significant changes expected in the next period; TEMPO means for temporary periods of up to 60 minutes between the times stated).
- ☐ **Relevant items like SNOCLO** (closure of airport due to heavy snow on runways or during snow clearance by ground vehicles).

A typical VOLMET could be:

> Liverpool at one six two zero.
>
> Surface wind two six zero degrees, one two knots.
>
> visibility one five kilometres.
>
> Cloud – scattered at one thousand feet, broken at two thousand feet.
>
> Temperature plus two, dewpoint minus one.
>
> QNH one zero two five.
>
> Thunderstorms to the north-west at two zero miles.
>
> London/Gatwick at one five five zero.
>
> Surface wind............ etc. etc.

NOTE If you have private access to a suitable radio receiver, you may be able to listen to a nearby ATIS (on VHF) and to VOLMETs (on VHF and HF/SW) in your spare time. You could take advantage of this to become familiar with the language used in these broadcasts, the speed at which they are made, and also to write down the important information in shorthand form.

Another example of an actual VOLMET is:

> This is London VOLMET South.
>
> Norwich at one one five zero zulu.
>
> Wind two four zero degrees, one one knots, varying between one eight zero degrees and two six zero degrees.
>
> Ten kilometres or more.
>
> Light rain.
>
> Few at one thousand five hundred, broken at seven thousand.
>
> Temperature one six, dewpoint one five.
>
> One zero one five.
>
> Becoming broken at one thousand.
>
> Stansted at one one five zero zulu.
>
> Wind.......

Voice Radio

The ATSU will use normal voice communications to update you with any significant changes from the ATIS that you have reported receiving, or of any current information that may be of operational value to you, such as runway condition (damp, wet, water patches, flooded), any potential wake turbulence (vortex wake) from a preceding aircraft taking off or landing that may affect you. The ATSU may also suggest a recommended spacing, any reported wind shear, flocks of birds, etc.

If you have *not* received the ATIS, then the ATSU will pass the information to you as **departure information** or **landing information** as appropriate (however, you should always try to copy the ATIS if there is one, to reduce everyone's workload). The information passed to you by the ATSU might be a reduced version of the ATIS, containing runway in use, wind, QNH, and temperature.

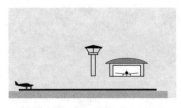
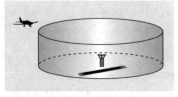

🛩 .... *Radar*
Golf Bravo Alpha Tango Charlie
Request departure information

🛩 *Golf Bravo Alpha Tango Charlie*
Departure Runway two three
Surface wind two five zero at six knots
QNH one zero zero eight
Temperature plus six, dewpoint minus three

🛩 .... *Tower*
Golf Bravo Alpha Tango Charlie
Request landing information

🛩 *Golf Bravo Alpha Tango Charlie*
Landing Runway one eight
one nine zero at one five knots
QNH one zero one five
Temperature one five
CAVOK

■ *Figure 4-8* **Requesting departure information (left); and requesting landing information (right)**

Now complete: **Exercises 4 – Aerodrome Information.**

Flying Further
Airspace Classification

The demands made on certain volumes of airspace by air traffic, especially around major aerodromes and along major airways, is quite enormous. For this reason, some control is exerted
over air traffic in these three-dimensional volumes. To avoid too
many restrictions in airspace that is not so busy, however, an international classification system has been developed to separate the
not-so-busy where less control (or no control) is considered necessary. In this chapter we look at:

☐ **types of aerodromes** (summarising what you already know);
   and
☐ **classes of airspace.**

Types of Aerodromes

The various aerodrome types were discussed in Chapter 3, *Aerodrome Operations.* You will remember that the main division is
between those that are:

☐ **aerodromes with ATC** (Air Traffic Control), where ATC *clearances* are required to operate on the aerodrome (i.e. to take off,
   and land); and
☐ **aerodromes with either FIS** (Flight Information Service) or
   A/G (Air/Ground radio) to provide information. There may
   of course be **no radio** at all. At FIS, A/G or no-radio aerodromes, *you* are completely responsible for aerodrome operations and ATC clearances are not required (nor available); however, you should *advise* others of your movements.

*Make contact with the
appropriate ATSU.*

The Air Traffic Service Unit (ATSU) situated at an aerodrome
(be it ATC, FIS or A/G) should know about operations within the
ATZ (Aerodrome Traffic Zone) surrounding that aerodrome. You
should be in radio contact with the aerodrome ATSU when operating in its ATZ, even if you are en route and not planning to land
at that aerodrome.

Classes of Airspace

As well as the type of aerodrome you are operating at, it is also
very important to be aware of the class of airspace that your aerodrome and training area lie within – check in the Aeronautical
Information Publication (AIP AD and ENR – UK ATS Airspace
Classifications Chart).

Airspace is divided into classes for reasons of safety and orderly
air traffic flow. The airspace around London/Heathrow and along

major airways obviously requires more control than the airspace over remote parts of the country or small aerodromes. To facilitate this, all airspace has been allocated to one of seven classes, named by the letters A to G.

The classes of airspace are listed below. Those most relevant to VFR pilots operating at aerodromes are **controlled Class D airspace** around some less-busy major aerodromes; and **uncontrolled Class G airspace,** which is often referred to as the *Open FIR*. There is no need for you to remember all the details, but you should take note of what class of airspace your aerodrome and training area lie within, and what the requirements for that particular class of airspace are. These classes of airspace are used internationally (sometimes with minor national differences, often benefiting the pilots, to allow for special situations).

All airspace is classified A to G.

The Aerodrome Traffic Zone (ATZ) around an aerodrome is not allocated a specific airspace classification, but adopts the classification of the airspace in which it is located. For example, Haverfordwest aerodrome has an Air/Ground (A/G) radio station and lies in uncontrolled Class G airspace. Swansea aerodrome also lies within uncontrolled Class G airspace, but is ATC. An ATC clearance is required for runway operations at Swansea, but not at Haverfordwest (since there is no ATC).

Each aerodrome ATZ adopts the classification of the airspace in which it is located.

However, you may find that permission is required to enter an ATZ, even though it is in Class G airspace (uncontrolled). Refer to Rule 39 of The Rules of the Air in the Air Navigation Order (ANO). See also page 47 of this book and Vol. 2 of *The Air Pilot's Manual.*

Of course, you might be en route to a destination airport and be cruising along well away from any aerodrome or aerodrome traffic zone; however, you still need to be aware of the class of airspace you are in, or are about to enter. The main division of airspace is into:

☐ **controlled airspace** – classes A, B, C (not used in UK), D and E;
☐ **uncontrolled airspace** – classes F and G.

Controlled Airspace

CLASS A AIRSPACE: Allocated to the busiest airspace, e.g. London-Heathrow, and to major upper level airways, and not available to VFR pilots.

CLASS B AIRSPACE: Upper airspace above FL 245 (24,500 feet), and so of no concern to most VFR pilots.

CLASS C AIRSPACE: Not applicable to the UK, but used in the Republic of Ireland and other European countries, often around very busy aerodromes.

> *VFR pilots (you) require an ATC route clearance to operate in Class D (and higher) airspace.*

CLASS D AIRSPACE: Allocated to less-busy controlled airspace: VFR flights should give flight notification prior to entry and require **ATC route clearances** to enter and operate in this airspace. For example, Teesside lies within Class D airspace.

CLASS E AIRSPACE: Only allocated to the Scottish CTR (including ATZs in the control zone), the Scottish TMA at and below 6,000 feet amsl, and the Belfast TMA. Class E airspace is similar to Class D airspace (it is controlled airspace), but differs from Class D in that prior flight notification is *not* required for VFR flights, ATC route clearances are *not* required for VFR flight (but ATC clearances are required for aerodrome operations at ATC aerodromes irrespective of the surrounding airspace classification), and a reduced traffic information service only is available from ATC.

Uncontrolled Airspace

CLASS F AIRSPACE: Advisory routes 10 nm wide between navigation aids on reasonably busy upper level routes (same width as the controlled Class A airways).

CLASS G AIRSPACE: All previously unallocated airspace, uncontrolled (except for runway operations at ATC airports), and known as the **Open FIR** (i.e. Open Flight Information Region). ATC clearances are *not* required to operate in Class G airspace. Haverfordwest aerodrome and Swansea aerodrome both lie in Class G airspace; the first is A/G, the second is ATC.

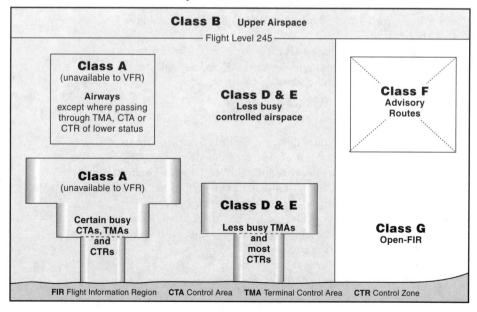

■ *Figure 5-1* **Summary of UK airspace classifications**

Air Traffic Services (ATS)

There are many Air Traffic Service Units (ATSUs) spread throughout the UK whose function it is to assist the passage of aircraft by providing information before and during flight.

Area Control Centre (ACC) Services

An Area Control Centre (ACC) provides the following Air Traffic Services:

- ☐ **an Air Traffic Control Service** to aircraft operating in controlled airspace on Airways (IFR flights), and in controlled Aerodrome Traffic Zones (ATZs);
- ☐ **an Air Traffic Advisory Service** to aircraft flying on Advisory Routes;
- ☐ **a Flight Information Service (FIS) and Alerting Service** (Distress and Diversion).

Radar Services

Within most *controlled* airspace (Classes A–E), ATC can provide a **radar control service** enabling separation from other traffic, radar vectoring around danger areas or onto final approach, etc., and any other form of navigation assistance you might require.

> Radar control is usually available in controlled airspace.

The controllers can also provide special radar services *outside controlled airspace* (i.e. in Classes F and G airspace) if you request them, such as the **Lower Airspace Radar Service (LARS).** The two services that comprise LARS are:

> Radar information and advisory services may be available outside controlled airspace.

- ☐ **Radar Advisory Service (RAS)** – provides information on other traffic and advisory avoiding action. RAS is available to IFR traffic only.
- ☐ **Radar Information Service (RIS)** – provides traffic information only (avoiding action not given). RIS is available to all traffic on request, controller workload permitting.

For more about RAS and RIS see pages 80 to 81.

Procedural Service

Radar is generally used to provide separation between aircraft on busy controlled airways and on advisory routes. If radar is not available, then ATC can offer a procedural service which separates aircraft at the same level by horizontal distance or time. This requires regular and accurate **position reports** from aircraft. On some routes, *compulsory* reporting points are marked on charts with a solid triangle, and *on-request* reporting points are marked with an outlined triangle (see page 84).

The procedural service is a control service in controlled airspace, and an advisory service in uncontrolled airspace.

A POSITION REPORT is given in the format:
- [ ] **Callsign**.
- [ ] **P Position** over which you are reporting.
- [ ] **T Time** at which you were overhead that position.
- [ ] **L Level**.
- [ ] **E Estimated** time at next position.

> Golf Tango Charlie
> Melton Mowbray at two seven
> Three thousand feet
> Bottesford at three four

■ Figure 5-2 **A position report**

Information Services

Some air traffic service units (ATSUs) have no control (ATC) functions, but rather serve to provide information to pilots. **London Information** and **Scottish Information,** whose frequencies are clearly marked on visual charts, and flight information service (FIS) units are all information providers.

Alerting Service

All air traffic service units (ATSUs) are capable of alerting emergency services (such as the fire brigade, search and rescue (SAR) authorities, sea rescue, hospitals, doctors, etc.) if an aircraft is known to be in an urgency or emergency situation. To be able to alert the appropriate people, the ATSU must know at least some of the aircraft's details, such as position, problem, and callsign if possible. The availability of this alerting service is one reason why it is good airmanship to be in touch with an ATSU, even when it is not required.

Now complete: **Exercises 5 – Airspace Classification.**

Flying Further
R/T in Uncontrolled Airspace

Uncontrolled airspace refers to Class F (Advisory Routes) and Class G (Open FIR). Private pilots generally spend a lot of their flight time in Class G airspace. In this chapter, we look at typical radio calls outside controlled airspace, covering various scenarios you are likely to encounter during your training.

*Make use of the **information** and other services.*

No en route control service is required in uncontrolled airspace; however, you should take advantage of the information services, and other services, that are offered. The services that are available to you in uncontrolled airspace are shown below. In many areas, you may operate without being in contact with an ATSU; however, it shows good airmanship if you do remain in contact with one if possible and make use of the services offered. You may at any time request information pertinent to your flight from these services, such as weather, the time of end-of-daylight, the serviceability of aerodromes, known traffic in your area, Danger Area Activity Information and so on.

Area Control Centre (ACC) Services in Uncontrolled Airspace

Not only is ATC active in controlled airspace, it also offers specific services in *uncontrolled* airspace (where ATC route clearances are *not* required). These services include:

- [ ] an Air Traffic **Advisory** Service to aircraft flying on Advisory Routes (i.e. Class F airspace);
- [ ] a **Flight Information Service and Alerting Service** (Distress and Diversion).

Air Traffic Advisory Service

The Air Traffic *Advisory* Service is offered to aircraft in uncontrolled airspace by various Air Traffic Service Units. The particular ATSU may, or may not, have the advantage of radar. Not all traffic will be known to the ATSU, so vigilance is required at all times in uncontrolled airspace. Air traffic services provided to flights in uncontrolled airspace include:

- [ ] **information and warnings** on meteorological conditions;
- [ ] **changes of serviceability** in navigational and approach aids;
- [ ] **condition** of aerodrome facilities;
- [ ] **aircraft proximity** warnings (i.e. known traffic); and
- [ ] **other information** pertinent to the safety of air navigation.

The Lower Airspace Radar Service (LARS)

When flying in UK uncontrolled airspace up to and including FL95 within the limits of radio/radar coverage, pilots are recommended to use the Lower Airspace Radar Service (LARS). LARS is a structured national system whereby nominated civil and military ATSUs, if their primary duties permit, may provide the Radar Advisory Service (RAS) or the Radar Information Service (RIS), on request, within approximately 30 nm of each unit. If three attempts to establish radio contact with a LARS station are made without success, assume that the station is not operating.

Radar Advisory Service (RAS)

The **Radar Advisory Service (RAS)** is available on request to IFR (Instrument Flight Rules) traffic only. The radar controller will use radio communications to provide:

> RAS provides traffic avoidance instructions.

- ▣ **traffic information** (bearing, distance and level if known); and
- ▣ **advisory avoiding action** instructions necessary to maintain separation from the other aircraft.

1. Requesting RAS

➤ *Shawbury Approach*
Golf Bravo Alpha Tango Charlie
Request Lower Airspace Radar Service

➤ *Golf Bravo Alpha Tango Charlie*
Shawbury Approach
Pass your message

➤ *Golf Bravo Alpha Tango Charlie*
PA-28
P *Overhead Shrewsbury*
H *Heading three four five*
A *Flight level four five*
E *En route Wrexham*
R *Request Radar Advisory Service*

➤ *Golf Tango Charlie*
Roger, squawk four six six five

➤ *Four six six five*
Golf Tango Charlie

➤ *Golf Tango Charlie is identified four miles northeast of Shrewsbury Radar Advisory*

➤ *Radar Advisory*
Golf Tango Charlie

2. Traffic Advice

➤ *Golf Tango Charlie*
Pop-up traffic left eleven o'clock
Eight miles, crossing you left to right
Fast moving one thousand feet above, descending,
If not sighted turn left heading two seven zero

Note *'Pop-up' traffic is traffic that suddenly appears on the radar screen, possibly due to climbing out of a radar shadow area.*

➤ *Left heading two seven zero*
Golf Tango Charlie

➤ *Golf Tango Charlie*
Clear of traffic, resume own navigation for Wrexham

➤ *Wilco*
Golf Tango Charlie

3. Advising a Descent

➤ *Golf Tango Charlie*
Ready for descent

Note *We are not **requesting** a descent here. Under Air Traffic Control, you would have to request a descent. However, under Radar Advisory, you use the word "Ready," although "Request" is also acceptable.*

➤ *Golf Tango Charlie*
Descend to altitude two thousand feet
QNH one zero one two
Report passing three thousand feet

➤ *Descending to altitude two thousand feet, one zero one two*
Wilco
Golf Tango Charlie

➤ *Golf Tango Charlie*
Passing three thousand feet
Descending to altitude two thousand feet

■ *Figure 6-1* **Using the Radar Advisory Service (RAS)**

The Radar Advisory Service (RAS) affords the highest level of protection in terms of being kept clear of other known aircraft.

Though RAS is available only to IFR traffic, you may elect to use it by flying Instrument Flight Rules (IFR) in Visual Meteorological Conditions (VMC) outside controlled airspace (see Vol. 2 of *The Air Pilot's Manual*).

However, be aware that if you are not licensed to fly in cloud you must not accept an instruction from a controller that would take you into cloud, i.e. remain in VMC at all times. Under RAS, controllers will expect you to accept radar vectors or level changes that may require flight into IMC conditions. Therefore, if any doubt exists that the flight can be continued in VMC, pilots *not* qualified to fly in IMC should not accept a RAS.

Advisory avoiding action will be given if deemed prudent by the controller, or on the pilot's request. *Advisory* avoiding action is just that, not instructions. The radar controller should be advised immediately of any instructions (heading or level changes) that are not acceptable to the pilot

If you are in good VMC and consider the other traffic to be of no risk you may disregard the avoiding action and continue on track, e.g. "G-TC, good VMC, happy to continue." You are then responsible for your own avoiding action. The controller should inform you if he still considers the traffic to be a threat.

Any self-initiated changes in heading or altitude by the pilot should be immediately advised to the radar controller, since it may affect separation from other aircraft.

RAS will not be available below terrain-safe levels, but remember that at all times the pilot is responsible for terrain clearance.

Radar Information Service (RIS)

RIS provides traffic information only.

The Radar Information Service (RIS) is available on request. The radar controller will use radio communications to provide:

- **traffic information only** (bearing, distance and level if known – no avoiding action will be offered).

The Radar Information Service is useful in good VMC conditions to the VFR pilot, where the radar controller can provide an extra pair of eyes, without repeated avoiding action which may be unnecessary in good conditions and time-wasting for the flight. The pilot should advise the radar controller if he is changing heading, level or level-band (e.g. operating between 2,000 and 4,000 ft). A RIS may be offered if RAS is impracticable.

RIS will not be available below terrain-safe levels, but remember that at all times the pilot is responsible for terrain clearance.

Both RAS and RIS are described in detail in AIP ENR, Radar Services and Procedures.

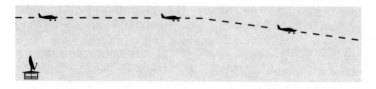

1. Advising a Descent

 Golf Tango Charlie is leaving flight level four five Descending to altitude two thousand feet

 Roger Nothing known to affect your descent QNH one zero one two

 One zero one two Golf Tango Charlie

2. Traffic Advice

 Golf Tango Charlie Traffic in your right two o'clock, right–left, slow moving, no height information

 Roger Golf Tango Charlie

Note *No avoiding action has been given as this is your responsibility under RIS – unlike RAS where the controller would have initiated avoiding action by giving you a heading and/or altitude change.*

■ *Figure 6-2* **Using the Radar Information Service (RIS)**

The Surveillance Radar Approach (SRA)

The *surveillance radar approach* (SRA) is a means by which air traffic controllers with high-quality radar can vector an aircraft to a runway. If you unintentionally get into cloud, which of course you should never do, this is a useful standby.

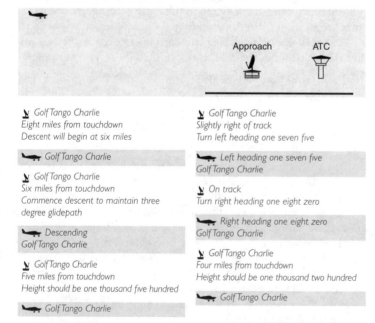

 Golf Tango Charlie Eight miles from touchdown Descent will begin at six miles

 Golf Tango Charlie

 Golf Tango Charlie Six miles from touchdown Commence descent to maintain three degree glidepath

 Descending Golf Tango Charlie

 Golf Tango Charlie Five miles from touchdown Height should be one thousand five hundred

 Golf Tango Charlie

 Golf Tango Charlie Slightly right of track Turn left heading one seven five

 Left heading one seven five Golf Tango Charlie

 On track Turn right heading one eight zero

 Right heading one eight zero Golf Tango Charlie

 Golf Tango Charlie Four miles from touchdown Height should be one thousand two hundred

 Golf Tango Charlie

■ *Figure 6-3* **A surveillance radar approach**

The radar controller will normally request you to set runway QFE so that your altimeter indicates height above the runway. However, should you operate using QNH, the controller will adjust the altitudes accordingly. Then heading instructions and slope guidance will be given. Figure 6-3 shows a typical example, and pages 150 to 151 illustrate an SRA in more detail. These radar instructions are given until the pilot is visual with the runway in sight or until the pilot has initiated a missed approach.

Before making an SRA check your aerodrome approach minima in AIP AD (Aerodrome Operating Minima) or *Pooley's Flight Guide*.

Flight Information Service (FIS)

The Flight Information Service (FIS) is available to all aircraft in both UK Flight Information Regions (FIRs) through London Information and Scottish Information ATSUs. The Flight Information Service (FIS) existed before the advent of radar services and is still available. The service is a valuable one, and provides local information on weather, serviceability of navigation aids, aerodrome conditions and other known traffic.

REPORTING POINTS. In a radar environment, your position will be shown on a radar screen; in a *non-radar* environment it will not. You are then encouraged to periodically report your position in the form of a **position report,** which follows the pattern:

- ☐ **Callsign.**
- ☐ *P* **Position** over which you are reporting.
- ☐ *T* **Time** at which you were overhead that position.
- ☐ *L* **Level.**
- ☐ *E* **Estimated** time at next position.

For example, you may be in contact with *London Information* en route between Gloucester and Shobdon via Worcester. You may be asked by London Information for a position report.

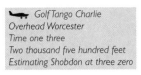

Golf Tango Charlie
Overhead Worcester
Time one three
Two thousand five hundred feet
Estimating Shobdon at three zero

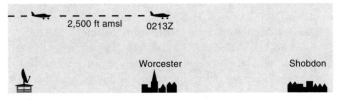

2,500 ft amsl   0213Z

Worcester   Shobdon

■ *Figure 6-4* **Typical position report**

Do not be concerned about getting the R/T call in immediately as you may be busy carrying out a heading change and then filling in your flight log, or the R/T may be blocked by other calls. The actual time you were overhead the reporting point is what is important to ATSU, and you have a note of that time on your flight log.

On some specific routes there are **compulsory reporting routes,** indicated on charts by a filled-in triangle (▲), where you are *required* to make a position report. There are also some **on-request reporting points,** indicated by an outlined triangle (△), where you should make a position report if requested to do so by the ATSU.

*In a **non-radar** environment, periodically report your position.*

 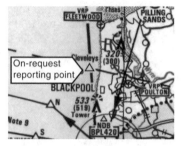

■ *Figure 6-5* **Reporting points on a CAA 1:500,000 aeronautical chart**

Danger Areas

Danger Areas are defined airspace in which activities dangerous to flight may occur, often of a military nature such as weapons firing, heavy military activity, target towing, parachute jumping and so on. Danger Areas are specified in AIP ENR and are shown on the Chart of Airspace Restrictions and Hazardous Areas.

In general, you should assume that a danger area is active, and stay out of it unless you have approval to go through it or are absolutely certain that it is not active.

Assume Danger Areas are active.

There are two services that can assist you if you wish to fly within a danger area:

☐ **Danger Area Crossing Service (DACS),** pronounced *"dacks"*. DACS is able to issue *clearances* to cross a particular danger area under certain circumstances, but you still need to keep a good lookout and listening watch for other aerial activity; and

☐ **Danger Area Activity Information Service (DAAIS),** pronounced *"day-iss"*. DAAIS can *advise* if a particular danger area is active or not, but is not authorised to issue a crossing clearance – you must take the responsibility if you want to fly through the danger area.

The frequencies of ATSUs that can provide these services are found on CAA 1:500,000 aeronautical charts (see Figure 6-6), in AIP AD & ENR and in *Pooley's Flight Guide*.

Typical calls when making use of the Danger Area Crossing Service or Danger Area Activity Information Service are shown in Figure 6-7. You may use the full names or the abbreviated pronunciations *("dacks" or "day-iss")*.

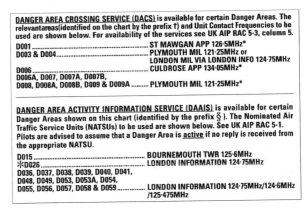

■ *Figure 6-6* **Extract of DACS and DAAIS information on a CAA 1:500,000 aeronautical chart**

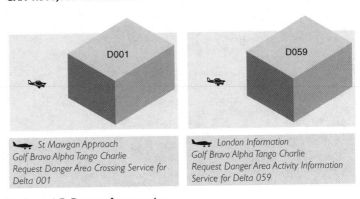

■ *Figure 6-7* **Danger Area services**

VDF

Some aerodromes are equipped with VHF direction-finding equipment (VDF) which can sense the direction of VHF-COM (voice) signals received from aircraft. VDF is old-fashioned and not as good as radar. VDF allows the pilot to request headings or bearings using a conventional VHF-COM radio. The pilot requests the heading or bearing using a "Q-code", and the controller replies advising it. Using VDF you can request:

- QDM – **magnetic heading** to be steered by the aircraft to reach the VDF station (assuming no wind).
- QDR – **magnetic bearing** of the aircraft from the VDF station (assuming no wind).
- QTE – **true bearing** of the aircraft from the VDF station (assuming no wind) – used for plotting purposes or orientation to VDF stations.

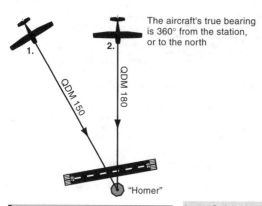

The aircraft's true bearing is 360° from the station, or to the north

"Homer"

1. QDM

🛬 Carlisle Homer
Golf Bravo Alpha Tango Charlie
Request QDM

Note "Homer" is used here, but "Approach" or "Tower" would also be acceptable.

✈ Golf Bravo Alpha Tango Charlie
Carlisle Approach
QDM 150 Class Bravo

🛬 QDM 150 Class Bravo
Golf Bravo Alpha Tango Charlie

This heading plus or minus an allowance for wind will get you to Carlisle.

2. QTE

To obtain a bearing from the field, ask for a true bearing (QTE). A QTE is easy to plot on a chart against the (true) meridians of longitude, since magnetic variation does not have to be applied.

🛬 Carlisle Homer
Golf Bravo Alpha Tango Charlie
Request true bearing

✈ Golf Bravo Alpha Tango Charlie
Carlisle Approach
True bearing 360 Class Bravo

🛬 True bearing 360 Class Bravo
Golf Bravo Alpha Tango Charlie

QGH

There is a controller-interpreted let-down procedure that uses VDF. You may hear the tower asking you to transmit for DF. This would be used for the QGH procedure, or to confirm your bearing for the controller who may not have a radar. For example:

✈ Golf Bravo Alpha Tango Charlie
Transmit for DF

Your response would be:

🛬 Golf Bravo Alpha Tango Charlie
Transmitting for DF

Refer to Vol. 5 of The Air Pilot's Manual for more about QGH procedures.

■ Figure 6-8 **Various QDMs**

Figure 6-8 shows examples of requesting a QDM or magnetic heading *to* the station. The longer your transmission takes, the easier it is for the VDF to get a good bearing, so it is usual to use your full callsign at both the beginning and end of your transmission. After receiving the QDM heading and accuracy classification, you should read back both of them, e.g. "QDM one five zero degrees, Class Bravo", followed by your callsign.

QDM is the VDF procedure that VFR pilots would generally use, rather than QDR, QTE or QGH.

The accuracy of each VDF service is classified as follows:

VDF SERVICE	ACCURACY
Class A	within ±2°
Class B	within ±5°
Class C	within ±10°
Class D	poorer than Class C

NOTE Normally no better than Class B bearings will be available. If conditions are unsatisfactory for VDF, no bearings will be given, but the controller will give the reason.

See AIP AD for stations that offer a VDF service, and note that some stations stipulate that the service is not available for en route navigation, except in emergencies.

Pilot Reports

Pilot reports can be useful.

While ATSUs can be a valuable source of information, so can pilots! You should, if you feel it could be relevant to some other pilot or of interest to some authority, report things such as:

☐ **unusual or unforecast weather;**
☐ **flooded runways;**
☐ **windshear;**
☐ **turbulence;**
☐ **birdstrikes;**
☐ **oil pollution** (for instance large oil slicks at sea);
☐ **airprox** (near misses with other aircraft);
☐ **any other aircraft or vessel** that appears to be in trouble;
☐ **your position and level** (in the form of a position report).

Class G Airspace – ATC Departure

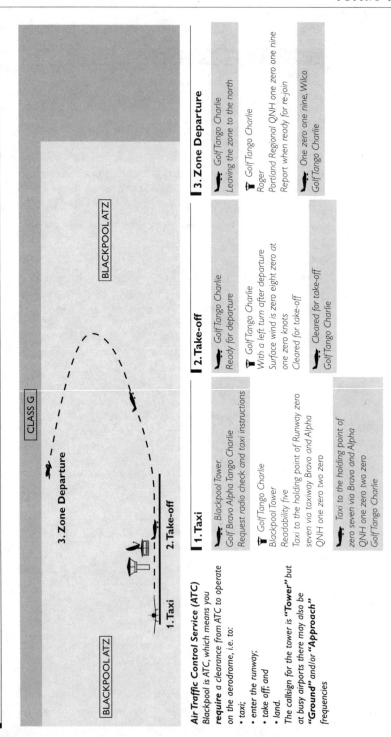

CLASS G

BLACKPOOL ATZ

BLACKPOOL ATZ

3. Zone Departure

2. Take-off

1. Taxi

Air Traffic Control Service (ATC)
Blackpool is ATC, which means you **require** a clearance from ATC to operate on the aerodrome, i.e. to:
• taxi;
• enter the runway;
• take off, and
• land.
The callsign for the tower is **"Tower"** but at busy airports there may also be **"Ground"** and/or **"Approach"** frequencies

1. Taxi

Blackpool Tower
Golf Bravo Alpha Tango Charlie
Request radio check and taxi instructions

Golf Tango Charlie
Blackpool Tower
Readability five
Taxi to the holding point of Runway zero seven via taxiway Bravo and Alpha
QNH one zero two zero

Taxi to the holding point of zero seven via Bravo and Alpha
QNH one zero two zero
Golf Tango Charlie

2. Take-off

Golf Tango Charlie
Ready for departure

Golf Tango Charlie
With a left turn after departure
Surface wind is zero eight zero at one zero knots
Cleared for take-off

Cleared for take-off
Golf Tango Charlie

3. Zone Departure

Golf Tango Charlie
Leaving the zone to the north

Golf Tango Charlie
Roger
Portland Regional QNH one zero one one nine
Report when ready for re-join

One zero one nine, Wilco
Golf Tango Charlie

Class G Airspace – ATC Arrival

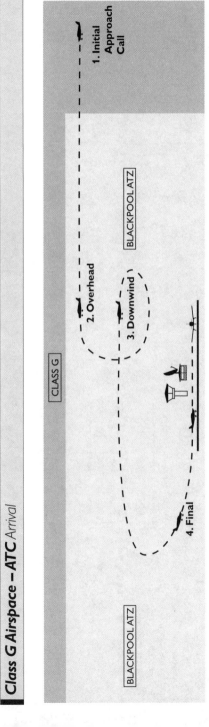

CLASS G

BLACKPOOL ATZ

BLACKPOOL ATZ

1. Initial Approach Call

2. Overhead

3. Downwind

4. Final

1. Initial Approach Call

You should make your initial call at 15 nm or 5 minutes flying time from the ATZ. This gives both the controller and yourself time to plan your arrival. The initial PACER call is shortened because you are already in contact with Blackpool.

Blackpool Tower
Golf Bravo Alpha Tango Charlie
P One five miles north
A Two thousand five hundred feet
R Request standard overhead join

Golf Tango Charlie
Report in the overhead for
Runway zero seven, left-hand
QFE one zero zero nine

Runway 07, QFE one zero zero one nine
Wilco, Golf Tango Charlie

2. Overhead

Golf Tango Charlie
Overhead for zero seven, left-hand

Golf Tango Charlie
Descend dead side and report downwind
You are number two following
a Cherokee on final

Wilco
Golf Tango Charlie

3. Downwind

Golf Tango Charlie
Downwind to land

Golf Tango Charlie
Report final

Wilco
Golf Tango Charlie

4. Final

Golf Tango Charlie
Final

Golf Tango Charlie
Surface wind is zero six zero at
eight knots
Cleared to land Runway 07

Cleared to land Runway 07
Golf Tango Charlie

Class G Airspace – FIS Departure

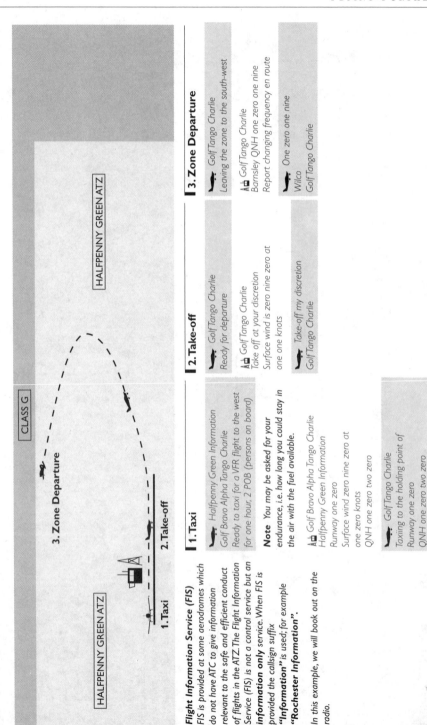

HALFPENNY GREEN ATZ

CLASS G

3. Zone Departure

1. Taxi   2. Take-off

HALFPENNY GREEN ATZ

Flight Information Service (FIS)

FIS is provided at some aerodromes which do not have ATC to give information relevant to the safe and efficient conduct of flights in the ATZ. The Flight Information Service (FIS) is not a control service but an **information only service**. When FIS is provided the callsign suffix **"Information"** is used; for example **"Rochester Information"**.

In this example, we will book out on the radio.

1. Taxi

🗣 Halfpenny Green Information
Golf Bravo Alpha Tango Charlie
Ready to taxi for a VFR flight to the west
for one hour, 2 POB (persons on board)

Note You may be asked for your endurance, i.e. how long you could stay in the air with the fuel available.

🛩 Golf Bravo Alpha Tango Charlie
Halfpenny Green Information
Runway one zero
Surface wind zero nine zero at
one zero knots
QNH one zero two zero

🗣 Golf Tango Charlie
Taxiing to the holding point of
Runway one zero
QNH one zero two zero

2. Take-off

🗣 Golf Tango Charlie
Ready for departure

🛩 Golf Tango Charlie
Take off at your discretion
Surface wind is zero nine zero at
one one knots

🗣 Take-off my discretion
Golf Tango Charlie

3. Zone Departure

🗣 Golf Tango Charlie
Leaving the zone to the south-west

🛩 Golf Tango Charlie
Barnsley QNH one zero one nine
Report changing frequency en route

🗣 One zero one nine
Wilco
Golf Tango Charlie

Class G Airspace – FIS Arrival

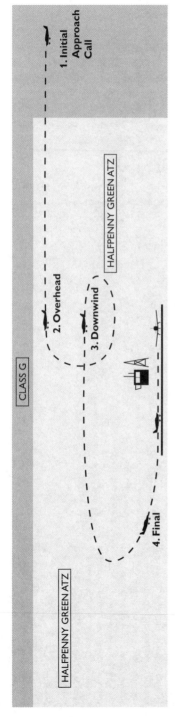

HALFPENNY GREEN ATZ

CLASS G

1. Initial Approach Call

2. Overhead

3. Downwind

4. Final

HALFPENNY GREEN ATZ

For arrival information, the full radio procedure is as follows. However, if you have not left the original frequency, it would be a shortened version of this.

1. Initial Arrival Call

🛩 Halfpenny Green Information
Golf Bravo Alpha Tango Charlie
Inbound

🏢 Golf Bravo Alpha Tango Charlie
Halfpenny Green Information
Pass your message

🛩 Golf Bravo Alpha Tango Charlie
P PA-28, Telford inbound
A Three thousand feet
C VFR
E Estimating the field at two five
R Request joining information

Note In this case the FISO knows where you are (Telford) and that you are heading towards Halfpenny Green aerodrome, so no heading is required.

🏢 Golf Tango Charlie
Runway one zero left-hand
Surface wind zero eight zero at one one knots
QFE one zero zero one zero
Two in the circuit.

You may be asked for additional information such as number of persons on board (POB).

You are expected to carry out a standard overhead join unless otherwise requested. See page 58 for standard overhead joins.

2. Overhead

🛩 Golf Tango Charlie
Overhead

🏢 Golf Tango Charlie
There are two aircraft in the circuit

🛩 Roger
Golf Tango Charlie

3. Downwind

🛩 Golf Tango Charlie
Downwind to land

🏢 Golf Tango Charlie
Report final

🛩 Golf Tango Charlie

4. Final

🛩 Golf Tango Charlie
Final

🏢 Golf Tango Charlie
Land at your discretion
Surface wind zero nine zero at one one knots

🛩 Golf Tango Charlie

Note It may be prudent to say "Landing", for the FISO's benefit. "Land at your discretion" means exactly that. The onus is on you to decide whether it is safe to land or not. The FISO may pass you relevant information such as "The runway is obstructed", but will not tell you to go around – that is up to you.

Class G Airspace – A/G or No Radio Departure

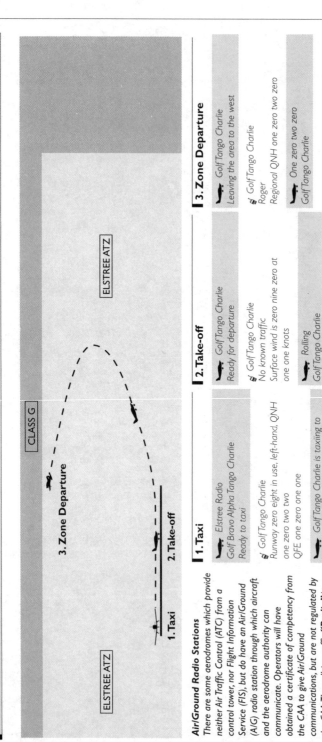

1. Taxi

🧍 Elstree Radio
Golf Bravo Alpha Tango Charlie
Ready to taxi

✈ Golf Tango Charlie
Runway zero eight in use, left-hand, QNH
one zero two two
QFE one zero one one

🧍 Golf Tango Charlie is taxiing to
Runway zero eight

2. Take-off

🧍 Golf Tango Charlie
Ready for departure

✈ Golf Tango Charlie
No known traffic
Surface wind is zero nine zero at
one one knots

🧍 Rolling
Golf Tango Charlie

3. Zone Departure

🧍 Golf Tango Charlie
Leaving the area to the west

✈ Golf Tango Charlie
Roger
Regional QNH one zero two zero

🧍 One zero two zero
Golf Tango Charlie

Air/Ground Radio Stations
There are some aerodromes which provide neither Air Traffic Control (ATC) from a control tower, nor Flight Information Service (FIS), but do have an Air/Ground (A/G) radio station through which aircraft and the aerodrome authority can communicate. Operators will have obtained a certificate of competency from the CAA to give Air/Ground communications, but are not regulated by the CAA. The callsign suffix **"Radio"** is used to distinguish A/G stations, for example "Elstree Radio".

No Radio
If there is **no radio** station active at the aerodrome, you would make a "*(place name)* Radio" call, e.g. "Elstree Radio".

Class G Airspace – A/G or No Radio Arrival

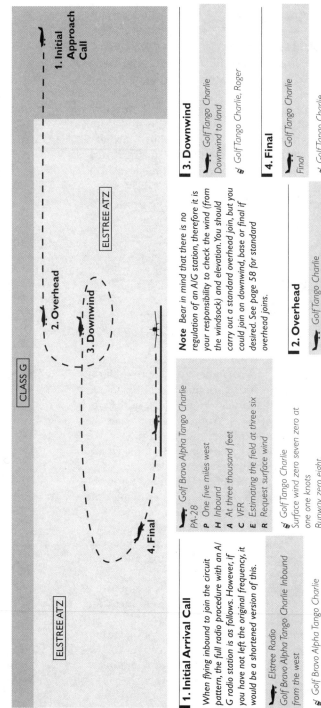

CLASS G

ELSTREE ATZ

ELSTREE ATZ

1. Initial Approach Call

2. Overhead

3. Downwind

4. Final

1. Initial Arrival Call

When flying inbound to join the circuit pattern, the full radio procedure with an A/G radio station is as follows. However, if you have not left the original frequency, it would be a shortened version of this.

🛫 Elstree Radio
Golf Bravo Alpha Tango Charlie Inbound from the west

📻 Golf Bravo Alpha Tango Charlie
Elstree Radio
Runway zero eight, left-hand

🛫 Golf Bravo Alpha Tango Charlie
PA-28
P One five miles west
H Inbound
A At three thousand feet
C VFR
E Estimating the field at three six
R Request surface wind

📻 Golf Tango Charlie
Surface wind zero seven zero at one one knots
Runway zero eight,
QFE one zero one one

🛫 Runway zero eight
QFE one zero one one
Golf Tango Charlie

Note Bear in mind that there is no regulation of an A/G station, therefore it is your responsibility to check the wind (from the windsock) and elevation. You should carry out a standard overhead join, but you could join on downwind, base or final if desired. See page 58 for standard overhead joins.

2. Overhead

🛫 Golf Tango Charlie
Overhead, descending dead side

📻 Golf Tango Charlie, Roger

3. Downwind

🛫 Golf Tango Charlie
Downwind to land

📻 Golf Tango Charlie, Roger

4. Final

🛫 Golf Tango Charlie
Final

📻 Golf Tango Charlie
Surface wind zero seven zero at six knots

🛫 Roger
Golf Tango Charlie

Note You may receive no response to any of these calls. In this case, precede the calls with "(place name) Radio" and the station name, e.g. "Elstree Radio, Golf Tango Charlie downwind to land".

Class G Airspace Surrounding a MATZ

Military Air Traffic Zones (MATZ)

Sometimes you may have to enter a Military Aerodrome Traffic Zone (MATZ). A MATZ is specified airspace surrounding many UK military aerodromes:

☐ **from the surface up to 3,000 feet** above aerodrome level within a radius of 5 nm; and usually

☐ **with a stub (or stubs),** width 4 nm, extending out a further 5 nm along final approach path(s) for the main instrument runway(s) between 1,000 and 3,000 ft above aerodrome level (aal).

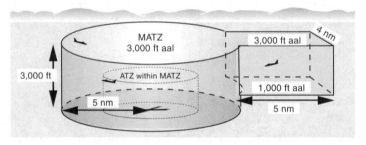

■ *Figure 6-9* **Dimensions of a typical Military Air Traffic Zone (MATZ)**

Pilots of civil aircraft wishing to penetrate a Military Air Traffic Zone are strongly advised to do so under the control of the MATZ ATC authority, in accordance with published procedures. These are detailed in AIP ENR, *Pooley's Flight Guide* and Aeronautical Information Circulars (AICs). A good lookout must be maintained because, as well as the military aircraft in the MATZ that will be known to the controller, there may also be civil aircraft in the zone that are *not* known to the controller.

Prior to entering a MATZ, communication should be established with the controller either 15 nm or 5 minutes flying time from the boundary, whichever is sooner. When flying within a Military Air Traffic Zone, comply with the controller's instructions and maintain a listening watch on the appropriate frequency. Notify the controller before changing level, heading, and when leaving the MATZ.

The controller may pass you a *clutch* QFE. This is a pressure setting common to closely situated military aerodromes, and equates to the QFE of the highest aerodrome.

If entering a MATZ outside the published hours of operation, you may proceed with caution if you receive no answer to two consecutive calls, on the assumption that ATC is not operating.

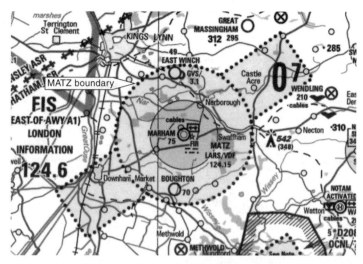

■ *Figure 6-10* **Marham MATZ, on the 1:500,000 aeronautical chart**

NOTE Even if you choose to ignore the MATZ airspace (which technically is uncontrolled), there is, within the MATZ, an Aerodrome Traffic Zone (ATZ) which must be observed at all times (most are 'H24', i.e. continuous). You require permission to enter the ATZ enclosed within the MATZ. See page 47.

An example of a MATZ penetration follows.

Class G Airspace MATZ Penetration

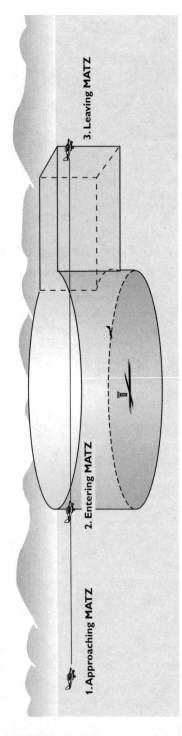

1. Approaching MATZ

2. Entering MATZ

3. Leaving MATZ

Make your first call at 15 nautical miles or 5 minutes from the boundary of the MATZ.

1. Approaching MATZ

🗣️ *Warton Approach*
Golf Bravo Alpha Tango Charlie
Request MATZ penetration

📡 *Golf Bravo Alpha Tango Charlie*
Warton Approach
Pass your message

🗣️ *Golf Bravo Alpha Tango Charlie*
PA-28,
P *Overhead Skelmersdale*
H *Heading three five five*
A *Two thousand five hundred feet on Regional QNH one zero zero five*
E/R *En route Lancaster*

📡 *Golf Tango Charlie*
Roger, are you transponder equipped?

🗣️ *Negative*
Golf Tango Charlie

📡 *Golf Tango Charlie*
Cross the MATZ on the Warton QFE one zero zero four
Report entering the zone

🗣️ *Cross the MATZ on Warton QFE one zero zero four*
Wilco
Golf Tango Charlie

Note QFE is used for a MATZ transit, which means your altimeter will indicate height above the military aerodrome.

2. Entering MATZ

📡 *Golf Tango Charlie*
Entering the zone, maintaining two thousand five hundred feet

📡 *Golf Tango Charlie*
Report leaving the zone

🗣️ *Wilco*
Golf Tango Charlie

3. Leaving MATZ

🗣️ *Golf Tango Charlie*
Zone boundary outbound

📡 *Golf Tango Charlie*
Roger Holyhead Regional QNH one zero zero five
Report changing frequency

🗣️ *QNH one zero zero five*
Wilco
Golf Tango Charlie

Note A MATZ penetration may be linked with a Lower Airspace Radar Service (LARS), see page 80. For information about transponders see page 14.

Class G Airspace Overflying/Transiting an ATZ

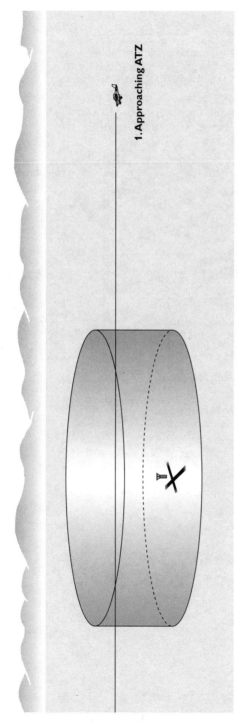

1. Approaching ATZ

There are occasions where you may wish to fly overhead or through (transit) an ATZ. To transit an ATZ you will have to either obtain permission, or at least let the appropriate station know. Again, make your call 15 nm or 5 minutes before reaching the ATZ boundary.

For example, to overfly the Cambridge ATZ the following calls would be used.

Approaching Zone

Cambridge Approach
Golf Alpha Bravo Charlie Delta

Golf Alpha Bravo Charlie Delta
Cambridge Approach
Pass your details

Golf Alpha Bravo Charlie Delta
Warrior
P One zero miles east of Cambridge
airfield
H Heading two seven zero
A Two thousand feet on
Regional QNH one zero two five
C VFR
E Estimate Cambridge at four eight
R Request overfly Cambridge at
two thousand, destination Bourn

Golf Alpha Bravo Charlie Delta
Cross the ATZ
Cambridge QNH one zero two four
Report entering and leaving the zone
Report overhead Cambridge

Cleared to Bourn at two thousand
Cambridge QNH one zero two four
Heading two seven zero
Wilco
Golf Alpha Bravo Charlie Delta

Class F Airspace

Class F airspace applies to Advisory Routes. These are equivalent
to airways in uncontrolled airspace. Aircraft can receive an Advisory Service from the responsible ATS unit. Separation is applied
to participating IFR traffic. If an Advisory Service is required an
IFR flight plan must be filed. The radio calls for participating IFR
traffic are the same as those used in Class A airspace. Note that
advice given to participating aircraft relates *only* to known traffic.

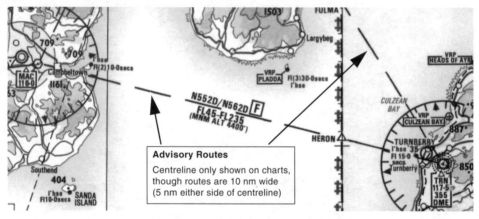

■ *Figure 6-11* **Advisory routes shown on a 1:500,000 chart**

Now complete: **Exercises 6 – R/T in Uncontrolled Airspace.**

Flying Further
R/T in Controlled Airspace

This chapter covers typical calls for Class A, D and E airspace and shows an Airways Crossing Clearance. As Class B airspace is high-level, and Class C airspace is not allocated in the UK, they are of little interest to UK VFR pilots. We will introduce controlled airspace before starting on the radio calls.

Controlled Airspace

In controlled airspace, Air Traffic Control is provided to all flights. UK controlled airspace is made up of various aerodrome Control Zones (CTR), Terminal Control Areas (TMA), Control Areas (CTA) and Airways.

A Control Zone extends from the surface to a specified altitude.

A CONTROL ZONE (CTR) is airspace around certain aerodromes in which Air Traffic Control (ATC) is provided to all flights. A Control Zone extends from ground level to a specified altitude or a specified flight level (FL), depending on height. The exceptionally busy London/Heathrow airport is situated in a Class A Control Zone (VFR flight not permitted in Class A); however, most UK CTRs (such as Edinburgh, Newcastle, East Midlands, London/Gatwick, Belfast and Cardiff) are Class D Control Zones.

A Control Area exists between specified vertical limits, and does not extend to the surface.

A CONTROL AREA (CTA) is a portion of airspace in which Air Traffic Control is provided, and which extends upwards from a specified base altitude or flight level to an upper limit expressed as a flight level. The busy Control Areas in the UK (e.g. Cotswold, Daventry and Worthing CTAs) are Class A, and the less busy ones (such as the Birmingham, Luton and Stansted CTAs) are Class D airspace.

Terminal Control Areas are near major aerodromes.

A TERMINAL CONTROL AREA is a Control Area established at the confluence of controlled airspace routes in the vicinity of one or more major aerodromes. *Terminal Control Area* is sometimes abbreviated as TCA, but more commonly as TMA (from the earlier designation *Terminal Manoeuvring Area).* There are currently four TMAs in the United Kingdom, with the busy London and Manchester TMAs allocated Class A, the Belfast TMA Class E, and the Scottish TMA Class D above notified levels and Class E below.

AN AIRWAY is a corridor-shaped Control Area and is delineated by radio navigation aids. Each Airway has an identification code (e.g. A25 or *Alpha Two Five*, R8 or *Romeo Eight)*, and extends 5 nm each side of a straight line joining certain places, with specified vertical limits.

> *Airways are route corridors 10 nm wide between specified vertical limits.*

All Airways are Class A except where they pass through a TMA, CTA or CTR of lower status. They are used by airliners (and other Instrument Flight Rules traffic) travelling between the principal aerodromes. As it approaches an aerodrome, the lower level of an Airway is usually stepped down to provide controlled airspace protection for air traffic on climb and descent.

As VFR flight is not permitted in Class A airspace, Class B is only upper airspace (above FL245), and Class C is not currently allocated in the UK, **VFR operations in controlled airspace** in the UK will usually be confined to Classes D and E. Class C airspace is used in the Republic of Ireland and other parts of Europe. Remember to fly within the limitations of your licence.

> *VFR flights in UK controlled airspace will usually be confined to Classes D or E airspace.*

Depiction of Controlled Airspace on Charts

The Chart of UK ATS Airspace Classifications (AIP ENR section) shows the boundaries and vertical extent of controlled airspace (CTRs, CTAs, TMAs and Airways). The AIP also contains listings of Controlling Authorities and Communications Channels for all UK controlled airspace.

Controlled airspace up to FL245 (24,500 ft), and its classification, is depicted on CAA 1:500,000 charts. For more about charts and airspace, see Vol. 2 of *The Air Pilot's Manual*.

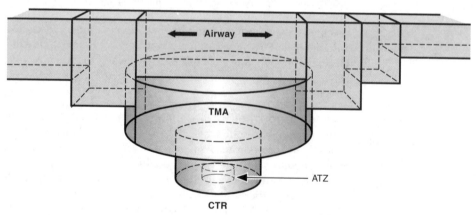

■ *Figure 7-1* **A Control Zone (CTR), Terminal Control Area (TMA), and an Airway**

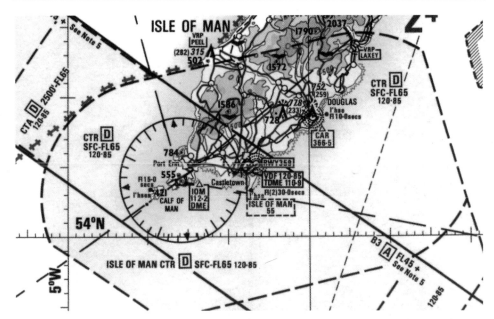

■ *Figure 7-2* **Isle of Man CTR and CTA boundaries, and Airway B3 on the 1:500,000 chart**

Class E

Class E airspace does not require an ATC clearance for VFR flights.

You do not require an ATC clearance to enter Class E controlled airspace on a VFR flight. It is, however, good airmanship to liaise with ATC and advise them of your intentions. Typical radio calls for a flight entering Class E airspace begin on page 102.

Class D

Class D airspace requires an ATC clearance.

Class D airspace surrounds some of the major airports such as Birmingham, Liverpool and Newcastle. An ATC clearance is required to operate in Class D airspace. Typical radio calls for a flight entering Class D airspace begin on page 104.

Class E Airspace *Departure*

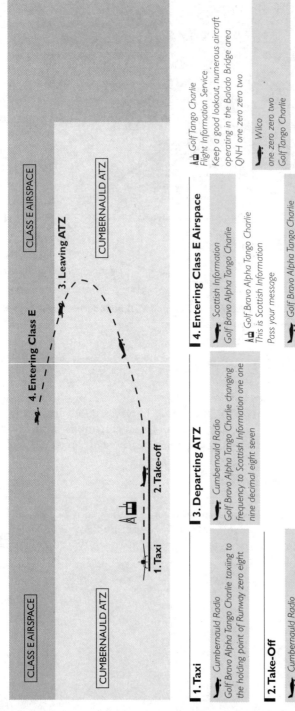

CLASS E AIRSPACE

CUMBERNAULD ATZ

CLASS E AIRSPACE

CUMBERNAULD ATZ

4. Entering Class E

3. Leaving ATZ

1. Taxi

2. Take-off

1. Taxi

🎤 *Cumbernauld Radio*
Golf Bravo Alpha Tango Charlie taxiing to the holding point of Runway zero eight

2. Take-Off

🎤 *Cumbernauld Radio*
Golf Bravo Alpha Tango Charlie taking off and departing the zone to the north, climbing to three thousand feet

3. Departing ATZ

🎤 *Cumbernauld Radio*
Golf Bravo Alpha Tango Charlie changing frequency to Scottish Information one one nine decimal eight seven

4. Entering Class E Airspace

🎤 *Scottish Information*
Golf Bravo Alpha Tango Charlie

🎤 *Golf Bravo Alpha Tango Charlie*
This is Scottish Information
Pass your message

🎤 *Golf Bravo Alpha Tango Charlie*
PA-28
P *Three miles north of Cumbernauld*
H *Heading north*
A *Four thousand feet*
C *VFR*
R *Request Flight Information Service*
Am operating in the Balado Bridge area on a training detail

🎤 *Golf Tango Charlie*
Flight Information Service.
Keep a good lookout, numerous aircraft operating in the Balado Bridge area
QNH one zero zero two

🎤 *Wilco*
one zero zero two
Golf Tango Charlie

You could talk to Edinburgh, Glasgow or Scottish Radar for a radar service instead of Scottish Flight Information, if you wish.

Class E Airspace Arrival

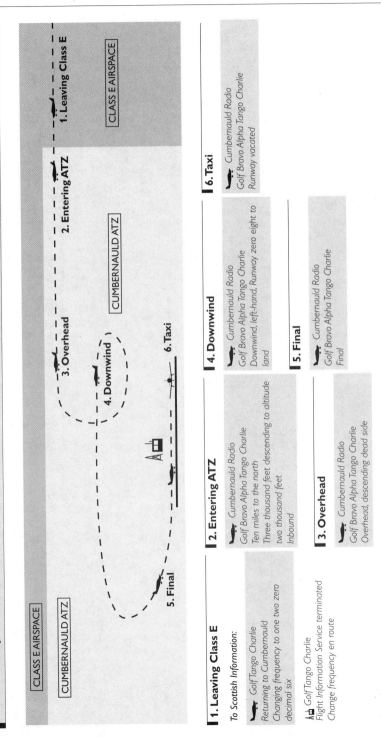

CLASS E AIRSPACE

CUMBERNAULD ATZ

1. Leaving Class E

2. Entering ATZ

3. Overhead

4. Downwind

CUMBERNAULD ATZ

CLASS E AIRSPACE

5. Final

6. Taxi

1. Leaving Class E

To Scottish Information:

🛩 *Golf Tango Charlie*
Returning to Cumbernauld
Changing frequency to one two zero
decimal six

Ⓐ *Golf Tango Charlie*
Flight Information Service terminated
Change frequency en route

2. Entering ATZ

🛩 *Cumbernauld Radio*
Golf Bravo Alpha Tango Charlie
Ten miles to the north
Three thousand feet descending to altitude
two thousand feet
Inbound

3. Overhead

🛩 *Cumbernauld Radio*
Golf Bravo Alpha Tango Charlie
Overhead, descending dead side

4. Downwind

🛩 *Cumbernauld Radio*
Golf Bravo Alpha Tango Charlie
Downwind, left-hand, Runway zero eight to
land

5. Final

🛩 *Cumbernauld Radio*
Golf Bravo Alpha Tango Charlie
Final

6. Taxi

🛩 *Cumbernauld Radio*
Golf Bravo Alpha Tango Charlie
Runway vacated

Class D Airspace *Departure*

MANCHESTER CTA

LIVERPOOL CTR

MANCHESTER CTA

LIVERPOOL CTR

LOW LEVEL ROUTE

4. En Route

3. Departure

1. Taxi   2. Take-off

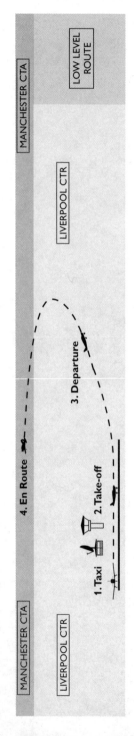

1. Taxi

Note An ATC route clearance is required for Class D airspace, which **must** be read back. This route clearance is separate from clearances from a control tower to operate on a runway at an ATC aerodrome. The ATC route clearance may be requested earlier, say in the parked position or while taxiing, to give you time to consider it with a request like "GolfTango Charlie, are you ready to copy your clearance?".

🎙 *Liverpool Tower*
Golf Bravo Alpha Tango Charlie
Request airfield information and taxi instructions

🗼 *GolfTango Charlie*
Surface wind zero five zero at one five
Temperature plus six
QNH one zero one four
Taxi to Holding Point Delta Runway zero nine via the northern taxiway

🎙 *Taxi to Holding Point Delta Runway zero nine via the northern taxiway*
QNH one zero one four
GolfTango Charlie

2. Take-Off

🎙 *GolfTango Charlie*
Ready for departure

🗼 *GolfTango Charlie is cleared to leave the Liverpool zone VFR via Aintree not above one thousand five hundred feet on the QNH*

🎙 *GolfTango Charlie*
Cleared to leave the zone VFR via Aintree not above one thousand five hundred feet on the QNH

🗼 *GolfTango Charlie*
Readback correct
Surface wind zero six zero at zero eight, with a left turn out
Cleared for take-off

🗼 *Cleared for take-off with a left turn out, GolfTango Charlie*

Note the two separate clearances.
1. ATC route clearance to enter and fly in Class D airspace.
2. Take-off clearance "Cleared for take-off".

3. Departure

🗼 *GolfTango Charlie*
Contact Liverpool Approach one one nine decimal eight five

🎙 *Changing frequency to Liverpool Approach one one nine decimal eight five*
GolfTango Charlie

Note "To" is followed by the name of the station to avoid confusion with the numbers (as would occur with "Changing to one one ......".

🎙 *Liverpool Approach*
This is Golf Bravo Alpha Tango Charlie

🗼 *Golf Bravo Alpha Tango Charlie*
Liverpool Approach
Report at Aintree
Traffic – a helicopter approaching Seaforth from the north at one thousand five hundred feet

🎙 *Wilco*
GolfTango Charlie

4. En Route

🎙 *GolfTango Charlie*
Overhead Aintree, helicopter in sight

🗼 *GolfTango Charlie*
No height restriction
Holyhead QNH one zero one two
Report when you wish to re-enter the zone

🎙 *Wilco*
Holyhead QNH one zero one two
GolfTango Charlie

Class D Airspace Arrival

MANCHESTER CTA

LIVERPOOL CTR

MANCHESTER CTA

LIVERPOOL CTR

1.Approaching ATZ

LOW LEVEL ROUTE

2.Joining Circuit

3.Taxi

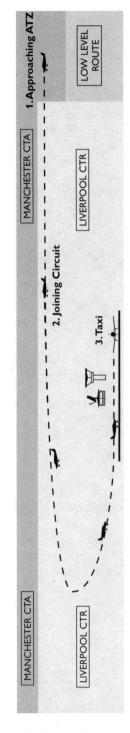

1. Approaching ATZ

✈ Liverpool Approach
Golf Bravo Alpha Tango Charlie

☎ Golf Bravo Alpha Tango Charlie
Liverpool Approach
Pass your message

✈ Golf Bravo Alpha Tango Charlie
PA-28
P Burscough
H Heading south
A Two thousand feet
C VFR
E Estimating Seaforth time one eight
R Request joining instructions

☎ Golf Tango Charlie
Report approaching Seaforth

✈ Wilco
Golf Tango Charlie

Note Remember that you may need to request a zone entry clearance, it won't necessarily be given automatically.

✈ Golf Tango Charlie
Approaching Seaforth

☎ Golf Tango Charlie is cleared to enter the zone at Seaforth not above one thousand five hundred feet Liverpool QNH one zero one five

✈ Golf Tango Charlie
Cleared to enter the zone at Seaforth not above one thousand five hundred feet, Liverpool QNH one zero one five

Note You now have the ATC clearance to enter the Class D controlled airspace.

☎ Golf Tango Charlie
Route via the east bank of the Mersey
Your clearance limit is the old north airfield
Expect Runway zero nine
QFE one zero one two. Report field in sight

✈ Golf Tango Charlie
Route via east bank of Mersey
Clearance limit the old north airfield
Expecting Runway zero nine
QFE one zero one two
Will report field in sight, Golf Tango Charlie

✈ Golf Tango Charlie
Contact Tower now on one one eight decimal one

✈ Golf Tango Charlie
Changing to frequency one one eight decimal one
Golf Tango Charlie

2. Joining Circuit

✈ Liverpool Tower
Golf Bravo Alpha Tango Charlie

☎ Golf Tango Charlie
Join and report approaching base for zero nine
QFE one zero one two
You are number two following a DC-9
Caution vortex wake, recommended spacing six miles

✈ Wilco, number two, visual with DC-9
Golf Tango Charlie

✈ Golf Tango Charlie, Base

☎ Golf Tango Charlie, Report final

✈ Wilco, Golf Tango Charlie

✈ Golf Tango Charlie, On final

☎ Golf Tango Charlie
Cleared to land, wind zero eight zero at zero six

✈ Cleared to land, Golf Tango Charlie

3. Taxi

☎ Golf Tango Charlie
Vacate next left onto the high-speed turn-off to Foxtrot and the western entrance to the main apron and follow the marshaller's instructions

✈ Golf Tango Charlie
Via Foxtrot and western entrance to main apron, further with marshaller
Golf Tango Charlie

Special VFR

The Special VFR Clearance

Special VFR is a concession (not a right) for pilots to fly within a
Control Zone when weather is below VMC minima, even though
they are unable to comply with Instrument Flight Rules (IFR)
procedures. Special VFR is designed to facilitate flights that would
otherwise be restricted due to weather. A Special VFR clearance
is usually given when traffic conditions allow (as determined by
the appropriate ATC unit).

> Special VFR is a concession for VFR pilots to operate in a Control Zone in poor weather conditions.

Many UK aerodromes have Special VFR Routes and/or
Entry/Exit Access Lanes established with published minimum
weather conditions (flight visibility and, in some cases, cloud ceiling) applicable to the route or lane. These are listed in AIP AD
and *Pooley's Flight Guide.*

Note that the issue of a Special VFR clearance by ATC to fly
in a Control Zone does not absolve you from the responsibility to
observe the Rules of the Air, where applicable. For example, a
Special VFR clearance to fly across London at 1,000 feet in the
London CTR may cause you to contravene the 'land clear'
requirements of Rule 5 of the Rules of the Air. If this is the case,
it is your responsibility to determine the breach of rules and reject
the clearance. See also Vol. 2 of *The Air Pilot's Manual.*

> On an Special VFR clearance, you must still obey the Rules of the Air.

When given a Special VFR clearance, you must:
- comply with **ATC clearances;**
- **remain clear of cloud,** determine your flightpath with reference to the ground, and keep clear of obstructions;
- **fly within the limitations of your licence;**
- **comply with low flying regulations** (note that this is *your*
responsibility, not the controller's);
- **avoid entering Aerodrome Traffic Zones** unless prior permission has been obtained from the appropriate Air Traffic
Services Unit.

There is also a requirement that, if you experience radio failure
when on a Special VFR clearance in a Control Zone, you should
squawk 7600 on your transponder and depart the Control Zone
(i.e. do not continue to the busy airport).

Further information on Special VFR is contained in AIP
ENR, and *Pooley's Flight Guide.* Finally, refer to your instructor
before embarking on your first Special VFR flight.

Departure

An example flight, which is Special VFR due to the weather being below the VFR minimum, begins on page 108.

The bigger the airport, the more people you have to speak to. For example, at East Midlands, you will first have to listen to the ATIS for the airfield information and ATIS code letter (see page 63), then call the Ground frequency for taxi instructions and clearance, telling them that you have received the latest ATIS by giving its code letter. Then you will change to the Tower frequency to obtain a clearance to enter the runway and take off. When airborne, you will call the Approach/Departures frequency.

Class D Airspace *Special/VFR Departure*

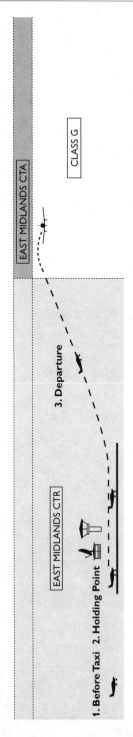

EAST MIDLANDS CTR

EAST MIDLANDS CTA

CLASS G

1. Before Taxi   2. Holding Point

3. Departure

---

1. Before Taxi

🛫 *East Midlands Ground*
Golf Bravo Alpha Tango Charlie, PA-28,
On the main apron with Information
Foxtrot
Request taxi instructions

📡 *GolfTango Charlie*
Information Foxtrot correct
Taxi to Holding Point Alpha, Runway zero
nine via the eastern taxiway

🛫 *Taxi to holding point Alpha,*
Runway zero nine
QNH one zero one nine
GolfTango Charlie

2. Holding Point

📡 *GolfTango Charlie*
Your clearance when ready

🛫 *Affirm*
GolfTango Charlie

Note *In this case, "Go ahead" is*
typically used instead of "Pass your
message". Also, the words used for the ATC
route clearance varies slightly in different
countries. For instance, you may hear,
"Ready to copy ATC".

📡 *GolfTango Charlie is cleared to leave*
the zone Special VFR by the Shepshed Lane
Exit not above two thousand feet, QNH
one zero one nine

🛫 *GolfTango Charlie cleared to leave*
the zone Special VFR by Shepshed Lane
exit not above two thousand feet, QNH
one zero one nine

📡 *GolfTango Charlie*
Readback correct
Contact Tower one two four decimal zero

🛫 *East Midlands Tower one two four*
decimal zero
GolfTango Charlie

3. Departure

📡 *Tower*
Golf Bravo Alpha Tango Charlie
Ready for departure

📡 *GolfTango Charlie*
After the landing Shorts 360, line-up and wait

🛫 *After the landing Shorts 360, line-up*
and wait
GolfTango Charlie

📡 *GolfTango Charlie*
Surface wind one hundred at sixteen knots
With a right turn out after departure,
cleared for take-off

🛫 *Right turn out after departure,*
cleared for take-off
GolfTango Charlie

📡 *GolfTango Charlie*
Contact Approach one one nine decimal six
five

🛫 *Contact Approach one one nine*
decimal six five
GolfTango Charlie

3. Departure

🛫 *East Midlands Approach*
Golf Bravo Alpha Tango Charlie

📡 *GolfTango Charlie*
East Midlands Approach
Report Shepshed

🛫 *Wilco*
GolfTango Charlie

📡 *GolfTango Charlie is now clear*
of the zone
Barnsley Regional QNH one zero one
seven
Report changing frequency en route

🛫 *Radar Control Service, Barnsley*
QNH one zero one seven
Wilco
GolfTango Charlie

Class D Airspace *Special VFR Arrival*

EAST MIDLANDS CTA

EAST MIDLANDS CTR

2. Joining Circuit

3. Taxi

1. Approaching ATZ

CLASS G

Before calling Approach for your zone entry clearance and joining instructions, listen to the ATIS to obtain the code letter.
* *For this example the conditions inside the zone are below the specified weather minima.*

1. Approaching ATZ

🦶 *East Midlands Approach*
Golf Bravo Alpha Tango Charlie
PA-28 inbound with Information Juliett

↘ *Golf Bravo Alpha Tango Charlie*
East Midlands Approach
Pass your message

🦶 *Golf Bravo Alpha Tango Charlie*
PA-28
P *Southwest of Leicester*
A *Two thousand feet, one zero one seven*
C *VFR*
E *Estimating Shepshed at five seven*
R *Request Special VFR zone entry*
clearance and joining instructions

↘ *Golf Tango Charlie*
Enter the zone Special VFR not above two thousand feet
Aerodrome QNH one zero one nine
Expect to join right base for Runway zero nine QFE one zero zero nine

🦶 *Golf Tango Charlie is cleared to enter the zone Special VFR not above two thousand feet*
Aerodrome QNH one zero one nine
Expecting a right base join for Runway zero nine QFE one zero zero nine

↘ *Golf Tango Charlie*
Report approaching Shepshed

🦶 *Wilco Golf Tango Charlie*

🦶 *Golf Tango Charlie*
Approaching Shepshed

↘ *Report field in sight*

🦶 *Wilco Golf Tango Charlie*

↘ *Golf Tango Charlie*
Field in sight

↘ *Golf Tango Charlie Call Tower on one two four decimal zero*

🦶 *Tower one two four decimal zero*
Golf Tango Charlie

2. Joining Circuit

🦶 *East Midlands Tower*
Golf Bravo Alpha Tango Charlie
Approaching right base Runway zero nine

↘ *Golf Tango Charlie*
Report on final
QFE one zero zero nine

🦶 *Golf Tango Charlie*
Wilco one zero zero nine

↘ *Golf Tango Charlie final*

📻 *Golf Tango Charlie*
Surface wind one one zero at one two two knots
Cleared to land

🦶 *Cleared to land*
Golf Tango Charlie

3. Taxi

📻 *Golf Tango Charlie*
Vacate next right Charlie taxiway
Contact Ground on one two one decimal nine

🦶 *Next right Charlie*
one two one decimal nine
Golf Tango Charlie

🦶 *Ground*
Golf Bravo Alpha Tango Charlie
Runway vacated at Charlie

Ground will then give you further taxi instructions.

Class A Airspace – Airways Crossing Clearance

Crossing an Airway

Crossing the Base of an Airway

A basic PPL holder (i.e. no IMC or Instrument Rating) may fly at right-angles across the base of an en route section of Airway where the lower limit is defined as a *flight level* (and not an *altitude*), but must not enter the Airway without permission. Weather conditions must be at least VMC. For example, if the lower limit of an Airway running east-west is FL75, then the pilot may cross it by flying north or south not above FL75.

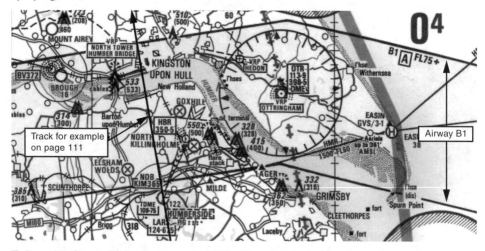

■ *Figure 7-3 Airway B1 (as shown on the half-million chart) can be crossed at right angles at FL75 in VMC. Track for Airway crossing example given on page 111 is marked from Humberside.*

Penetrating an Airway

Pilots who hold a valid Instrument Rating, even in an aeroplane not fully equipped for IFR flight, may penetrate and cross an Airway in Visual Meteorological Conditions (VMC) by day provided they:

☐ **file a flight plan** either before departure or when airborne; and

☐ **request a** *'crossing clearance'* from the responsible Air Traffic Control unit when at least 10 minutes from the intended crossing point, and subsequently receive that ATC crossing clearance. See page 111.

Except where otherwise authorised by ATC, aircraft are required to cross an Airway by the shortest route (normally at right-angles) and to be in level flight at the cleared level on entering the Airway.

Class A Airspace Airways Crossing

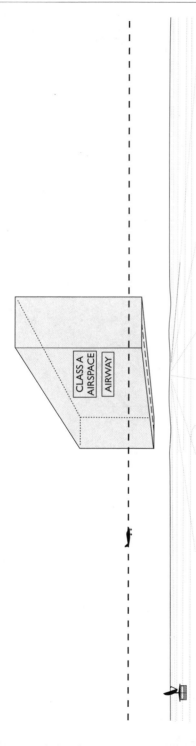

CLASS A AIRSPACE

AIRWAY

1. Requesting Crossing Clearance

Manchester Control
Golf Bravo Alpha Tango Charlie
Request cross Bravo One at Humberside

Golf Bravo Alpha Tango Charlie
Manchester Control
Pass your message

Golf Bravo Alpha Tango Charlie
PA-28
P Over Binbrook
H Heading three four five
A Flight level eight five
C VFR
E/R Estimating Bravo One at four six to cross flight level eight five

Golf Bravo Alpha Tango Charlie is cleared to cross Bravo One at Humberside Maintain flight level eight five whilst in controlled airspace

Cleared to cross Bravo One at Humberside maintaining flight level eight five
Golf Bravo Alpha Tango Charlie

Golf Tango Charlie
Readback correct, report entering

Wilco
Golf Tango Charlie

2. Entering Airway

Golf Tango Charlie
Entering Bravo One at Humberside, maintaining flight level eight five

Golf Tango Charlie
Roger

Note You may be given a transponder code to squawk while crossing the airway.

3. Leaving Airway

Golf Tango Charlie
You are just leaving controlled airspace, report changing frequency

Changing frequency to Linton one two nine decimal one five
Golf Tango Charlie

Now complete: **Exercises 7 – R/T in Controlled Airspace.**

When Things Go Wrong
Emergency Procedures

As pilot-in-command, you are responsible for the safety of yourself, your passengers, and the aircraft. If you do find yourself in real difficulty, waste no time in requesting assistance. Two straightforward means by which you can immediately alert others to an emergency situation which you are experiencing are:

You can communicate "emergency" using voice radio, and your transponder (code 7700).

☐ **a voice message** over the radio (on the frequency you are currently using with an Air Traffic Service Unit or on the VHF international aeronautical emergency frequency 121·5 megahertz); and/or

☐ **squawk code 7700** on your transponder if you feel it is advisable (which will alert a radar controller both visually and aurally, provided you are within radar range).

NOTE Even though this is a 'radio book', the use of the transponder as a means of communication is discussed here since the transponder is often combined with voice messages, or used to replace or reduce them.

Fly the Aeroplane
Even during an emergency your first priority must be to fly the aeroplane. Your second priority is to navigate, i.e. to be heading in a suitable general direction at a safe altitude. Your third priority is to communicate.

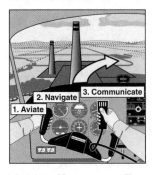

■ Figure 8-1 **Aviate, navigate, then communicate**

Making Known an Emergency Situation

Speak slowly and clearly.

You should make an emergency radio call whenever there is any serious doubt regarding the safety of a flight. This might be to request assistance for yourself, or to pass on information regarding another flight you believe to be experiencing difficulties. Transmissions should be slow and distinct, with each word pronounced clearly so that there is no need for repetition. This of course should apply to all radio transmissions but is more important in emergency situations. The emergency itself should be described concisely and accurately.

The recommended procedures to follow in an emergency situation are as illustrated. The procedures differ slightly depending upon whether you are already in radio contact with an Air Traffic Service Unit (ATSU), either civil or military, or not.

☐ **If you are already in radio contact with an ATSU,** then proceed with your voice message on that frequency initially (or 121·5 if you receive no response), and continue squawking the transponder code already assigned to you (other than the conspicuity code 7000) or squawk the emergency code 7700.

☐ **If you are *not* in radio contact with an ATSU,** then squawk the emergency code 7700 on your transponder to alert a radar controller visually and aurally that an emergency situation exists, that an emergency voice call on the frequency in use or on 121·5 MHz is likely, and to highlight your position on the radar screen.

Declaring an Emergency	Declaring an Emergency
Already in VHF Contact	Not in VHF Contact

▐ 1. Pass your message on frequency in use.

🔊 *Mayday, Mayday, Mayday*
....
....

▐ 2. Continue to squawk the code currently set on your transponder or 7700.

▐ 1. Squawk code 7700 on your transponder.

▐ 2. Pass your message on 121·5 MHz.

🔊 *Mayday, Mayday, Mayday*
....
....

■ *Figure 8-2* **Making known an emergency situation**

The Emergency or Guard Frequency 121·5 Mhz

The VHF frequency 121·5 megahertz is reserved right around the world as the **international aeronautical emergency frequency.** It is also known as the *guard* frequency. It should not be used for normal voice messages or general conversation.

In the UK, the emergency frequency 121·5 MHz is 'guarded' (listened to continuously) by two dedicated **Distress and Diversion (D&D) Sections,** manned by Royal Air Force controllers

121·5 MHz is the emergency frequency.

located at the London Air Traffic Control Centre and at the Scottish Air Traffic Control Centre. Their primary functions are to provide pilots with:

☐ **a search and rescue service (SAR);**

☐ **emergency services** if required (fire trucks, rescue launches, doctors, etc.); or

☐ **a position-fixing service** (i.e. Where am I?).

If you are making an emergency call on 121·5 MHz, you should (if you remember in the heat of the moment) address your calls to **London Area Control Centre** when south of latitude N55°, and **Scottish Area Control Centre** when north of latitude N55°.

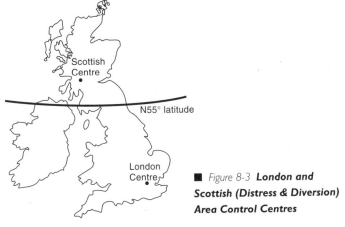

■ *Figure 8-3* **London and Scottish (Distress & Diversion) Area Control Centres**

People likely to hear emergency calls on 121·5 MHz:
• London/Scottish Centres
• ATSUs guarding 121·5
• pilots guarding 121·5

ELT signals are transmitted on 121·5.

As well as the D&D Sections, many **Air Traffic Service Units** (ATC and FIS) maintain a listening watch on 121·5, as do many pilots flying aircraft with more than one VHF radio (VHF-1 selected to the normal communications frequency; VHF-2 or VHF-3 selected to the emergency frequency 121·5). Even if you are too low or too remote for a D&D Section or an ATSU to receive your voice transmission, an aircraft flying overhead listening out on 121·5 MHz may hear your emergency call and relay it.

If you have more than one VHF set, then it is good airmanship for you to listen out on 121·5 MHz on the second set, while using the first set for normal communications (provided it is not a distraction). As well as emergency voice messages on 121·5, you may also hear the wailing sound of an activated **emergency locator transmitter (ELT)**. You should consider relaying these voice messages and report ELT transmissions if they have not already been acknowledged by someone in authority. Sometimes an ATSU will try to establish contact with an aircraft on 121·5 in a non-emergency situation if for some reason it is out of contact on the normal VHF frequency.

Radio and the transponder can play vital roles in an emergency when assistance is required, but remember always to fly the aircraft first. The order of priorities is aviate, navigate, and then communicate.

> Aviate, navigate, then communicate.

Classification of Emergency Situations

Depending on the seriousness of the situation, emergency radio calls are classified into two states – distress (Mayday), which is the more serious, and urgency (Pan-Pan), which is an emergency, but less serious.

- ☐ **Distress ("Mayday, Mayday, Mayday"):** the aircraft is threatened by serious and/or imminent danger, and requires *immediate* assistance. Absolute top priority message!
- ☐ **Urgency ("Pan-Pan, Pan-Pan, Pan-Pan"):** the caller has a very urgent message to transmit concerning the safety of an aircraft (own aircraft or another), or of a person on board or in sight, but which does *not* require immediate assistance.

The Distress Message or Mayday Call

The distress message is the absolute top priority call. It has priority over all others, and the word Mayday should force everyone else into immediate radio silence. Mayday is the Anglicised spelling of the French phrase *m'aidez!* which means "Help me!"

> A Mayday call takes priority above all others.

Some situations that would justify making a Mayday call include:

- ☐ **single-pilot incapacitation;**
- ☐ **engine failure,** fire, structural damage or failure;
- ☐ **a forced landing;**
- ☐ **being lost,** (very) uncertain of your position, or very low on fuel;
- ☐ **weather conditions deteriorating below** what you are able to fly in safely (cloud, poor visibility, etc.);
- ☐ **darkness, when you are not qualified to fly at night** and/or the aeroplane is not suitably equipped.

NOTE The equivalent written signal for Mayday is **SOS**, which in morse code is transmitted as "· · ·   — — —   · · ·" (*dit-dit-dit dah-dah-dah dit-dit-dit*).

Mayday Call Procedure

Make a Mayday call when you require immediate assistance and are being threatened by grave and immediate danger.

are already in direct contact with an ATSU when the ᵕy arises, transmit the Mayday call on the air-ground ᴑu are currently using. You may then be instructed ᵘuency to 121·5 MHz. In this case, any trans-

> Communicate on ATSU frequency in use.

ponder code setting previously assigned by ATC (other than the conspicuity code 7000) should be retained until you are instructed otherwise.

Squawk 7700.

2. **If you are *not* in direct radio contact with an ATSU** and your aircraft is transponder-equipped, squawk Mode A code 7700 (the emergency code), with Mode C (altitude-reporting) if available, before making the emergency call on the relevant ATSU frequency or on 121·5. If you are in a radar environment, squawking 7700 causes a special symbol to appear around your aircraft on the ATC radar screen, immediately alerting the ATC radar controllers.

Use 121·5 MHz.

3. **The Mayday distress message can be transmitted** on 121·5 MHz to "London Centre" when south of latitude N55° and "Scottish Centre" when north of N55°. (If you are uncertain about which centre to call, the station name may be omitted.) Once two-way communication has been established, you must not leave 121·5 MHz without notifying the controller.

Mayday Call Content

The distress message should contain as much of the following information as time and circumstances permit, and if possible be spoken in the order below. Commit this to memory – it will help you in a real emergency (and will be tested in your radio test).

MAYDAY CALL CONTENT
a. Mayday, Mayday, Mayday
b. Name of the station addressed (when appropriate)
c. Callsign
d. Type of aircraft
e. Nature of the emergency
f. Intention of the pilot-in-command
g. Present or last known position
h. Flight level/altitude
i. Heading
j. Pilot qualifications (see following note) state whether: 1. Student pilot (TYRO); 2. No instrument qualification; 3. IMC rating; or 4. Full instrument rating
k. Any other useful information, e.g. endurance remaining and number of people on board (written as POB and pronounced "pee-oh-bee")

NOTE Including the pilot's qualification is not mandatory, but it will help controllers to issue instructions appropriate to your experience. Inexperienced or student civil pilots should use the word "TYRO" when communicating with a military station or the Distress and Diversion centre. This code word indicates their lack of experience to the controller. Other descriptions include Basic PPL, CPL, and instrument-rated.

You must of course use your operational judgement and not delay transmission of the distress message (say by trying to determine your position too precisely in the absence of suitable landmarks or in conditions of poor visibility). Early advice to an ATSU of your emergency situation may assist in more rapid assistance. If you become confused regarding order and content of the Mayday message, then pass the information as best you can.

Typical Mayday Call

A typical Mayday call is illustrated below showing a situation where you have been in radio contact with Caernarfon ATSU previously and have now experienced an engine failure. You would make a Mayday call on the frequency in use, and squawk code 7700.

> *Make your initial Mayday call on the ATSU frequency in use.*

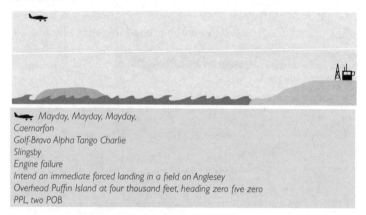

Mayday, Mayday, Mayday,
Caernarfon
Golf-Bravo Alpha Tango Charlie
Slingsby
Engine failure
Intend an immediate forced landing in a field on Anglesey
Overhead Puffin Island at four thousand feet, heading zero five zero
PPL, two POB

■ *Figure 8-4* **A typical Mayday call**

If no response is received on the Caernarfon ATSU frequency which you have been using, squawk 7700 on your transponder and call London Centre on 121·5, repeating the call. (If you are north of latitude 55°N, you would call Scottish Centre on the same frequency.)

> *Squawk 7700 and call on 121·5 MHz.*

The reply from London Centre would be:

Golf Bravo Alpha Tango Charlie
London Centre
Roger your Mayday

Appropriate Search and Rescue (SAR) action would then be commenced.

Repeat your message if necessary.

If there is no immediate response from a ground station acknowledging your call, then the distress message should be repeated at intervals. Other aircraft hearing the Mayday call will have imposed radio silence on themselves, but, having noted that the distress call was not acknowledged by a ground station, may at this stage be able to assist by relaying the distress call to a ground station.

The Urgency Message or Pan-Pan Call

The urgency or Pan-Pan message is made over the air-ground frequency in use, or 121·5 MHz if considered more prudent, when an emergency exists that does not require immediate assistance.

Typical situations when a Pan-Pan urgency message is appropriate include:

- **if you are experiencing navigational difficulties** (i.e. uncertain of position), and require the urgent assistance of ATC;
- **if you have a passenger on board** who has become seriously ill and will require urgent medical attention;
- **rough-running engine,** electrical fault or other technical problems;
- **deteriorating weather or light** with no appropriate instrument rating;
- **if you see another aeroplane or a ship** whose safety is threatened and urgent action is perhaps needed;
- **if you are making an emergency change of level** in controlled airspace and you may conflict with traffic below. (This could be a Mayday call, for instance if you are in IMC where there is greater risk of collision with other aircraft.)

Pan-Pan is the second priority, after a Mayday call which always has top priority.

The *urgency* or Pan-Pan takes priority over all other calls except a Mayday call. If you want to make a Pan-Pan call, but a Mayday call and its follow-up are already in process, or if a Mayday call interrupts your Pan-Pan call, then standby with your Pan-Pan call, or select another suitable VHF frequency. Do not interrupt a Mayday call!

If you are already in direct contact with an ATSU, make your emergency call on that frequency. If you are not in direct contact with an ATSU, then squawk 7700 and make your emergency call on the relevant ATSU frequency or on 121·5 MHz.

NOTE The equivalent written signal for Pan-Pan is **XXX**, which in morse code is transmitted as: "– · · –   – · · –   – · · –" (*dah-dit-dit-dah   dah-dit-dit-dah   dah-dit-dit-dah).*

Pan-Pan Call Content

The Pan-Pan call should contain the same information in the
same order as the Mayday call.

PAN-PAN CALL CONTENT
a. Pan-Pan, Pan-Pan, Pan-Pan
b. Name of the station addressed (when appropriate)
c. Callsign
d. Type of aircraft
e. Nature of the emergency
f. Intention of the pilot-in-command
g. Present or last known position
h. Flight level/altitude
i. Heading

j. Pilot qualifications – state whether:
   1. Student pilot (military term TYRO);
   2. No instrument qualification;
   3. IMC rating; or
   4. Full instrument rating

k. Any other useful information, e.g. endurance remaining and number of persons on board (POB)

Typical Pan-Pan Call

A typical Pan-Pan call is shown in Figure 8-5. The situation is that
you are in radio contact with Shawbury Radar and are now experiencing a rough-running engine which could lead to further
problems (e.g. total engine failure).

As a precautionary measure, you decide to land at the nearest
suitable airfield. The aircraft is *not* in grave and imminent danger,
hence a Mayday call is not appropriate. You would make a Pan-
Pan call on the frequency in use, and continue to squawk the code
already assigned to you on your transponder until otherwise
instructed. Not being familiar with the area, you request guidance
to the nearest suitable airfield. If you were familiar with the area
and did not require assistance to locate the airfield, you would just
advise the ATSU in your Pan-Pan call where you intended to
land.

If no response is received on the Shawbury Radar frequency
which you have been using, squawk 7700 on your transponder
and call London Centre on 121·5 and repeat your urgency message. (If you are north of latitude N55°, you would call Scottish
Centre on the same frequency 121·5).

- Pan-Pan, Pan-Pan, Pan-Pan
- Shawbury Radar
- Golf Bravo Alpha Tango Charlie
- Slingsby
- Rough running engine
- Request diversion heading to the nearest airfield
- Northwest abeam Whitchurch
- Two thousand five hundred feet
- Heading three four zero
- Student
- One person on board

Golf Bravo Alpha Tango Charlie
Roger your Pan call, standby

Golf Tango Charlie
The nearest suitable airfield is Sleap,
which is one zero miles to the south of you
Turn left onto a heading of two zero zero degrees
I will pass your details to Sleap now, Standby

Turn left, head two zero zero Standing by
Golf Tango Charlie

Golf Tango Charlie
Contact Sleap radio now on one two two decimal four five

Sleap Radio one two two decimal four five
Golf Tango Charlie

■ *Figure 8-5* **A typical Pan-Pan call**

A Training-Fix or Pan Call when Uncertain of Position

The Distress and Diversion (D&D) Sections located at London
Centre and Scottish Centre, and some ATSUs, can assist you in
locating your position if necessary and in guiding you to your destination or to a diversion airfield.

Radar can fix your position.

If you are in radar coverage and have a **transponder,** then they
can determine your position almost immediately using their radar
screen, and perhaps by asking you to squawk a particular code or
to squawk *ident.*

D/F can fix your position.

If you are not in radar coverage, then D&D can determine your
position by an older method known as VHF direction finding
(VDF or D/F). A number of different ground stations note the
direction from which your radio voice messages are received
(using radio D/F equipment). With information from two or
more ground stations equipped with VDF, position lines can be
plotted on a map (automatically or manually at one of the ground
stations or elsewhere), with their point of intersection showing
your position. This means of fixing position is known as triangu-
lation. The accuracy of the position lines depends to some extent
on the height of the aircraft above terrain (so that your radio signals are not inhibited because of high ground) and your proximity
to several ground stations equipped with VDF.

In some areas your D/F position can be determined very quickly automatically (auto-triangulation); in other areas it may have to be plotted manually on a chart by the ATSU and may take a little longer.

For a practice emergency requiring only confirmation of your position, you can request a Training-Fix on 121·5 MHz. This call takes precedence over a Practice-Pan, but not over a real Mayday or Pan call.

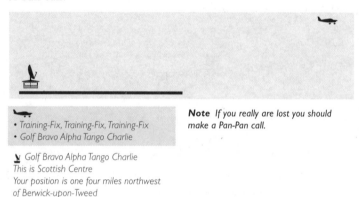

• Training-Fix, Training-Fix, Training-Fix
• Golf Bravo Alpha Tango Charlie

Note *If you really are lost you should make a Pan-Pan call.*

➘ Golf Bravo Alpha Tango Charlie
This is Scottish Centre
Your position is one four miles northwest
of Berwick-upon-Tweed

■ Figure 8-6 **A Training-Fix call when you are simulating uncertain of your position**

A Practice-Pan Call

To gain experience with making emergency calls, you are permitted to make a Practice-Pan call in which you simulate the call you would make in an *urgency* situation. You preface this call with the words "*Practice-Pan, Practice-Pan, Practice-Pan*". Under no circumstances are you allowed to use the word Mayday except in a *genuine* distress situation (hence you are *not* permitted to make practice distress calls.)

To give you practice in urgency calls at little cost in time or fuel, you could make a Practice-Pan call on the way back from the training area to your airfield or as part of a cross–country flight, perhaps even asking for a heading for your destination airfield. You should make a practice call at some stage during your training; the experience will be valuable should you ever need to use the service in a real situation.

Before making the Practice-Pan call, listen out on 121·5 MHz to ensure that no real emergencies or other practice calls are in progress. Make sure you begin your call with "Practice-Pan". Should the Distress and Diversion centre be unable to take your practice call at that time, they will instruct you to call back.

Practice-Pan, Practice-Pan, Practice-Pan
London Centre, this is Golf Bravo Alpha Tango Charlie
requesting Practice-Pan

↘ Golf Bravo Alpha Tango Charlie
This is London Centre
Roger your Practice-Pan, Standby

↘ Golf Bravo Alpha Tango Charlie
London Centre
Continue with your Practice-Pan

When the Practice-Pan call is accepted, pass your details. Transponder Mode A Code 7700 should not be selected during a practice emergency unless required by the controller. Mode C (altitude reporting) should be switched on, if available.

• Practice-Pan, Practice-Pan, Practice-Pan
• London Centre
• This is Golf Bravo Alpha Tango Charlie
• Slingsby
• I have a passenger who has become unconscious
• Request headings to the nearest aerodrome with medical facilities available
• Northeast of Great Yarmouth
• Three thousand feet
• Heading two seven zero
• PPL with three POB

↘ Golf Bravo Alpha Tango Charlie
The nearest suitable aerodrome is
Norwich, which is one five miles to the northwest of you
Turn right, heading three two five degrees

✈ Right heading three two five
Golf Tango Charlie

↘ Golf Tango Charlie
Contact Norwich Radar on one one nine decimal three five
They have your details and are arranging medical assistance
Cancelling Practice-Pan
Golf Tango Charlie

■ Figure 8-7 **A typical Practice-Pan call**

Imposition of Radio Silence

Do not interrupt Mayday calls.

Distress Mayday calls have priority over all others. On hearing an emergency call, you must maintain radio silence unless you can render assistance, and continue to listen on the frequency concerned until it is apparent that assistance is being provided. Copy down the details of the call in case you are required to help.

The aircraft in emergency or the ATSU in control of an emergency may impose radio silence on all stations in the area or on any particular station that interferes with emergency transmissions. In the example in Figure 8-8, Bristol Tower imposes radio silence on all aircraft except the aircraft experiencing the emergency. The imposition of radio silence will be initially directed at all aircraft on the frequency, or specifically at one aircraft if it inconveniently breaks the radio silence.

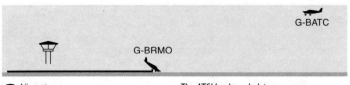

<table>
<tr><td>

🛩 All stations
Bristol Tower
Stop transmitting
Mayday
or:

🛩 Golf Bravo Alpha Tango Charlie
Stop transmitting
Mayday

</td><td>

The ATSU acknowledging an emergency
message may transfer all other aircraft on
that frequency to another convenient
frequency to avoid disruption of the
emergency transmissions. For example:

🛩 Mayday Golf Bravo Romeo Mike Oscar
All other aircraft contact Bristol Radar on
one two four decimal three five, out.

</td></tr>
</table>

■ Figure 8-8 **Imposing radio silence**

Relaying Emergency Messages

If you hear an emergency call that is not acknowledged, perhaps
because the transmitting aircraft is out of range of a ground station, you should relay the emergency message.

Whenever you hear a Mayday call, you should note the details
down, just in case you have to relay the message. Try and note the
details when you first hear them because the pilot in distress may
not be able to transmit them a second time. Having heard another
pilot make a Mayday call, you should self-impose radio silence for
an appropriate period so as not to impede communication
between the aircraft in distress and the ATSU.

If you see someone else in distress, say a ditched aircraft or a
boat on fire, you should transmit an urgency message on their
behalf. To make it clear that the transmitting aircraft is not in distress, but that the call is on someone else's behalf, you should
repeat their identity.

<table>
<tr><td>

🛩 Mayday, Mayday, Mayday
Shawbury Radar
Golf Bravo Alpha Tango Charlie
Have intercepted Mayday from
Golf Bravo Alpha India Romeo
I say again Golf Bravo Alpha India Romeo
Mooney
Engine fire forced landing two miles north
of Whitchurch
CPL, over

</td><td>

Your call would be acknowledged:

🛩 Golf Bravo Alpha Tango Charlie
Shawbury Radar
Roger your relayed **Mayday** from
Golf Bravo Alpha India Romeo

</td></tr>
</table>

■ Figure 8-9 **Relaying an emergency message**

Cancellation of Emergency Communications and Radio Silence

When your aircraft is no longer experiencing an emergency condition, then you can make a call to cancel the condition and also to inform the ground station of your further intentions. When an emergency situation has been resolved, the controlling station will notify all stations that normal transmissions can be resumed.

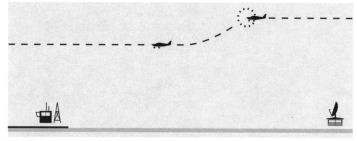

Golf Bravo Alpha Tango Charlie
*Cancel **Mayday***
Engine restarted
Diverting to Caernarfon aerodrome
I have the field in sight

 All stations London Centre
***Mayday** traffic ended*

■ *Figure 8-10* **Cancelling emergency communications and radio silence**

Now complete: **Exercises 8 – Emergency Procedures.**

When Things Go Wrong
Radio Failure Procedures

If you experience a loss of radio communications, you should:
- ☐ **try to restore communications,** then proceed normally; or
- ☐ **if communications cannot be restored,** then follow standard radio failure procedures according to your best judgement.

Radio failure?
1. Try to restore communications.
2. Otherwise follow standard radio failure procedures.

■ *Figure 9-1* **Loss of radio communications**

Aeroplanes Can Still Fly Without a Radio
The Wright brothers never thought to install a radio in their first aeroplane, yet it still flew. Radio is simply a modern aid to flying that we make great use of to improve the safety and efficiency of flight.

Fly the aeroplane accurately at all times.

Whether the radio is working or not does not affect the flying characteristics of the aeroplane. If the radio fails and you lose communications, it does not mean that the aeroplane stops flying. You should continue to fly the aeroplane accurately, navigate safely (i.e. head in a suitable direction at a safe altitude), and then try to restore communications. If that is not possible, then follow reasonable radio failure procedures according to good airmanship and your own best judgement. The golden rule is: *aviate, navigate, communicate.*

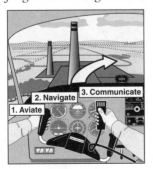

■ *Figure 9-2*
Aviate, navigate, communicate

Loss of Communications due to Human Error

Loss of communications is typically caused by human error.

With modern equipment, actual radio failure radio is a rare event. However, loss of communications or failure to establish communications still occurs from time to time, usually due to some human error.

These errors, once you are aware of them, can usually be remedied. They include:

- ☐ **wrong frequency selected;**
- ☐ **audio panel selected incorrectly** (e.g. wrong VHF-COM set selected to speaker/headset);
- ☐ **volume too low** (no incoming calls heard);
- ☐ **squelch too low** (blocking out desired signals as well as unwanted noise);
- ☐ **microphone or headset** not firmly plugged in;
- ☐ **stuck mike** (yours or someone else's);
- ☐ **out of range** of ground station being called;
- ☐ **ground station being called off the air** (see hours of service in AIP AD or NOTAMs).

Once these human errors are remedied, what you thought was a radio failure turns out to have been merely a temporary loss of communications. Everything can then proceed normally.

Loss of Communications due to Equipment Failure

Occasionally, however, you may experience a *genuine* failure of the radio set, or a complete electrical failure in the aircraft which of course will mean that the radios will not function. Other genuine problems could be a faulty microphone or headset, or popped circuit breakers or blown fuses which protect the radios from electrical overloads or overheating. Sometimes you can remedy this, by resetting the popped CB or replacing the blown fuse (once only), or replacing the faulty microphone or headset, or switching to an alternative radio.

> *Loss of communications can be caused by equipment failure.*

> *Attempt to restore electrical power once only.*

You should *not* reset a popped CB or replace a blown fuse more than once, since a second occurrence will usually indicate that there is a genuine electrical problem with the equipment. If you try to restore it repeatedly, say by holding the CB in, this could lead to more serious electrical problems or a fire.

Sometimes a radio can experience a partial failure rather than a complete failure. If the transmitter fails, you can still receive messages. If the receiver fails, you can still transmit messages (known as *transmitting blind).*

■ *Figure 9-3* **Reset a popped CB once only**

ATSU Actions Following Suspected Aircraft Radio Failure

The Air Traffic Service Unit will make several calls to the aircraft to try and regain or establish communications. If not successful, the ground station will then check that its own equipment is operating normally by making a radio check with other aircraft, or checking the equipment. If the ground station equipment is unserviceable, then the ATSU will switch to other standby equipment (if available).and resume normal operations.

*Relaying messages
is possible.*

Usually the ground station equipment is serviceable. In that case, the ATSU will ask other aircraft to try and communicate with the aircraft that is out of radio contact. The target aircraft might *not* have had a radio failure, but be simply shielded from line–of–sight contact with the ATSU by high terrain. If contact is made, then messages can be relayed via the other aircraft.

➘ *Golf Bravo Alpha Tango Charlie
Contact Eglinton on one two three decimal
six two*

No response from G-BATC

➘ *Shamrock 341
Belfast Radar
Could you relay a message to Golf Bravo
Alpha Tango Charlie to contact Eglinton on
one two three decimal six two*

✈ *Shamrock three four one
Wilco*

✈ *Golf Bravo Alpha Tango Charlie
from Shamrock three four one*

✈ *Shamrock three four one
Golf Bravo Alpha Tango Charlie*

✈ *Golf Bravo Alpha Tango Charlie
Relay from Belfast Radar to contact
Eglinton on one two three decimal six two*

✈ *Eglinton on one two three decimal
six two
Golf Bravo Alpha Tango Charlie*

✈ *Belfast Radar
Shamrock three four one
Message relayed*

➘ *Shamrock three four one
Belfast Radar
Roger*

■ *Figure 9-4* **Relaying a message**

If communication is *not* established, the ATSU will transmit blind to the aircraft that is out of contact on the frequency that it is believed to be listening (the frequency in use or the emergency frequency 121·5 MHz). The content of these blind transmissions will include:

▢ **the level, route, and estimated times of arrival** of the aircraft according to what the ATSU assumes the aircraft is adhering; and

▢ **the weather conditions** at the destination airport and suitable alternate airports.

Failure of ATSU Ground Equipment

*Transfer frequencies if
a ground station goes
off the air.*

Ground stations do occasionally experience radio failure, perhaps following a lightning strike. Failure of ground equipment is a rare event, though, and most ATC ground stations have emergency power backup and standby transmitters that can be used if required. If necessary you can often regain communications by transferring to the frequency of another ground station. An A/G or FIS radio station is unlikely to have emergency power backups.

Other Means of Communicating

A loss of *voice* communications does not mean a loss of *all* communications.

> Means of communication from the aircraft include:
> • voice radio;
> • partial voice radio;
> • transponder;
> • light signals;
> • speechless code;
> • mobile telephone.

☐ **First of all,** you may have a **partial radio failure.** You might be able to *receive* but not *transmit*, or vice versa, in which case you can still make use of what remains.

☐ **You can use your transponder** (provided it still has electrical power and you are within range of a radar station) to indicate radio failure by squawking code 7600. Further still, there are **light signals** with specific meanings that can be beamed at you from a tower, such as a steady green light which means "Clear to land". You can flash your landing lights on and off to indicate "I am compelled to land".

☐ Also, *carrier wave transmissions only* (no superimposed voice messages) can be used to pass simple messages like *yes* or *no* using the **speechless code** – a single 1-second press of the transmit button meaning "yes", and two 1-second presses of the transmit button meaning "no". (Carrier waves are explained on page 162.)

The specific *light signals*, and the *speechless code* are explained in detail at the end of the chapter.

To determine wind direction and the landing runway at your diversion or destination airport, you may be able to hear the ATIS on a VOR frequency using the VHF-NAV radio, or you could use visual means such as the wind indicator and/or the signals square at the airport which you can observe as you overfly. You can also determine circuit direction from the flight paths of other aircraft. Remember that *see-and-be-seen* applies, so make yourself visible (landing lights on), transmit blind, and keep a very good lookout. In general, the safest procedure is to overfly the nearest suitable airfield at 2,000 feet aal (or as appropriate to the airfield), make a standard join of the circuit pattern, transmit blind at the usual reporting points (downwind and final – you may also consider it worthwhile to make a call turning base), flash your landing lights, and make a normal safe landing.

Radar Assistance

Transponder squawk for radio failure is 7600.

If you are within radar coverage and experience a radio failure, **squawking 7600** on your transponder will bring up a special message on radar screens that alerts radar controllers to your radio failure.

■ *Figure 9-5* **Radio failure – squawk 7600**

Radar assistance can be most useful.

The radar controller may try to determine if you are able to *receive* (i.e. transmitter failure only but receiver OK) by issuing instructions to you such as "Turn right onto heading 180", or "If you are receiving this message squawk ident", and then observing if you comply. If you *do* comply, then the radar controller will assume that you can receive messages and will then proceed to provide you with assistance and clearances if required. If you do *not* comply, then the controller will assume total radio failure, will alert other relevant ATSUs and aircraft to your situation, and will monitor your flight path and try to keep it clear. The ATSU will use your callsign if known, otherwise will refer to the *speechless aircraft*. The ATSU will attempt to establish your callsign.

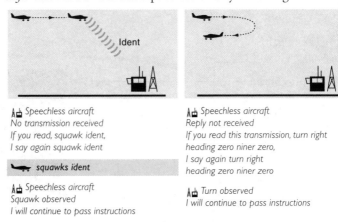

*Speechless aircraft
No transmission received
If you read, squawk ident,
I say again squawk ident*

squawks ident

*Speechless aircraft
Squawk observed
I will continue to pass instructions*

*Speechless aircraft
Reply not received
If you read this transmission, turn right
heading zero niner zero,
I say again turn right
heading zero niner zero*

*Turn observed
I will continue to pass instructions*

■ *Figure 9-6* **Radar assistance**

An old-fashioned and little-used procedure to attract the attention of a radar controller to your radio failure (if you do not have a transponder) is to fly a triangle with 2-minute legs. This is described in detail at the end of the chapter. It is a time-consuming manoeuvre that may not bring results (unlike squawking 7600 in a radar environment).

Loss of Communications Procedures

1. Try to Restore Communications

- ☐ Fly the aeroplane accurately.
- ☐ Check correct frequency and in range of active ATSU.
- ☐ Check your radio setup:
    - Electrical master switch, avionics switch, and individual radio switch – on.
    - Audio selector panel selected correctly.
    - Volume correctly set.
    - Squelch correctly set.
    - Microphone PTT button not stuck.
    - Microphone plugged in firmly.
    - Headset plugged in firmly: consider swapping headsets or transferring to speaker (or, if you are already on speaker, transferring to a headset).
- ☐ CBs/fuses – check (if easily accessible without distraction to normal flight), reset once only.
- ☐ Try another VHF-COM set.
- ☐ Ask for a *relay* from another aircraft.
- ☐ Try another frequency, e.g. another ATSU or the emergency frequency 121·5 MHz.
- ☐ If communications are re-established, continue with normal operations. If you *cannot* restore communications, then follow loss of communications procedures (listed below) according to your best judgement.

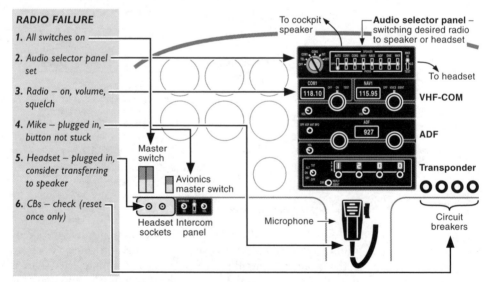

■ Figure 9-7 **Try to restore normal communications**

2. Assume Loss of Communications

☐ **Fly the aeroplane accurately.**

☐ **Squawk 7600** on your transponder.

☐ **Transmit blind** (just in case you have a *receiver* failure only: address the station, identify yourself, pass your message, then repeat the whole call.

☐ **If *transmitter* failure only** – answer any messages you receive with transponder squawks or heading changes as requested, or with speechless code (see later). Follow received instructions as appropriate.

☐ **Stay in Visual Meteorological Conditions (VMC)** and land at the nearest suitable airport. Remember that there is no hurry – the aircraft is not in danger and can fly normally. Overfly the airfield to check wind direction and landing runway if necessary. *See-and-be-seen* applies, so keep an especially good lookout. Do not continue on a Special VFR clearance (SVFR) into a busy airport in controlled airspace, since the need for an SVFR clearance indicates that conditions might be less than VMC, but turn around and depart the control zone if you consider that to be a safe option.

☐ **After landing,** contact the relevant ATSU by telephone, by radio from another aircraft, or face-to-face, and advise them of your situation.

☐ **Get the radio repaired.**

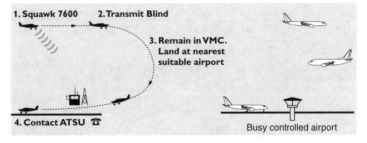

I 1. Squawk 7600

I 2. Transmit Blind

> 🛩 *Shoreham Approach*
> *Golf Bravo Alpha Tango Charlie*
> *Transmitting blind*
> *No reception on one two three decimal one five*
> *I am remaining Victor Mike Charlie and returning to the overhead*
> *I say again, am remaining in VMC and returning to the overhead*

I 3. Remain in VMC and Land at Nearest Airport

I 4. Contact ATSU

■ *Figure 9-8* **Follow standard radio failure procedures**

General Plans if you experience Radio Failure In Flight

If you are in VMC and outside controlled airspace, then squawk 7600, stay in VMC, stay outside controlled airspace, transmit blind if you think there is any chance of your message getting out, and land at the nearest suitable airport.

If you are in VMC and with a clearance to enter or are already in controlled airspace, then squawk 7600, stay in VMC, transmit blind if you think there is any chance of your message getting out, and land at the nearest suitable airport. You should not enter the controlled airspace unless you already have a clearance to enter.

If you are on a Special VFR (SVFR) clearance to enter controlled airspace: squawk 7600; remain clear of the controlled airspace or depart it if it is safe to do so (even though you have an SVFR clearance); stay in VMC; transmit blind if you think there is any chance of your message getting out; and land at the nearest suitable airport.

Light Signals from the Tower

Having returned to an airport in an aircraft known to have experienced radio failure, the ATSU may beam light signals that convey special instructions at your aircraft. You should remember these light signals, and occasionally during your training (and afterwards) ask tower controllers to demonstrate them to you. The light signals differ in meaning according to whether you are in flight or on the ground. Green flashes, for instance, when beamed at an aircraft in flight mean "Return for a landing", whereas when beamed to an aircraft on the ground they mean "Authorised to taxi".

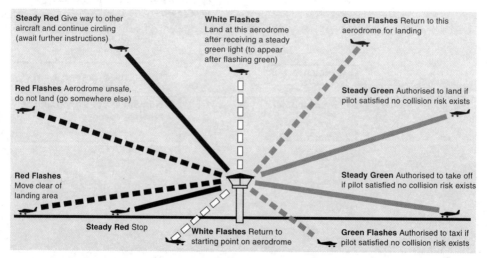

■ Figure 9-9 **Light signals beamed to an aircraft from an ATSU**

There are also light signals which can be sent *from* an aircraft, but the equipment (such as flares) is rarely available for a pilot to use. The one signal that can be used in almost any aircraft, however, is the flashing on and off of the landing lights or of the position navigation lights (usually visible from the ground only at night) to indicate "I am compelled to land".

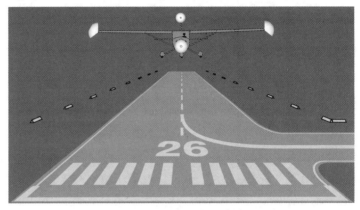

■ *Figure 9-10* **Flashing landing and/or navigation lights: "I am compelled to land"**

Rarely used light signals from an aircraft are:
- ☐ **a red pyrotechnic light** or red flare sent from an aircraft indicating "Immediate assistance is requested"; or
- ☐ **a continuous green light,** or green flashes, or green pyrotechnic light sent from an aircraft indicating by night: "May I land?"; and by day: "May I land in a direction different from that indicated by the landing T?"

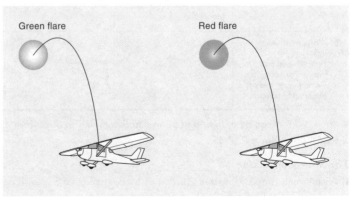

■ *Figure 9-11* **Rarely used light signals from an aircraft**

Characteristic and colour of light beam or pyrotechnic	From an aerodrome		From an aircraft in flight to an aerodrome
	to an aircraft in flight	to an aircraft or vehicle on the aerodrome	
(a) Continuous red light	Give way to other aircraft and continue circling	Stop	—
(b) Red pyrotechnic light, or red flare	Do not land; wait for permission	—	Immediate assistance is required
(c) Red flashes	Do not land; aerodrome is not available for landing	Move clear of landing area	—
(d) Green flashes	Return to aerodrome; wait for permission to land	To an aircraft: You may move on the manoeuvring area and apron To a vehicle: You may move on the manoeuvring area	—
(e) Continuous green light	You may land	You may take off	—
(f) Continuous green light, or green flashes, or green pyrotechnic light	—	—	By night: May I land? By day: May I land in direction different to that indicated by landing T?
(g) White flashes	Land at this aerodrome after receiving continuous green light and then, after receiving green flashes, proceed to the apron	Return to starting point on the aerodrome	I am compelled to land
(h) White pyrotechnic lights Switching on and off the navigation lights Switching on and off the landing lights	—	—	I am compelled to land

■ Figure 9-13 **Meaning of light and pyrotechnic signals – extract from the CAA publication CAP 85**

The Speechless Code

If your voice message is *unintelligible* to a controller, or if you have *carrier wave* transmission only with no voice message superimposed, then you may be instructed to use the speechless code. This is a series of simple transmissions, which you can make by pressing your *press-to-transmit* button, with the following meanings:

THE SPEECHLESS CODE

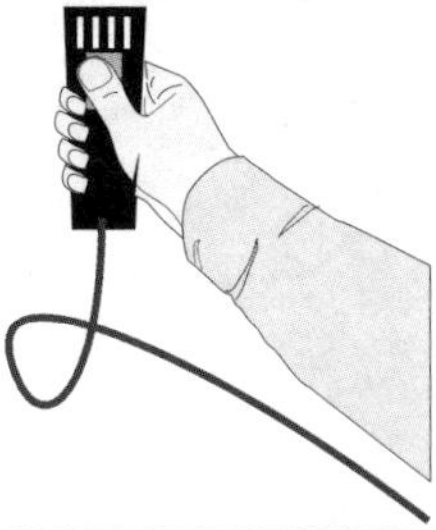

Number of Transmissions	Meaning
One short	**"Yes"** or an acknowledgement.
Two short	**"No"**
Three short	**"Say again"** (To be used by the pilot when he/she has not fully heard the controller's transmission, or the transmission was an instruction and the pilot is unable to comply).
Four short (letter H in morse code)	**"Request homing"** (to an airfield), or used for initial alerting (a civil pilot should only use the four short transmissions if he/she is aware, or suspects before attempting to make initial contact with the Emergency Controller, that his/her own aircraft microphone is unserviceable. The Emergency Controller will then interrogate the pilot, using the callsign "Speechless aircraft" if the identity of the aircraft is unknown).
One long (2 seconds)	**"Manoeuvre complete"** (e.g. steady on heading).
One long, two short and one long (− .. − letter X in morse)	**"My aircraft has developed another emergency."**

- Yes
- ■ No
- ■ ■ Say again
- ■ ■ ■ Require homing
- ■ Manoeuvre complete
- ■ ■ ■ A further emergency

■ Figure 9-15 **The speechless code**

The 2-minute-leg Radio Failure Triangle

A little-used (and not-recommended) procedure to indicate to a radar controller that you have experienced radio failure is to fly a **radio failure triangle**. (A much easier means is to squawk 7600 on your transponder, but this may not be available to you if your aircraft has experienced electrical failure.)

Right triangle: receiver is OK (transmitter has failed).

A situation where a radio failure triangle *might* be useful is if you have experienced a **transmitter failure** (but you can still receive) and are lost, or trapped above clouds, and need assistance from a radar controller whose attention you first have to attract. You should then fly a clockwise radio failure triangle to the right, i.e. all turns to the *right*, with each leg at light aircraft speeds being 2 minutes long. Allow for wind effect so that the track over the ground, and that painted on the radar screen, is indeed a triangle. Fly the pattern at least twice, which means it will take at least two times six minutes, i.e. 12 minutes, plus times for the turns, which should be fairly tight (say 30° bank angle). The aim is to paint an unusual picture on the radar screen that attracts the eye of the radar controller. Since you are able to receive transmissions from the ATSU, the controller can send you voice instructions and information.

If you have experienced a total radio failure, then you would fly an anticlockwise triangle to the *left*. Since you can neither send nor receive, there is not much the radar controller can do to assist you directly, other than to be aware of your situation and to alert others, and in an extreme situation despatch another aircraft to guide you down.

Left triangle: total radio failure (transmitter and receiver have failed), i.e. "left hand = nothing left".

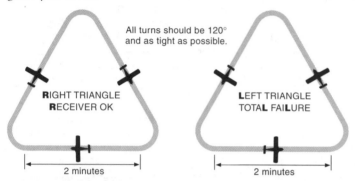

All turns should be 120° and as tight as possible.

RIGHT TRIANGLE
RECEIVER OK

LEFT TRIANGLE
TOTAL FAILURE

|← 2 minutes →|

|← 2 minutes →|

■ *Figure 9-16* **The 2-minute-leg radio failure triangles**

The radio failure triangle is really a 'desperation' manoeuvre. Normally, following a radio failure that cannot be remedied, you should just **stay in VMC and land at the nearest suitable airport**, using your transponder (7600) and the other radio failure procedures detailed above using good airmanship and your best judgement.

Some Radio Failure Situations

Each radio failure situation will be different, but some examples of procedures which you could follow are illustrated below. The main things to remember are fly the aeroplane accurately, squawk 7600 on your transponder, and act upon your best judgement. Stay in VMC and land at the nearest suitable airport, then contact an ATSU by any means and advise them of your situation.

A Suspected Receiver Failure Only

If you make radio calls and your transmissions sound normal (other signals and noise are cut out, and you hear your own transmission through your headset), but receive no response, then you may be out of radio range of the station being called, or you may have a receiver failure. To establish this, you could make a number of transmissions directed first of all to the relevant ATSU, then perhaps to "all stations" or a specific aircraft that you have heard on the frequency. Make these calls at least ten seconds apart to allow for a response.

Fly accurately.

If the ATSU responds, then continue normal operations. If another aircraft responds, then ask the pilot to relay your message to the ATSU. If no one answers, then you may have a radio failure of some sort (transmitter only, receiver only, or total). You would, of course, first try to remedy the failure. If that did not succeed, then you would follow standard radio failure procedures according to your best judgement. Remember that your first priority is to fly the aircraft accurately. At all times display good airmanship (common sense), and keep a very good lookout.

Transmit blind.

If it is only your receiver that has failed, you may still be able to *transmit* messages, which may be valuable even though you will not hear any responses. To alert others (the ATSU and other aircraft) to your situation, you should **transmit blind.** Transmit on the frequency in use, or any other usable frequency, or the emergency frequency 121·5 MHz. Start each of your radio calls with "Golf (your registration).................. Transmitting blind due to receiver failure." State your message, and then repeat it. It would also be good airmanship to state the time and/or place of your next intended call.

Squawk 7600.

If your calls are received by an ATSU, they may then issue requests or instructions to see if you can receive them. These could be instructions to:

☐ **squawk ident** or a particular transponder code;
☐ **turn onto a specific heading;** or
☐ **reply with the speechless code** using the transmit button of your microphone.

No response from you to their requests will indicate to the ATSU that you are *not* receiving their messages.

Squawk 7600 to alert radar controllers to your radio failure.

Stay in VMC and land at the nearest suitable airport.

In general, aim to stay in VMC and land at the nearest suitable airfield. Continue to transmit blind (messages twice). The ATSU will listen to any transmissions from you, and alert other relevant ATSUs and aircraft to your situation. At a suitably equipped airport, they will prepare to beam light signals at you at an appropriate time (e.g. green flashes for "Return for a landing", followed by steady green for "Authorised to land"). Periodic messages from you, even though transmitted blind, will be of value to the ATSU and to other nearby aircraft. When approaching an airport, be on the lookout for light signals beamed at you. It would be good airmanship to overfly the airfield to observe the windsock and/or the signals area to determine landing direction, and then join the circuit pattern in the normal manner. After landing, contact the ATSU and advise them of your situation. Plan on getting the radio repaired.

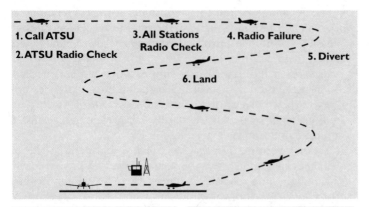

1. Call ATSU

Shoreham Approach
Golf Bravo Alpha Tango Charlie

2. ATSU Radio Check

Shoreham Approach
Golf Bravo Alpha Tango Charlie
Radio check on one two three decimal one
five

3. All Stations Radio Check

All stations
Golf Bravo Alpha Tango Charlie
Radio check on one two three decimal one
five

4. Radio Failure!

- Unable to fix.
- Squawk 7600.
- Listen out.
- Stay in VMC and land at nearest suitable
  airport.
- Transmit blind (messages twice).
- If receiving messages, use given
  transponder squawks or speechless code
  on your microphone to acknowledge.

5. Divert

Golf Bravo Alpha Tango Charlie
Transmitting blind due to receiver failure
I will proceed to overhead Seaford at two
thousand feet, then divert to Shoreham
airport, ETA 56
I say again, I will proceed to overhead
Seaford at two thousand feet, then divert
to Shoreham airport, ETA 56

- Look for light signals from ATSU.
- Overfly to check windsock and/or signals
  area for landing direction. Join circuit
  normally.

6. Land

Continue to transmit blind (messages
twice).

Golf Bravo Alpha Tango Charlie
Transmitting blind due to receiver failure
I am overhead Shoreham at two thousand
feet, and descending to join a left circuit for
Runway two one
I say again, I am overhead Shoreham at
two thousand feet, and descending to join
a left circuit for Runway two one

- Look for light signals.

■ Figure 9-17 **A suspected receiver failure only (transmitter OK)**

A Suspected Transmitter Failure Only

If you make radio calls where your transmissions sound abnormal
(other signals and noise *not* cut out, your own transmission *not*
heard through your headset), and you receive no response to your
calls, then you may have a *transmitter* failure.

Fly accurately.

If another aircraft responds, then ask the pilot to relay your message to the ATSU. If no one answers, then you may have a radio failure of some sort (transmitter only, receiver only, or total). If you can hear transmissions from the ATSU and other aircraft, then this confirms your receiver is operating. If not, then you might have a total radio failure (transmitter and receiver). You would, of course, first try to remedy the failure. If that did not succeed, then you would follow standard radio failure procedures according to your best judgement. Remember that your first priority is to fly the aircraft accurately. Display good airmanship at all times, and this includes keeping a very good lookout.

Transmit blind, just in case.

If it is only your transmitter that has failed, you may still be able to *receive* messages, which may be valuable even though you will probably not be able to transmit any response. All the same, you should still transmit blind just in case your messages are getting out, to alert others (the ATSU and other aircraft) to your situation. Transmit on the frequency in use, or any other usable frequency, or the emergency frequency 121·5 MHz. Start each of your radio calls with "Golf (your registration), Transmitting blind." State your message, and then repeat it. It would also be good airmanship to state the time and/or place of your next intended call.

If your calls are received by an ATSU, they may then issue requests or instructions to see if you can receive them. These could be instructions to:

☐ **squawk ident** or a particular transponder code;
☐ **turn onto a specific heading;** or
☐ **reply with the speechless code** using the transmit button of your microphone.

Respond to any instructions, if appropriate.

A response from you to their requests will indicate to the ATSU that you are receiving their messages, and so further instructions and advice will follow.

Radio failure transponder code is 7600.

If you are receiving messages directed at you, continue to squawk your current transponder code, unless asked to transfer to the radio failure code 7600 or to some other specific code. If you do not receive any messages, then assume a total radio failure, and squawk 7600.

Stay in VMC and land at the nearest suitable airport.

In general, aim to stay in VMC and land at the nearest suitable airport. If possible, follow any instructions issued to you, provided you consider them to be safe and appropriate. When approaching an airport, be on the lookout for light signals beamed at you. After landing, contact the ATSU and advise them of your situation. Plan on getting the radio repaired.

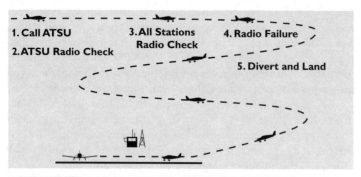

1. Call ATSU

🛩 *Shoreham Approach*
Golf Bravo Alpha Tango Charlie

2. ATSU Radio Check

🛩 *Shoreham Approach*
Golf Bravo Alpha Tango Charlie
Radio check on one two three decimal one five

3. All Stations Radio Check

🛩 *All stations*
Golf Bravo Alpha Tango Charlie
Radio check on one two three decimal one five

4. Radio Failure!

• *Unable to fix.*
• *Squawk 7600.*
• *Listen out.*
• *Stay in VMC and land at nearest suitable airport.*
• *Transmit blind (messages twice).*
• *If receiving messages, use given transponder squawks or speechless code on your microphone to acknowledge.*

5. Divert and Land

📡 *Station calling Shoreham on frequency one two three decimal one five.*
I am receiving carrier wave only.
If that is Golf Bravo Alpha Tango Charlie confirm by answering 'yes' using a one-second press on your transmit button.
If you are not Golf Bravo Alpha Tango Charlie, indicate by 'no' using two one-second presses on your transmit button.
Is that Golf Bravo Alpha Tango Charlie?

🛩 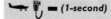 ▬ *(1-second)*

📡 *Yes, received Golf Bravo Alpha Tango Charlie*
Are you planning to return to Shoreham?

🛩 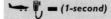 ▬ *(1-second)*

📡 *Yes, received Golf Bravo Alpha Tango Charlie*
Runway in use is two four, left-hand
Wind is two three zero at one zero knots
Join downwind for a left circuit
Acknowledge is you have received with a one-second press of your transmit button

🛩  ▬ *(1-second)*

■ *Figure 9-18* **A suspected transmitter failure only (receiver possibly OK)**

Radio Failure on the Ground

If you experience radio failure on the ground, then you should return to the parking position for repairs, keeping a good lookout for other aircraft, and transmitting blind your intentions.

Now complete: **Exercises 9 – Radio Failure Procedures.**

Putting It All Together
Example Flights

Most flights involve a series of very short radio conversations between the aircraft and the ATSU. The main points to remember if you want to develop a professional radio style are:

☐ **Place** your callsign correctly.
☐ **Read back** the required items.
☐ **Use** a good microphone technique.
☐ **Use** standard phraseology wherever possible.

The following five flights illustrate radio calls you can expect on a typical navigation exercise flight, including Danger Area crossings and a surveillance radar approach (SRA).

Follow the routes on a CAA 1:500,000 chart to help visualise the examples.

...rfordwest to Swansea

`HAVERFORDWEST ATZ`   `CLASS G`   A/G   `HAVERFORDWEST ATZ`

`HAVERFORDWEST ATZ`

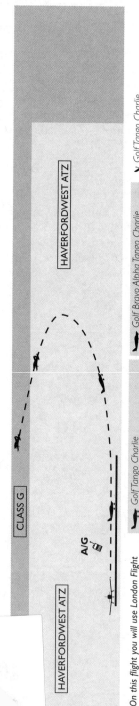

On this flight you will use London Flight Information Service and need to avoid the Danger Areas D117 and D118. Information on these areas including hours of operation and contact frequencies can be found in AIP ENR and Pooley's Flight Guide. Haverfordwest is Class G airspace and has an Air/Ground station. Swansea is also Class G, but has ATC in a control tower.

Departing Haverfordwest

Haverfordwest Radio
Golf Bravo Alpha Tango Charlie
Taxiing to the holding point of Runway zero nine for a VFR flight to Swansea

Golf Tango Charlie
Haverfordwest Radio
Roger, surface wind zero eight zero at one one knots
QNH one zero one five

Golf Tango Charlie
Lining up zero nine and taking off with a right turn out

Golf Tango Charlie
Roger, surface wind zero nine zero at nine knots

Golf Tango Charlie
Leaving the zone to the south-east and changing frequency to London Information one two four decimal seven five

Golf Tango Charlie, Roger

Enroute

London Information
Golf Bravo Alpha Tango Charlie
Request Flight Information Service

Golf Bravo Alpha Tango Charlie
London Information
Pass your message

Golf Bravo Alpha Tango Charlie
P PA-28
P Six miles southeast of Haverfordwest
H Heading one three five
A Altitude three thousand feet
C VFR
E Estimating Swansea time four six
R Request Flight Information Service

Golf Tango Charlie
Roger, Flight Information Service
Wessex Regional QNH one zero one four

Wessex QNH one zero one four
Golf Tango Charlie

Golf Tango Charlie
Request DAAIS for Deltas one one seven and one one eight

Golf Tango Charlie
Standby

Golf Tango Charlie
Delta one one seven and one one eight are active until one seven zero zero Zulu

Golf Tango Charlie, Roger
Routing via Carmarthen

Golf Tango Charlie
Request the Swansea weather

Golf Tango Charlie, Standby

Golf Tango Charlie
Swansea weather at time one zero two zero Zulu
Surface wind zero eight zero at one two knots
Greater than one zero kilometres visibility
Scattered at two thousand five hundred feet
Temperature plus one four, dewpoint plus six
QNH one zero two zero,
QFE one zero one zero
Runway two eight

Golf Tango Charlie, Runway two eight
QNH one zero two zero, QFE one zero one zero

Flight 1 continued

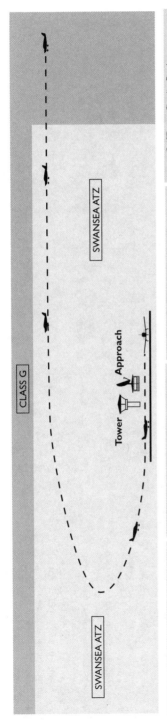

SWANSEA ATZ

CLASS G

SWANSEA ATZ

Tower

Approach

Golf Tango Charlie
Overhead Carmarthen
Changing frequency to Swansea one one nine decimal seven

Golf Tango Charlie
Wessex QNH one zero one nine
Flight Information Service terminated

Golf Tango Charlie
QNH one zero one nine
Golf Tango Charlie

Arriving at Swansea

Swansea Approach
Golf Bravo Alpha Tango Charlie
Inbound

Golf Bravo Alpha Tango Charlie
Swansea Approach
Pass your details

Swansea Approach
Golf Bravo Alpha Tango Charlie
PA-28
P One mile south-east of Carmarthen
A Altitude three thousand feet
C VFR
E Estimating you at time four nine
R Request joining instructions

Note The ETA has increased by three minutes because of the diversion via Carmarthen to avoid the Danger Areas

Golf Tango Charlie
Join and report left base, Runway one zero
QFE one zero zero zero

Wilco, Runway one zero, QFE one zero zero zero
Golf Tango Charlie

QDM, QDM, QDM
Golf Bravo Alpha Tango Charlie
Request QDM

Golf Tango Charlie
Your QDM is one five zero, Class Bravo

QDM one five zero
Golf Tango Charlie

Golf Tango Charlie
Joining left base, Runway one zero, to land

Golf Tango Charlie
Report final

Wilco, Golf Tango Charlie

Golf Tango Charlie, Final

Golf Tango Charlie
Surface wind zero eight zero at one zero knots
Cleared to land

Cleared to land
Golf Tango Charlie

At Swansea both Approach and Tower are on the same frequency, so there was no need to change frequencies.

Flight 2 Swansea to Compton Abbas

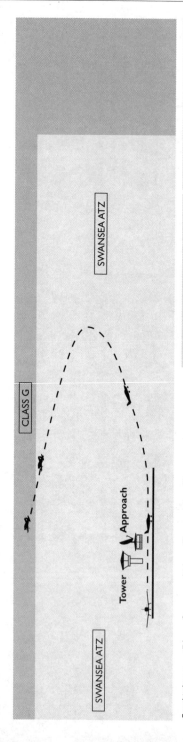

SWANSEA ATZ

CLASS G

SWANSEA ATZ

Tower

Approach

For this leg you will leave Swansea, which is an ATC aerodrome in the Open FIR Class G airspace, then call Cardiff Radar for Radar Information Service (RIS) and a clearance through the Cardiff Control Zone (Class D airspace, which has specified minimum weather provisions attached). Then on to Compton Abbas using a Lower Airspace Radar Service (LARS) from Cardiff and then Yeovilton Radar. This also means a MATZ penetration, as you will clip the north-east corner of the Yeovilton MATZ by Wincanton before arriving at Compton Abbas (FIS). Whilst en route you can make use of the VOLMET service to obtain the weather for adjacent fields Bournemouth, Bristol, Cardiff and Southampton as required.

Departing Swansea

Swansea Tower
Golf Bravo Alpha Tango Charlie
Request radio check and taxi instructions

Golf Tango Charlie
Readability five
Taxi to the holding point of Runway one zero via Charlie and Delta
QNH nine nine eight millibars

Taxi to the holding point of one zero via Charlie and Delta
QNH nine nine eight millibars
Golf Tango Charlie

Golf Tango Charlie
Request right turn after departure to set course from the overhead
Ready for departure

Golf Tango Charlie Right turn approved
Report overhead
Surface wind one zero zero at six knots
Cleared for take-off

Wilco
Cleared for take-off
Golf Tango Charlie

Golf Tango Charlie
Overhead two thousand three hundred feet setting course to the southeast

Golf Tango Charlie
Roger
Contact Cardiff Radar one two five decimal eight five

Cardiff radar one two five decimal eight five
Golf Tango Charlie

Flight 2 continued

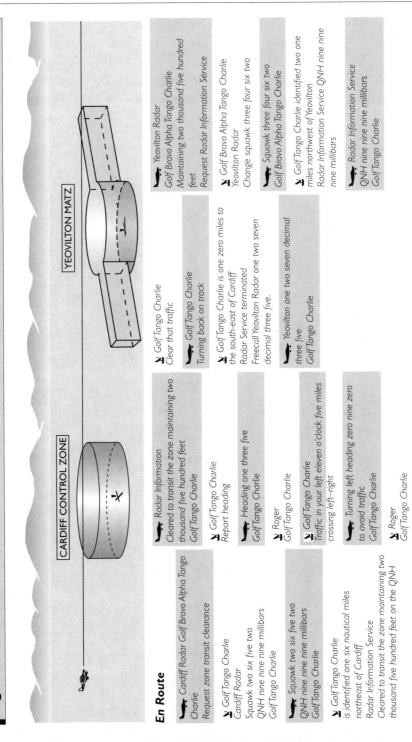

CARDIFF CONTROL ZONE

YEOVILTON MATZ

En Route

Cardiff Radar Golf Bravo Alpha Tango Charlie
Request zone transit clearance

Golf Tango Charlie
Cardiff Radar
Squawk two six five two
QNH nine nine nine millibars
Golf Tango Charlie

Squawk two six five two
QNH nine nine nine millibars
Golf Tango Charlie

Golf Tango Charlie
is identified one six nautical miles
northeast of Cardiff
Radar Information Service
Cleared to transit the zone maintaining two
thousand five hundred feet on the QNH

Radar Information
Cleared to transit the zone maintaining two
thousand five hundred feet
Golf Tango Charlie

Golf Tango Charlie
Report heading

Heading one three five
Golf Tango Charlie

Roger
Golf Tango Charlie

Golf Tango Charlie
Traffic in your left eleven o'clock five miles
crossing left–right

Turning left heading zero nine zero
to avoid traffic
Golf Tango Charlie

Roger
Golf Tango Charlie

Golf Tango Charlie
Clear that traffic

Golf Tango Charlie
Turning back on track

Golf Tango Charlie is one zero miles to
the south-east of Cardiff
Radar Service terminated
Freecall Yeovilton Radar one two seven
decimal three five.

Yeovilton one two seven decimal
three five
Golf Tango Charlie

Yeovilton Radar
Golf Bravo Alpha Tango Charlie
Maintaining two thousand five hundred
feet
Request Radar Information Service

Golf Bravo Alpha Tango Charlie
Yeovilton Radar
Change squawk three four six two

Squawk three four six two
Golf Bravo Alpha Tango Charlie

Golf Tango Charlie identified two one
miles northwest of Yeovilton
Radar Information Service QNH nine nine
nine millibars

Radar Information Service
QNH nine nine nine millibars
Golf Tango Charlie

Flight 2 continued

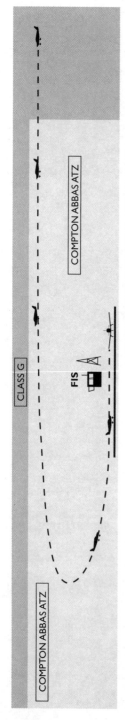

COMPTON ABBAS ATZ

CLASS G

FIS

COMPTON ABBAS ATZ

At this point you can listen to London VOLMET South on frequency 128·6. It gives the latest actual meteorological reports for selected aerodromes in the south of England for observations taken at 20 and 50 minutes past the hour. Of these, you may find useful the weather for Bournemouth, Bristol, Cardiff and Southampton.

VOLMET:

Bristol at one zero five zero Zulu
Surface wind zero nine zero at one zero knots
Visibility greater than one zero kilometres
Cloud scattered at two thousand seven hundred feet
Broken at four thousand eight hundred feet
Temperature plus one zero, dewpoint plus seven
QNH nine nine eight
No significant change

Having copied the weather, you are cleared by Yeovilton Radar through the MATZ. Even though the clearance has been given to you automatically in this case, you must remember it is the pilot-in-command's responsibility to obtain this clearance, and a clearance through the ATZ is a minimum requirement. If a required clearance is not offered to you, then you must request it at least 15 nm or 5 minutes before you reach the boundary of that airspace.

Golf Tango Charlie
You are cleared to penetrate the MATZ to the southeast of Wincanton, maintaining two thousand five hundred feet

Clear to transit the MATZ south of Wincanton
Maintaining two thousand five hundred feet
Golf Tango Charlie

Golf Tango Charlie
Four miles to the southeast of Wincanton, nothing further for you
Radar Service terminated
Squawk seven zero zero zero and freecall
Compton Information one two two decimal seven

Squawk seven zero zero zero,
Compton Information one two two decimal seven
Golf Tango Charlie

Arriving at Compton Abbas (FIS)

Compton Information
Golf Bravo Alpha Tango Charlie inbound

Golf Tango Charlie
Compton Information
Pass your message

Golf Bravo Alpha Tango Charlie
PA-28
Eight miles to the north-west
Three thousand feet
VFR
Estimating the overhead at time three four

Golf Tango Charlie
Runway zero eight
QFE nine nine seven five millibars
Two in the circuit

Golf Tango Charlie

Golf Tango Charlie
In the overhead, descending dead side

Golf Tango Charlie
One aircraft on final

Golf Tango Charlie

Golf Tango Charlie
Downwind left, zero eight to land

Golf Tango Charlie

Golf Tango Charlie
Final

Golf Tango Charlie
Land at your discretion
Surface wind zero nine zero at one one knots

Golf Tango Charlie

Golf Tango Charlie
Runway vacated

Flight 3 Compton Abbas to Eaglescott via Exeter

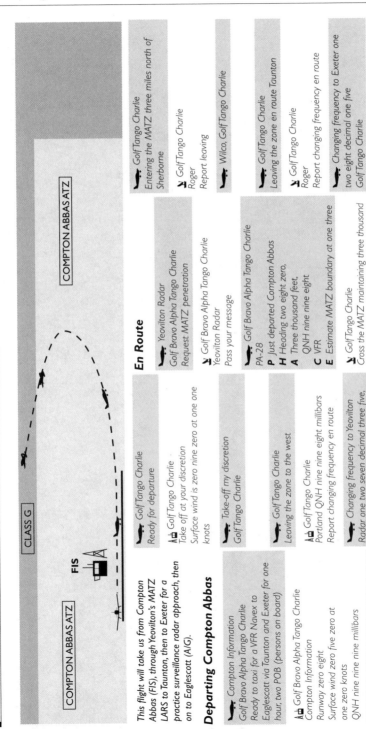

This flight will take us from Compton Abbas (FIS), through Yeovilton's MATZ LARS to Taunton, then to Exeter for a practice surveillance radar approach, then on to Eaglescott (A/G).

Departing Compton Abbas

Compton Information
Golf Bravo Alpha Tango Charlie
Ready to taxi for a VFR Navex to
Eaglescott via Taunton and Exeter for one
hour, two POB (persons on board)

Golf Bravo Alpha Tango Charlie
Compton Information
Runway zero eight
Surface wind zero five zero at
one zero knots
QNH nine nine nine millibars

Taxi holding point zero two eight
QNH nine nine nine millibars
Golf Tango Charlie

Golf Tango Charlie
Ready for departure

Golf Tango Charlie
Take off at your discretion
Surface wind is zero nine zero at one one
knots

Take-off my discretion
Golf Tango Charlie

Golf Tango Charlie
Leaving the zone to the west

Golf Tango Charlie
Portland QNH nine nine eight millibars
Report changing frequency en route

Changing frequency to Yeovilton
Radar one two seven decimal three five,
Portland QNH nine nine eight millibars
Golf Tango Charlie

Golf Tango Charlie
Roger

En Route

Yeovilton Radar
Golf Bravo Alpha Tango Charlie
Request MATZ penetration

Golf Bravo Alpha Tango Charlie
Yeovilton Radar
Pass your message

Golf Bravo Alpha Tango Charlie
PA-28
P Just departed Compton Abbas
H Heading two eight zero,
A Three thousand feet,
QNH nine nine nine eight
C VFR
E Estimate MATZ boundary at one three

Golf Tango Charlie
Cross the MATZ maintaining three thousand
feet on the QFE nine nine six millibars
Report entering and leaving the MATZ

Cross the MATZ, three thousand
feet, Yeovilton QFE nine nine six millibars
Golf Tango Charlie

Golf Tango Charlie
Entering the MATZ three miles north of
Sherborne

Golf Tango Charlie
Roger
Report leaving

Wilco, Golf Tango Charlie

Golf Tango Charlie
Leaving the zone en route Taunton

Golf Tango Charlie
Roger
Report changing frequency en route

Changing frequency to Exeter one
two eight decimal one five
Golf Tango Charlie

Golf Tango Charlie
Portland QNH nine nine seven
Radar Service terminated

QNH nine nine seven
Golf Tango Charlie

Flight 3 continued

EXETER ATZ

Radar

Arriving at Exeter (SRA)

Exeter Radar
Golf Bravo Alpha Tango Charlie

Golf Bravo Alpha Tango Charlie
Exeter Radar
Pass your message

Golf Bravo Alpha Tango Charlie
PA-28
P West abeam Dunkeswell
H Heading one nine zero
A Maintaining three thousand feet,
QNH nine nine eight
C VFR
E Estimating the ATZ at five five
R Request SRA Runway zero two eight

Golf Tango Charlie
Squawk three six four two

Three six four two
Golf Tango Charlie

Golf Tango Charlie is identified
nine miles north-east of Exeter
Radar Information
This will be a surveillance radar approach
to Runway zero two eight terminating at two
miles from touchdown
Check your minima, step down fixes and
missed approach point.

Golf Tango Charlie

Golf Tango Charlie
Turn right heading two six zero
Golf Tango Charlie

Golf Tango Charlie
Descend to altitude two thousand seven
hundred feet on the Exeter QNH nine nine
nine millibars
Weather when you are ready to copy

Descend to altitude two thousand
seven hundred feet, QNH nine nine nine
millibars
Go ahead with the weather
Golf Tango Charlie

Golf Tango Charlie
Exeter weather timed at one four two zero
Zulu
Surface wind one zero zero at seven knots
One zero kilometres
Cloud scattered at one thousand three
hundred feet, broken at three thousand feet
Temperature plus one zero, dewpoint plus six
QNH nine nine nine millibars
QFE nine nine nine six millibars
Runway in use zero two eight

QNH nine nine nine millibars,
QFE nine nine nine six millibars
Runway zero two eight
Golf Tango Charlie

Golf Tango Charlie
Turn left heading one eight zero, base leg,
you have twelve track miles to touchdown

Left heading one eight zero
Golf Tango Charlie

Golf Tango Charlie
Turn left heading one two zero
Closing final approach track from the left

Left heading one two zero
Golf Tango Charlie

Golf Tango Charlie
One zero miles from touchdown
Descend to height two thousand one
hundred feet, QFE nine nine nine six millibars

Descend height two thousand one
hundred feet, QFE nine nine nine six millibars
Golf Tango Charlie

Flight 3 continued

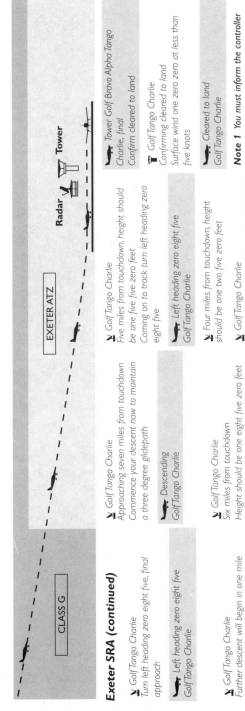

CLASS G | EXETER ATZ | Radar | Tower

Exeter SRA (continued)

↘ Golf Tango Charlie
Turn left heading zero eight five, final approach

🎙 Left heading zero eight five
Golf Tango Charlie

↘ Golf Tango Charlie
Approaching seven miles from touchdown
Commence your descent now to maintain a three degree glidepath

🎙 Descending
Golf Tango Charlie

↘ Golf Tango Charlie
Six miles from touchdown
Height should be one eight five zero feet

🎙 Golf Tango Charlie

↘ Golf Tango Charlie
Five miles from touchdown, height should be one five five zero feet
Coming on to track turn left heading zero eight five

🎙 Left heading zero eight five
Golf Tango Charlie

↘ Golf Tango Charlie
Further descent will begin in one mile

🎙 Golf Tango Charlie

↘ Golf Tango Charlie
Slightly left of track, turn right five degrees heading zero nine zero

🎙 Right heading zero nine zero
Golf Tango Charlie

↘ Golf Tango Charlie
Four miles from touchdown, height should be one two five zero feet

↘ Golf Tango Charlie
Advise at any time when you get the approach lights or runway in sight and check wheels

🎙 Wilco Golf Tango Charlie

↘ Golf Tango Charlie
Three miles from touchdown, height should be nine five zero feet
Cleared to land, surface wind zero nine zero at five knots

🎙 Runway in sight, cleared to land
Golf Tango Charlie

↘ Golf Tango Charlie SRA terminated, call Tower one one nine decimal eight

🎙 Tower one one nine decimal eight
Golf Tango Charlie

🎙 Tower Golf Bravo Alpha Tango Charlie, final
Confirm cleared to land

🗼 Golf Tango Charlie
Confirming cleared to land
Surface wind one zero zero at less than five knots

🎙 Cleared to land
Golf Tango Charlie

Note 1 You must inform the controller of any heading or altitude change which would take you into IMC.

Note 2 For SRAs terminating at less than two miles from touchdown, the controller is likely to say "Do not reply to further instructions." No response is expected from you to further heading changes as you will be busy enough controlling the aircraft.

Flight 4 *Exeter to Eaglescott*

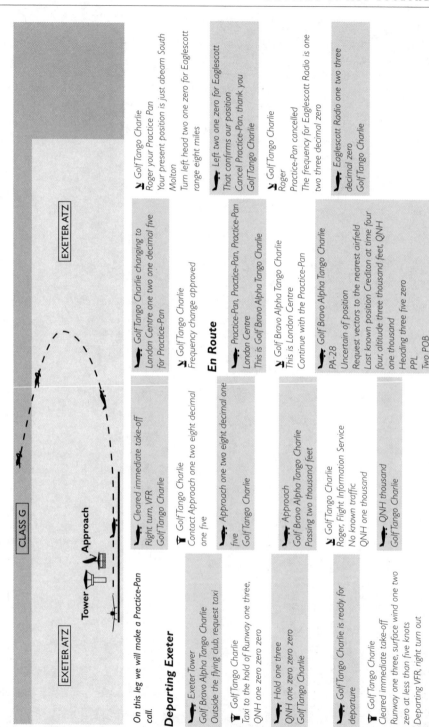

On this leg we will make a Practice-Pan call.

Departing Exeter

Exeter Tower
Golf Bravo Alpha Tango Charlie
Outside the flying club, request taxi

Golf Tango Charlie
Taxi to the hold of Runway one three,
QNH one zero zero zero

Hold one three
QNH one zero zero zero
Golf Tango Charlie

Golf Tango Charlie is ready for
departure

Golf Tango Charlie
Cleared immediate take-off
Runway one three, surface wind one two
zero at less than five knots
Departing VFR, right turn out

Cleared immediate take-off
Right turn, VFR
Golf Tango Charlie

Golf Tango Charlie
Contact Approach two eight decimal
one five

Approach one two eight decimal one
five
Golf Tango Charlie

Approach
Golf Bravo Alpha Tango Charlie
Passing two thousand feet

Golf Tango Charlie
Roger, Flight Information Service
No known traffic
QNH one thousand

QNH one thousand
Golf Tango Charlie

Golf Tango Charlie changing to
London Centre one two one decimal five
for Practice-Pan

Golf Tango Charlie
Frequency change approved

En Route

Practice-Pan, Practice-Pan, Practice-Pan
London Centre
This is Golf Bravo Alpha Tango Charlie

Golf Bravo Alpha Tango Charlie
This is London Centre
Continue with the Practice-Pan

Golf Bravo Alpha Tango Charlie
PA-28
Uncertain of position
Request vectors to the nearest airfield
Last known position Crediton at time four
four, altitude three thousand feet, QNH
one thousand
Heading three five zero
PPL
Two POB

Golf Tango Charlie
Roger your Practice Pan
Your present position is just abeam South
Molton
Turn left head two one zero for Eaglescott
range eight miles

Left two one zero for Eaglescott
That confirms our position
Cancel Practice-Pan, thank you
Golf Tango Charlie

Golf Tango Charlie
Roger
Practice-Pan cancelled
The frequency for Eaglescott Radio is one
two three decimal zero

Eaglescott Radio one two three
decimal zero
Golf Tango Charlie

Flight 4 continued

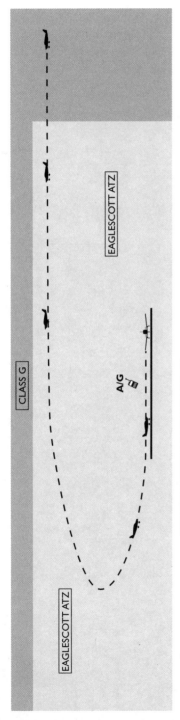

EAGLESCOTT ATZ

CLASS G

EAGLESCOTT ATZ

A/G

Arriving at Eaglescott

Eaglescott Radio
Golf Bravo Alpha Tango Charlie
South Molton inbound

No reply from Eaglescott Radio.

Eaglescott Radio
Golf Bravo Alpha Tango Charlie
PA-28
South Molton
Descending to altitude two thousand five hundred feet to join in the overhead
VFR

Eaglescott Radio
Golf Tango Charlie
Overhead descending dead side for
Runway zero eight

Eaglescott Radio
Golf Tango Charlie downwind left for
Runway zero eight to land

Eaglescott Radio
Golf Tango Charlie final

Eaglescott Radio
Golf Tango Charlie runway vacated

Note *For a standard overhead join the aircraft is required to join overhead at 1,000 feet above circuit height.
Circuit height for Eaglescott is 800 feet QFE (above aerodrome level), therefore the overhead joining height is 1,800 feet QFE or 2,500 feet QNH.
(Eaglescott's elevation is 655 ft amsl therefore circuit height is 1,455 ft [655 + 800], round up to 1,500 ft, so approach the overhead at 2,500 ft amsl.) Figure 3-28 on page 57 explains QNH and QFE.*

Flight 5 Eaglescott to Bristol

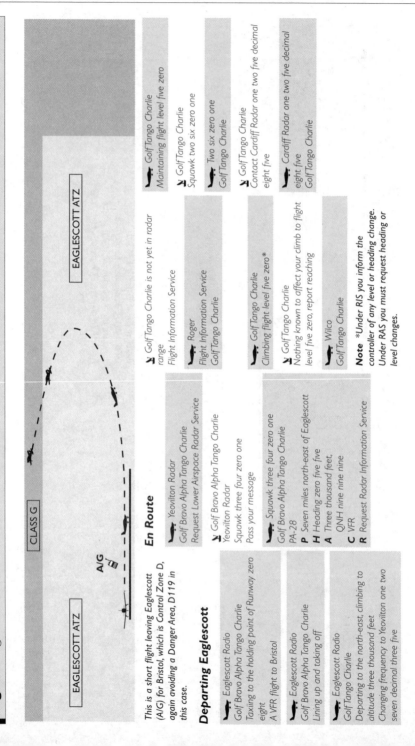

CLASS G

EAGLESCOTT ATZ

EAGLESCOTT ATZ

A/G

This is a short flight leaving Eaglescott (A/G) for Bristol, which is Control Zone D, again avoiding a Danger Area, D119 in this case.

Departing Eaglescott

Eaglescott Radio
Golf Bravo Alpha Tango Charlie
Taxiing to the holding point of Runway zero eight
A VFR flight to Bristol

Eaglescott Radio
Golf Bravo Alpha Tango Charlie
Lining up and taking off

Eaglescott Radio
Golf Tango Charlie
Departing to the north-east, climbing to altitude three thousand feet
Changing frequency to Yeovilton one two seven decimal three five

En Route

Yeovilton Radar
Golf Bravo Alpha Tango Charlie
Request Lower Airspace Radar Service

Golf Bravo Alpha Tango Charlie
Yeovilton Radar
Squawk three four zero one
Pass your message

Squawk three four zero one
Golf Bravo Alpha Tango Charlie
PA-28
P Seven miles north-east of Eaglescott
H Heading zero five five
A Three thousand feet,
  QNH nine nine nine
C VFR
R Request Radar Information Service

Golf Tango Charlie is not yet in radar range
Flight Information Service

Roger
Flight Information Service
Golf Tango Charlie

Golf Tango Charlie
Climbing flight level five zero*

Golf Tango Charlie
Nothing known to affect your climb to flight level five zero, report reaching

Wilco
Golf Tango Charlie

Golf Tango Charlie
Maintaining flight level five zero

Golf Tango Charlie
Squawk two six zero one

Two six zero one
Golf Tango Charlie

Golf Tango Charlie
Contact Cardiff Radar one two five decimal eight five

Cardiff Radar one two five decimal eight five
Golf Tango Charlie

Note *Under RIS you inform the controller of any level or heading change. Under RAS you must request heading or level changes.

Flight 5 continued

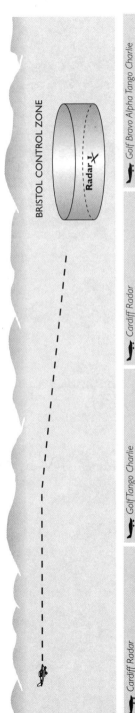

BRISTOL CONTROL ZONE

Radar

Cardiff Radar
Golf Bravo Alpha Tango Charlie
Maintaining flight level five zero

Golf Tango Charlie
Cardiff Radar, identified seven miles south of Minehead
Maintain flight level five zero
Radar Advisory Service

Wilco
Radar Advisory Service
Golf Tango Charlie

Golf Tango Charlie
Turn right one zero degrees heading zero six five to keep you clear of Delta one one nine

Right one zero, heading zero six five
Golf Tango Charlie

Golf Tango Charlie
Leaving the frequency for two minutes for a Training-Fix with London Centre one two one decimal five

Golf Tango Charlie
Report back on this frequency

Wilco
Golf Tango Charlie

Select one two one decimal five

Training-Fix, Training-Fix, Training-Fix
Golf Bravo Alpha Tango Charlie

Golf Bravo Alpha Tango Charlie
London Centre
Your position is six miles to the north-west of Taunton

Roger
Golf Tango Charlie
Changing frequency to Cardiff Radar one two five decimal eight five

---

Cardiff Radar
Golf Bravo Alpha Tango Charlie
Back on frequency
Maintaining flight level five zero

Golf Tango Charlie
Cardiff Radar
Maintain flight level five zero

Before talking to Bristol, listen to the ATIS on one two six decimal zero two five and note the code letter.

ATIS:
Bristol Information Juliett timed at one five zero Zulu
Surface wind one one zero at one three knots
CAVOK
Temperature plus one two, dewpoint plus six
QNH nine nine eight millibars
Runway zero nine QFE nine nine seven
Report aircraft type and information Juliett received with first contact with Bristol Approach

---

Golf Bravo Alpha Tango Charlie
Ready for descent

Golf Tango Charlie
Descend to altitude three thousand feet, QNH nine nine nine millibars

Descend three thousand
QNH nine nine nine millibars
Golf Tango Charlie

Golf Tango Charlie
Radar Service terminated
Squawk one four six two and contact Bristol Approach on one two zero decimal six

One four six two and Bristol
Approach one two zero decimal six
Golf Tango Charlie

Flight 5 continued

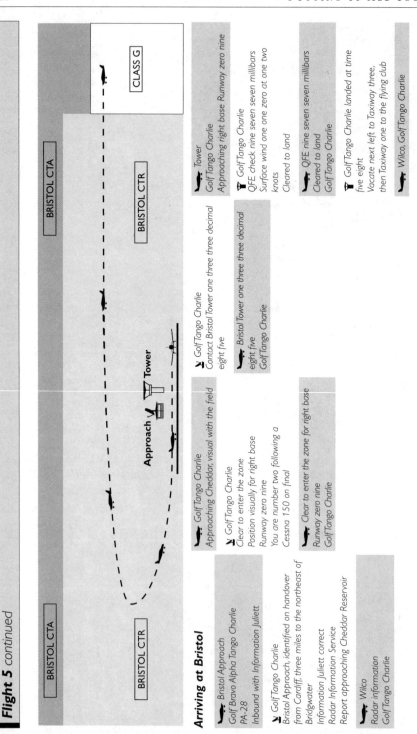

BRISTOL CTA

BRISTOL CTA

BRISTOL CTR

BRISTOL CTR

CLASS G

Approach

Tower

Arriving at Bristol

Bristol Approach
Golf Bravo Alpha Tango Charlie
PA-28
Inbound with Information Juliett

Golf Tango Charlie
Bristol Approach, identified on handover
from Cardiff, three miles to the northeast of
Bridgwater
Information Juliett correct
Radar Information Service
Report approaching Cheddar Reservoir

Wilco
Radar information
Golf Tango Charlie

Golf Tango Charlie
Approaching Cheddar, visual with the field

Golf Tango Charlie
Clear to enter the zone
Position visually for right base
Runway zero nine
You are number two following a
Cessna 150 on final

Clear to enter the zone for right base
Runway zero nine
Golf Tango Charlie

Golf Tango Charlie
Contact Bristol Tower one three three decimal
eight five

Bristol Tower one three three decimal
eight five
Golf Tango Charlie

Tower
Golf Tango Charlie
Approaching right base Runway zero nine

Golf Tango Charlie
QFE check nine seven seven millibars
Surface wind one one zero zero at one two
knots
Cleared to land

QFE nine seven seven millibars
Cleared to land
Golf Tango Charlie

Golf Tango Charlie landed at time
five eight
Vacate next left to Taxiway three,
then Taxiway one to the flying club

Wilco, Golf Tango Charlie

How Radio Works
Radio Fundamentals

Communication by Sound Waves

When you speak, your voice box sets up vibrations in the air, called sound waves. Air is the medium through which the sound waves travel to the ear of the listener.

■ *Figure 11-1* **Voice vibrations are transmitted through the air**

At the receiving end the sound waves strike the listener's ear drums, making them vibrate at the same frequency as the sound waves. The ears convert these vibrations into electrical signals that are sent to the brain.

Sound waves are like the waves you see form on the surface of a still pond when you throw a stone into the water. The waves spread outwards from the point of impact in ever-increasing circles. Like ripples on a pond, sound waves are *attenuated* (weakened or reduced in strength) quickly as they travel away from the source.

Sound waves can only travel short distances before becoming attenuated.

It is quite simple to cause minor variations in the atmospheric pressure surrounding you. For example, if you take a steel ruler, hold it on the edge of a table and make it vibrate, your ears will pick up the sound waves. By varying the length of the ruler that is allowed to vibrate, you can alter the **frequency** of these vibrations (i.e. the number of vibrations or oscillations per second) and, as a consequence, a different pitch of sound is heard.

The unit for frequency is the hertz (Hz).

The historical unit for frequency was *cycles per second (cps)*, but this was changed to *hertz* to honour the German physicist H. R. Hertz (1857–94), one of the first scientists to investigate radio-telegraphy. The unit hertz is abbreviated to Hz.

- **One wave per second** past a given point is called a frequency of **1 hertz.**
- **1,000 waves per second** past a given point is called 1,000 Hz or **1 kilohertz (kHz).**
- **1,000,000 waves per second** is called 1,000,000 Hz, 1,000 kHz or **1 megahertz (MHz).**

The human ear can respond to frequencies between approximately 20 hertz and 20,000 hertz (20 kHz). This is known as the audio frequency range. The range of human speech is normally between frequencies of approximately 100 Hz and 10,000 Hz.

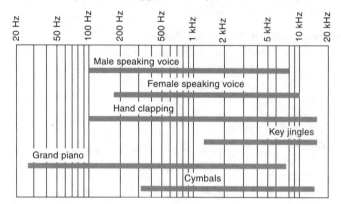

■ *Figure 11-2* **Sounds and their frequency ranges**

Wave Motion

Wave motion can be described by its shape and frequency. As you may have noticed from ripples on a pond, the normal wave shape is a smooth symmetrical shape (referred to in mathematical terms as a *sine wave* or *sine curve).*

■ *Figure 11-3* **The normal shape of energy waves is symmetrical (often described as sine waves)**

Water waves consist of water molecules moving up and down (and around) in a regular manner as the wave passes. *Sound waves* passing through the air consist of the air being compressed and expanded (i.e. pressure variations) in a regular manner. The water or air only vibrates as the wave passes; it does not travel outward from the source with the waves. Thus a cork floating on water only bobs up and down as a waves passes, it does not travel with the wave.

Radio waves, although similar to sound waves in some respects, do *not* require a medium to travel through – they can travel through a vacuum. Radio waves, unlike sound waves, can also travel very long distances without being noticeably attenuated. Radio waves travel at the speed of light.

Radio waves can be transmitted over long distances without being noticeably attenuated.

Wave Terminology

Wave energy is of a continuous nature in that it consists of many waves, one following the other at regular intervals, with the *wave-cycle* repeating itself over and over again as the wave motion passes a given point.

Wave motion can be described in fairly simple terms. The main points are:

WAVELENGTH: the length of one single wave (or of one complete cycle); it is also the distance travelled by the wave during transmission of one cycle.

FREQUENCY: the number of complete waves (or cycles) passing a point in one second. Note that the higher the frequency of radio waves, the shorter the wavelength. A high frequency (HF) radio is also know as a *short wave* radio.

AMPLITUDE: the distance from one extremity of the oscillation to the middle point or neutral value. With sound waves, the greater the amplitude, the louder the sound.

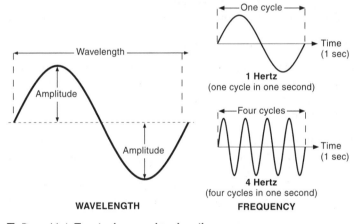

■ *Figure 11-4* **Terminology used to describe waves**

Radio Waves

Radio signals can be selectively tuned by a receiver.

As well as travelling long distances without becoming noticeably attenuated, radio waves can be selectively tuned, or 'picked up' by a receiving radio. Unlike the various pressure vibrations in the audio range (which our ears hear as a blend of sounds all mixed together), we can actually **tune** a radio receiver to one particular *frequency,* allowing it to receive messages on that frequency alone. All other unwanted radio frequencies, and the information being transmitted on them, are automatically screened out. This useful characteristic allows different radio frequencies to be used for different functions.

As we all know, the airwaves are full of millions of radio messages. When tuning a radio, we extract only those messages on the
frequency to which we are tuned. If our desired signal on the
selected frequency predominates over unwanted weak signals or
noise, then we have good radio reception (or a good *signal-to-noise*
ratio).

> Unwanted background
> hash or static is called
> **noise**.

Using Radio Waves to Carry Voice Messages

Radio waves can be used as the carrier that transports voice messages from one place to another because:

- ☐ **radio waves travel long distances** virtually instantaneously;
  and
- ☐ **radio waves are not attenuated** noticeably over long distances
  (i.e. the signal remains strong).

Radio waves consist of regular variations in the strength of
electric and magnetic fields. They can travel through a vacuum,
through outer space and even through walls; however, like sound
waves, radio waves are attenuated (weakened) by dense material
such as the earth and large buildings.

There are some fundamental differences between sound waves
and radio waves. Radio waves travel much faster, and at much
higher frequencies than sound waves.

SOUND WAVES are pressure waves. They travel at the *speed of sound*
– approximately 760 miles per hour (1,223 km/hr, 340 metres/
sec), depending on air temperature. Sound waves are in the audio
frequency range of 20 Hz to 20,000 Hz (20 kHz).

RADIO WAVES are electromagnetic waves. They travel much faster
than sound waves – at the *speed of light* – 186,000 statute miles per
second. (300,000 km/sec). This is equivalent to travelling around
the world 15 times in two seconds. Radio waves are in the radio
frequency range of 3,000,000 to 300,000,000 Hz (3 MHz to 300
MHz). A radio message is received practically at the same instant
it is transmitted, regardless of the distance travelled.

> Radio signals travel at the
> speed of light.

The difference in the speeds of light and sound is illustrated by
lightning and thunder during a storm. You see a lightning flash
practically at the same time it occurs, but there is a time interval
before you hear its associated peal of thunder – the time it takes
for the sound waves to reach you.

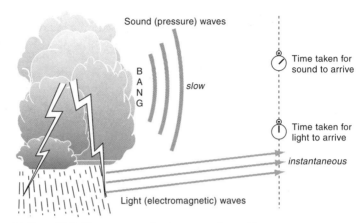

■ *Figure 11-5* **Electromagnetic waves travel very fast**

How Voice Messages are Carried by Radio Waves

Figure 11-6 illustrates the process of converting sound waves to an electrical signal, transmitting a voice message by radio, receiving it on another radio, and reproducing it with a speaker. The following text explains how sound waves are superimposed on radio waves, transmitted and received, then reproduced as sound waves.

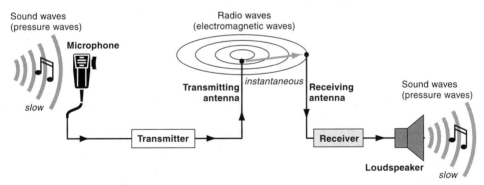

■ *Figure 11-6* **Transmitting a voice message by radio**

The electrical signals generated by a microphone from sound sources (such as a voice) are in the audio frequency *band* from 20 to 20,000 hertz. The frequency spread of radio signals suitable for transmission is much higher than this – between 3 MHz and 300 MHz (Figure 11-7).

This means that before an audio signal (containing a voice message) can be transmitted, it must be superimposed on a radio frequency called a **carrier wave**. The carrier wave is generated by your radio when you press the transmit button and the microphone accepts your voice signal to be superimposed on the carrier wave. This combination of the radio and audio signals is what the radio transmits.

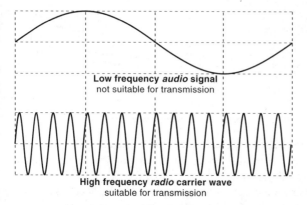

Low frequency *audio* signal
not suitable for transmission

High frequency *radio* carrier wave
suitable for transmission

Figure 11-7 **Audio signals are not in the radio frequency range**

The receiving radio is tuned to the radio frequency of the transmitted signal, receives it, removes the carrier wave, then feeds the remaining audio signal to a speaker or headset where it is converted to pressure waves in the air – and your message is heard. Because radio waves travel at the speed of light, your message is transmitted and reproduced virtually instantaneously.

A radio carrier wave is similar to a mail van that delivers a letter which contains a message. The radio carrier wave delivers an audio signal which contains a message. Just as a letter may travel in any one of a number of mail vans to reach you, a carrier wave may be on any one of a number of different frequencies.

The process of superimposing an audio signal onto a radio carrier wave is called **modulation**. The two most common methods of modulation are amplitude modulation (AM) and frequency modulation (FM).

Amplitude modulation (AM) modulates (varies) the *amplitude* of the carrier wave according to the frequency variations of the audio signal, whereas the frequency remains the same (Figure 11-8).

Frequency modulation (FM), on the other hand, modulates the *frequency* of the carrier wave according to the frequency variations of the audio signal, whereas the amplitude remains the same (Figure 11-9).

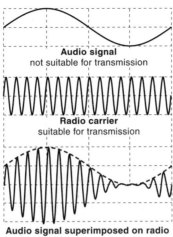

Figure 11-8 Amplitude modulation (AM) varies the amplitude of the carrier wave according to the audio signal

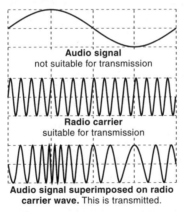

Figure 11-9 Frequency modulation (FM) varies the frequency of the carrier wave according to the audio signal

The process of *removing* the carrier wave from the audio signal by the receiving radio is called **demodulation.** Then the audio signal is **amplified** before being sent to the speaker.

Commercial radio stations use either amplitude modulation (AM) or frequency modulation (FM) to transmit their programmes. A radio carrier wave can be at any frequency within a certain range. It is the frequency of the carrier wave that you select when you tune to a station on your transistor radio.

Summary

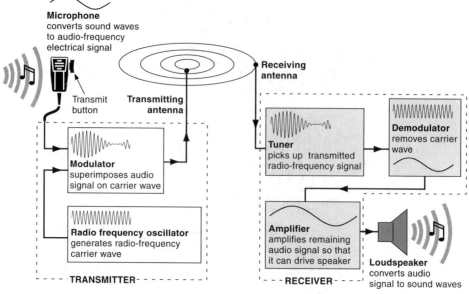

■ *Figure 11-10* **Radio transmission and reception**

Radio Frequency Bands

There are several radio frequency bands available for different purposes, but the most commonly used for voice communication is the very high frequency (VHF) band.

VHF is the most common form of radio communication in aviation.

Very high frequency (VHF) refers to a specific range of frequencies or radio frequency *band* (30 MHz to 300 MHz). The characteristics of VHF transmissions are such that communication systems operating in the VHF band are able to provide high-quality *line-of-sight* (and consequently short-range) communications between aircraft and ground stations, and between aircraft.

VHF is line-of-sight.

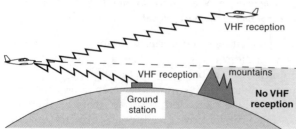

■ *Figure 11-11* **VHF communications are line-of-sight**

VHF Range

VHF radio waves are refracted (bent) slightly as they pass through the air and so, strictly speaking, the VHF range is slightly greater than straight line-of-sight.

Because of the restricted range, the same VHF frequency can be allocated to more than one ground station provided they are widely separated geographically (300 nm is more than adequate).

The VHF range of an aircraft will increase with altitude due to:
- the **line-of-sight horizon** being further; and
- **less obstruction** from mountains, etc.

Typical realistic VHF ranges are 60 nautical miles at 2,000 feet agl and 120 nm at 10,000 feet agl.

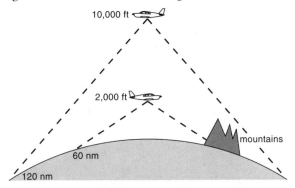

■ Figure 11-12 **VHF range increases with altitude**

Because VHF transmissions are line-of-sight, their effectiveness depends upon the proximity of the other station and whether or not there are obstructions between the two stations. The higher you go above the ground, the less chance there is of the signal being obstructed by mountains or buildings. Consequently the range of VHF transmissions increases with height. This makes it possible, if you are high enough, to accidentally contact a different ground station to your intended one, if it is on the same frequency, even though it is located in a different part of the country entirely.

Frequencies are allocated so that the following critical airspace volumes are protected from unwanted interference. See AIP GEN under *Communication Services – Types of Service*.

VHF COMMUNICATION RANGE LIMITS		
When contacting:	**Aircraft altitude limit (feet)**	**Range limit (nautical miles)**
Tower	*4,000 feet*	*25 nautical miles*
Approach	*10,000 feet*	*25 nautical miles*

Repeater (relay) stations on mountain tops (or in satellites in some countries) enable high-quality line-of-sight VHF reception over wider areas.

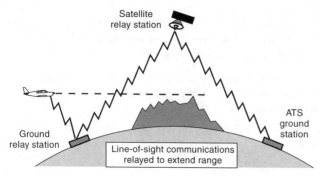

■ *Figure 11-13* **Although VHF is line-of-sight, long-range communications using VHF are possible through repeater stations and satellite links**

Long-range radio communications are possible on another frequency band, the high frequency (HF) band, and by satellite. HF is also known as *short wave,* since the higher the frequency, the shorter the wavelength. HF is used over remote areas such as the Atlantic Ocean and other oceanic areas, parts of India, Afghanistan, and much of Africa.

Now complete: **Exercises 11 – Radio Fundamentals.**

How Radio Works
Radio Wave Propagation &
Long-Range Communications

This chapter is for those who have a deeper interest in radio, and for those who might use long-range HF radio.

Radio Frequency Bands

As we have seen earlier, the part of the electromagnetic spectrum which contains radio waves has been subdivided into several different **radio frequency bands**. Just as certain characteristics of waves within the visible light spectrum vary from frequency to frequency (e.g. colour), many properties of radio waves also vary from one frequency band to another.

FREQUENCY BANDS USED IN AVIATION		
Band	Abbreviation	Frequency range (between 10 kHz and 3,000 MHz)
Very low frequency	VLF	10 to 30 kHz
Low frequency	LF	30 to 300 kHz
Medium frequency	MF	300 to 3,000 kHz
High frequency	HF	3 to 30 MHz
Very high frequency	VHF	30 to 300 MHz
Ultra high frequency	UHF	300 to 3,000 MHz

Each of the radio frequency bands has its own unique characteristics (affecting transmission, propagation and reception), and this largely determines its suitability for different applications.

For example, radio signals in the *very high frequency* (VHF) band are less susceptible to static interference than signals in the *high, medium* and *low frequency* (HF, MF, LF) bands, making VHF ideal for voice communications. VHF radio signals, however, travel in straight lines, and so must be able to pass directly from the transmitting antenna to the receiving antenna with no significant obstructions in between (i.e. 'line-of-sight' transmissions). This restricts VHF usage to relatively short-range applications.

Allocation of Frequency Bands

Because of the need by many organisations for good radio communication, it is obviously necessary that certain frequencies be allotted to various organisations for their sole use, to avoid interference from unwanted signals.

Frequency allocation has been done internationally, and aviation has certain specific groups of frequencies in the:

- ☐ low frequency (LF) band;
- ☐ medium frequency (MF) band;
- ☐ high frequency (HF) band;
- ☐ very high frequency (VHF) band; and
- ☐ ultra high frequency (UHF) band.

Very High Frequency (VHF)

VHF (30 MHz to 300 MHz) provides high quality line-of-sight radio signals and is used for short-range voice communication (118·00 to 135·95 MHz) and radio navigation aids such as the VOR and ILS (108·00 to 117·95 MHz).

VHF is the preferred method of voice communication in aviation. The curvature of the earth puts a natural limit on ground–aircraft VHF communication and navigation signals, although atmospheric refraction of the radio waves will extend their range slightly beyond line-of-sight. Line-of-sight gives us the *visible horizon*, and the slightly extended range for VHF radio transmissions gives us the *radio horizon*.

NOTE Line-of-sight does not mean that you have to be able to physically see the aeroplane – it could be in cloud or be night-time. It means there are no physical obstructions between the transmitter and the receiver.

VHF Range

The expected range of VHF radio transmissions is given approximately by the formula:

VHF range in nm = the square root of (1.5 × altitude in feet)

EXAMPLE 1 What is the expected range for air–ground communications if the aircraft is 1,000 feet higher than the ground antenna?

$$\text{VHF range in nm} = \sqrt{(1.5 \times 1,000)}$$
$$= \sqrt{1500}$$
$$= 39 \text{ nm}$$

Remember that this distance can be reduced by any obstacles between the aircraft and the ground station.

EXAMPLE 2 What is the expected VHF range (or the radio horizon) for air–ground communications if you fly at an altitude 5,000 feet higher than the antenna on the ground?

$$\text{VHF range in nm} = \sqrt{(1.5 \times 5,000)}$$
$$= \sqrt{7500}$$
$$= 87 \text{ nm}$$

EXAMPLE 3 What is the expected VHF range for air–ground communications if the aeroplane is 10,000 feet higher than the antenna on the ground?

$$\text{VHF range in nm} = \sqrt{(1.5 \times 10,000)}$$
$$= \sqrt{15,000}$$
$$= 122 \text{ nm}$$

HEIGHT OF AEROPLANE	EXPECTED VHF RANGE
1,000 feet	*39 nm, say 40 nm*
5,000 feet	*87 nm, say 90 nm*
10,000 feet	*122 nm, say 120 nm*

NOTE It is obvious that improved direct wave communications can be achieved by raising the height of the ground-based antenna or by increasing the altitude of the aeroplane.

High Frequency (HF)

HF is used for communications when you are outside VHF range and includes frequencies from 3,000 kHz to 30,000 kHz. The 3 MHz frequency (i.e. 3,000 kHz) is more suitable at night, and the higher frequencies (5, 6, 7 or 8 MHz) are more suitable during the day. Expected ranges may vary up to 2,000 nm.

Low and Medium Frequency (LF & MF)

LF and MF are used for non-directional beacons (NDBs). LF is from 30 kHz to 300 kHz, and MF is from 300 kHz to 3,000 kHz. The aeronautical allocation for NDBs covers a part of both bands from 200 kHz to 420 kHz.

Ultra High Frequency (UHF)

UHF (300–3,000 MHz) is used by the military for voice communications, in the glideslope (vertical guidance) of the ILS, and in the international (1,000 MHz) DME. *Secondary surveillance radar* (SSR) also operates in the UHF band, with the *mode* on 1,030 MHz and the *code* on 1,090 MHz.

Very Low Frequency (VLF)

VLF transmissions (10–30 kHz) are used by global navigation systems such as the Omega navigation units found in some aircraft. These systems compute position in latitude/longitude by comparing the signals from the closest of the VLF transmitters located around the world.

Properties of Radio Waves

Like light waves, radio waves interact with the medium through which they are travelling. They may be *reflected, refracted* (bent), *attenuated* (weakened), *absorbed* and *diffracted* (divided). The degree to which radio waves are affected by these processes is primarily dependent upon their frequency.

Reflection

Reflection occurs when a radio wave 'bounces' off a suitable reflecting surface, just as light waves are reflected from mirrors. This property is utilised in radar systems, but it is important to note that radio waves can be reflected from a wide variety of surfaces and not just metallic objects like aircraft and ships. Airborne weather radar, for example, depends upon the fact that radio waves from certain frequency ranges are reflected by water droplets in the atmosphere.

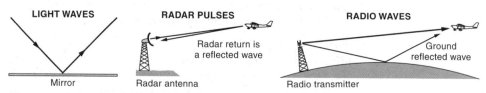

LIGHT WAVES   RADAR PULSES   RADIO WAVES

Radar return is
a reflected wave

Ground
reflected wave

Mirror   Radar antenna   Radio transmitter

■ *Figure 12-1* **Reflection is where a wave 'bounces off' an object at the same angle at which it strikes the object**

Refraction

Refraction is a 'bending' of the paths of radio waves as they move obliquely across the boundary between media of differing density. This bending occurs because the speed of electromagnetic waves varies slightly according to the density of the material through which they are moving (the speed of light is only constant in a vacuum).

A most important case involving the refraction of radio waves is that which occurs in the **ionosphere,** (a number of layers of ionised gases which envelop the earth at high altitude, extending from approximately 30 nm to 300 nm in height).

The variations in density between the layers within the ionosphere can bend and alter the paths of certain radio waves to such an extent that they return to the earth's surface. The ionosphere effectively re-directs them back into the lower atmosphere. Radio waves in the high frequency (HF) band are particularly susceptible to this process, which is termed **ionospheric refraction.**

The amount of refraction to which a particular radio signal is subject depends not only upon the frequency of the radio waves, but also upon the state of the ionosphere itself, which, as we shall see,

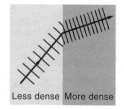

Less dense More dense

■ *Figure 12-2*

Refraction is the 'bending' of a wave when it passes from one medium to another

is extremely variable. Consequently, for any given HF frequency, the strength of the signals returned to the earth's surface by refraction can vary from hour to hour, and even minute to minute.

Attenuation

Attenuation is something which affects all radio signals, though its effect is not appreciable over short-range VHF transmissions. It is the process by which all radio transmissions are progressively weakened as they radiate further and further away from the transmitter.

To illustrate this, imagine a radio antenna transmitting a momentary signal of equal strength in all directions (i.e. an *omnidirectional* signal). This signal will radiate outwards as an expanding spherical surface. A fixed amount of radio energy, determined by the strength of the initial transmission, will be spread over this surface. The further the signal travels, the greater the area of the spherical surface and the more thinly the original signal energy is spread, i.e. signal strength is progressively reduced with increasing distance from the transmitter.

Higher transmitter power increases the range of reception of a radio station.

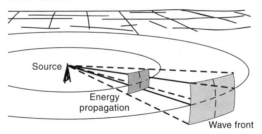

■ *Figure 12-3* **Signal strength is attenuated as distance from transmitter increases**

How Radio Carries Voice Messages

This was covered in Chapter 11, but we include some more information here for readers who are interested.

The electric and magnetic signals generated in a microphone from audio signals (such as a voice) are in the audio frequency band from 20 to 20,000 hertz. The frequency spread of radio signals suitable for transmission is much higher than this – from 3,000,000 to 300,000,000 hertz. Radio waves are illustrated as symmetrical (sine-curve) waves radiating outward from the source, and, as can be seen in the following diagram, the higher the frequency the more waves per second that are transmitted, and the shorter the wavelength.

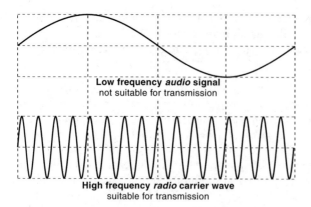

Low frequency *audio* signal
not suitable for transmission

High frequency *radio* carrier wave
suitable for transmission

■ *Figure 12-4* **Audio signals are not in the radio frequency range**

The electromagnetic voice signals from the microphone are not immediately suitable for transmission as radio waves. The audio signal is superimposed onto the radio frequency signal which acts as a carrier wave. This process is called *modulation,* and may be done in one of two ways:

1. By modulating (varying) the amplitude of the carrier wave (**amplitude modulation** or **AM**).

2. By modulating the frequency of the carrier wave (**frequency modulation** or **FM**), as used in VHF and UHF transmissions.

Amplitude modulation and frequency modulation are the usual means employed to allow the radio carrier wave to carry voice messages. The radio frequency (RF) carrier wave (CW) *carries* the audio frequency (AF).

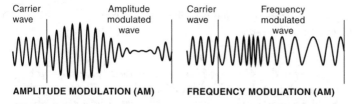

Carrier wave — Amplitude modulated wave — Carrier wave — Frequency modulated wave

AMPLITUDE MODULATION (AM)   **FREQUENCY MODULATION (AM)**

■ *Figure 12-5* **Modulating the carrier wave to carry a voice message using amplitude modulation (AM) and frequency modulation (FM)**

There is a simpler method of allowing the carrier wave to carry a signal less sophisticated than a voice message. This is known as **pulse modulation** and is achieved by interrupting the carrier wave, as is done in transmitting morse code. This process is also used in radar, where short bursts of the carrier wave are transmitted, followed by relatively long periods when no signals are transmitted and the radar dish is free to receive reflected signals.

no transmission   no transmission

■ *Figure 12-6* **Pulse modulation**

The Radio Transmitter and the Antenna

The carrier wave, modified by the audio signal superimposed upon it, is passed to the radio antenna and transmitted.

The fundamental components of a radio transmitter are:
- ☐ **a power supply** to provide direct current;
- ☐ **an oscillator** to generate a radio frequency (carrier wave) and a device for controlling the frequency of the generated signal;
- ☐ **an amplifier** to increase the output of the oscillator;
- ☐ **a modulator** to add the audio signals from the microphone to the carrier wave; and
- ☐ **an antenna** (or aerial) to transmit the signals out into space.

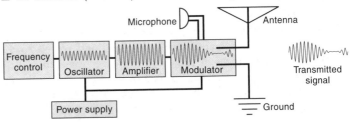

■ *Figure 12-7* **Schematic diagram of a radio transmitter**

The Antenna

The signal from the transmitter is sent to the antenna and radiated into space. The final signal from the transmitter is still in the form of an alternating current and it flows up and down the antenna. As the electrons in the alternating current race up and down the antenna, they generate electric and magnetic fields (or an electromagnetic field) in the area surrounding the antenna. This electromagnetic field radiates into space as radio waves of the same frequency as the alternating current sent to the antenna. (Common radio antenna installations are shown on page 2.)

Antenna theory is a subject of its own and we need do nothing more here than state that a really efficient antenna is about the same length as half the wavelength of the signal it is transmitting. To transmit a 6 MHz HF signal (i.e. 6,000 kHz or 6,000,000 Hz), the wavelength can be found from the formula:

Speed of propagation = frequency × wave length

For example:

300,000,000 metres per second = 6,000,000 Hz × wave length

Therefore: Wave length = $\dfrac{300,000,000}{6,000,000}$ = 50 metres

Thus a good half-wavelength antenna for this 6 MHz frequency would be 25 m.

For higher frequencies (with shorter wavelengths) the half-wave antenna would be shorter. Consequently, you would expect a VHF antenna to be shorter than an HF antenna. (This of course applies to the antennas on aircraft as well as those on the ground.)

For lower frequencies (with longer wavelengths) the half-wave antenna would be longer, and this is one of the disadvantages of low radio frequencies. Very low frequency (VLF) ground antennas, as are used in VLF Omega navigation transmitters, may be several hundred metres high. If a half-wave antenna is not realistic, then a quarter-wave antenna will be used, and so on.

The Radio Receiver

The receiver works in reverse to the transmitter. Radio signals from elsewhere are detected by the antenna and passed to the radio receiver. The receiver removes the carrier wave, then feeds the remaining audio signal to a speaker or headset where it is converted to pressure waves in the air – and your message is heard. Of course if the transmitted signal is not a voice message, but say a radio navigation signal, then it is passed to the appropriate navigation instrument in the cockpit and displayed there.

Many radios use common circuitry to both transmit and receive, and these are commonly known as *transceivers.*

Propagation Paths of Radio Waves

After transmission, radio waves may follow a number of different paths, called **propagation paths.** Radio waves arriving at a receiving antenna may, of course, have followed a *direct* path between the transmitter and the receiver. However, depending upon their frequency, some of the incoming waves may have followed a different path, e.g. they may have been *reflected* from nearby mountains, or *refracted* back to the earth from the ionosphere.

Radio waves arriving at a receiver's antenna can be divided into two principal groups, depending upon the propagation path which they have followed from the point of transmission to the point of reception:

☐ **ground waves:** which follow paths in close proximity to the earth's surface, and approximately parallel to it; and

☐ **sky waves:** waves that have been refracted by the ionosphere, and effectively re-directed back to the earth's surface.

Transmissions from a wide range of radio frequencies generate both ground waves and sky waves. However, the relative importance of each type of wave, as far as reception is concerned, varies with frequency.

Phase

If the radio waves intercepted by a particular receiving antenna have followed different paths in reaching that point, they will 'mix' together to produce a *resultant* signal. For instance, there may be one or more sky wave signals arriving at the receiver, which may be mixing with the ground wave signal from the same transmitter. In some cases, signals of the same frequency, but from different transmitters, can mix to form a resultant signal at the same receiver.

Under these circumstances, there are several possible effects on reception.

1. If two different waves arrive simultaneously at a receiver, and they are *in phase,* i.e. their peaks and troughs are exactly aligned, then the resultant signal will be increased, providing better reception.

 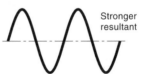

Stronger resultant

■ *Figure 12-8* **Two waves arriving in phase will reinforce the signal**

2. If two waves arrive totally *out of phase,* i.e. the peak of one wave arrives at exactly the same time as the trough of the other wave, they will tend to cancel each other out, giving a very weak or *null* resultant signal.

Weaker resultant

■ *Figure 12-9* **Two waves arriving out of phase will weaken or cancel the resultant signal**

3. If radio waves arrive so that their phase relationship is constantly changing (very often the case), then the resultant signal will be alternately reinforced and weakened. This variation in signal strength is commonly referred to as *fading*.

Ground Waves

Ground waves are waves which travel directly from the transmitter to the receiver, i.e. waves that follow a straight, line-of-sight path.

Signals received by a VHF navigation or communications receiver will consist almost entirely of ground waves. This is why VHF transmissions provide high-quality reception, because there are practically no out-of-phase waves mixing with the primary signal to cause fading or cancellation. However, VHF reception is restricted to approximately line-of-sight distances, and so is only suitable for use in relatively short-range navigation and communication systems.

Repeater stations may be used to increase the range of direct wave VHF transmissions. Antennas positioned at remote locations can, with the aid of satellite, microwave and/or land-line links, establish communications in areas well beyond the normal VHF horizon of the original transmitter.

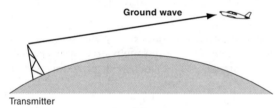

■ *Figure 12-10* **The ground wave**

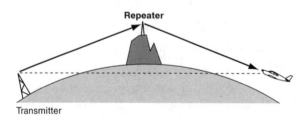

■ *Figure 12-11* **Repeater stations extend the VHF coverage**

NOTE Repeater stations are not suitable for extending the range of VHF *radio navigation* stations, because these systems depend upon there being only one source of signals. If, for example, an indicator needle in the cockpit points in a certain direction when tuned to a particular radio-navigation aid frequency, the pilot must be certain that it is actually pointing to the position of the original transmitter, and not at a repeater station positioned elsewhere.

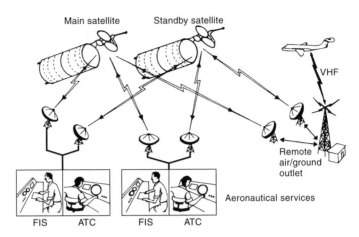

Figure 12-12 **Operation of VHF satellite repeater stations**

Sky Waves

When signals radiate outwards from a transmitting antenna, a proportion of the waves follow paths that are approximately parallel to the earth's surface, i.e. they are ground waves.

Other waves will travel upwards into the sky at all angles. In the absence of any significant obstacles to their passage, these waves would continue straight out into space. This is normally the case for waves in the VHF band and higher. However, radio waves within other frequency ranges (i.e. the HF band and below) are subjected to significant and varying amounts of *absorption* and *refraction* when they encounter the ionosphere during their upward passage.

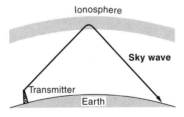

Figure 12-13 **Sky waves**

The Ionosphere

When ultra-violet (UV) radiation emitted by the sun strikes the upper levels of the earth's atmosphere, some of the constituent gas molecules and atoms suffer *ionisation* – a process in which negatively charged electrons are separated from their host atoms, which then become positively charged ions. The upper layers of the atmosphere that contain this mixture of electrically charged particles are known collectively as the **ionosphere**.

The height and thickness of the ionosphere is highly variable.

☐ **During daylight hours,** when the sun is overhead and the ion-ising radiation is intense, the ionosphere expands to its thickest extent and can stretch from a height of about 50 km up to 500 km or more above the earth's surface.

☐ **At night,** when ionising radiation is largely absent, the iono-sphere contracts, and usually extends between about 100 km to 400 km in height.

The extent of the ionosphere, and the degree of ionisation within it, varies on a daily (diurnal) basis. It varies, too, on a sea-sonal basis, i.e. it will be thicker during a summer day than during a winter day.

Also significant, as far as ionospheric intensity is concerned, is the 11-year *sunspot cycle.* At the peak of sunspot activity, enormous electrical and magnetic disturbances on the sun can generate exceptional emissions of ultra-violet radiation, causing more intense ionisation activity in the upper layers of the atmosphere.

During the hours immediately before and after sunrise and sunset, large and rapid fluctuations occur in the ionosphere, and consequently radio signals from frequency bands that are most affected by the ionosphere (i.e. LF, MF and HF bands) will become 'confused'.

Refraction of Radio Waves by the Ionosphere

Some radio waves are almost completely absorbed (attenuated) during their passage through the ionosphere. Other waves, which are not as significantly attenuated, may undergo refraction in the ionosphere, and some of these can be refracted or 'bent' so far that they bend back towards the earth's surface.

The amount of refraction that occurs to a radio wave during its passage through the ionosphere will depend upon:

☐ **the frequency** of the wave;

☐ **the angle** at which the wave enters the layers of the iono-sphere;

☐ **the intensity of the ionisation** (which varies both with time and between the constituent layers of the ionosphere).

When a radio wave encounters a layer of ionised gas, it tends to accelerate slightly. If the wave enters the ionised layer at an oblique angle, the top edge of the wave front will accelerate first, causing a change in the wave's direction of travel, i.e. it will undergo refraction.

After their paths have been altered by refraction within the ion-osphere, many waves simply continue on their way out into space. However, as the angle at which the radio waves enter the iono-sphere decreases, the amount of refraction which they undergo will increase. Eventually, at a particular angle of incidence, sufficient refraction will occur to re-direct the waves back towards the earth's surface, thereby producing the first sky waves for that particular transmission.

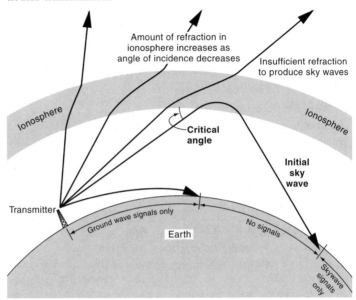

■ *Figure 12-14* **Not all waves refracted by the ionosphere produce sky waves**

Long-Range Communications

For signals on any given frequency, the angle of incidence that produces the initial sky waves is known as the **critical angle** for that frequency. Waves that enter the ionosphere at an angle less than the critical angle, will, of course, all produce sky waves.

Before continuing with further discussion on sky wave propagation, it would be appropriate at this point to consider more specifically how frequency determines the behaviour of radio waves when they encounter the ionosphere.

- ☐ **VHF and higher frequency bands:** radio waves within this frequency range suffer no appreciable attenuation or refraction during their passage through the ionosphere, and will continue out into space relatively undisturbed.
- ☐ **HF frequency band:** Many HF radio transmissions can produce strong sky wave signals both day and night. However, signals at the lower end of this frequency band undergo significant attenuation within a particular layer in the ionosphere during daylight hours. Consequently, there is almost a complete absence of sky waves for frequencies less than about 5 MHz,

virtually ruling them out for reliable long-range communications between sunrise and sunset. Sky waves will, however, be present throughout the *whole* HF band during the hours of darkness.

☐ **LF/MF band frequencies:** radio waves from these lower frequency bands are almost completely absorbed by the ionosphere during the day. However, at night, in the absence of this attenuating layer, quite strong sky waves are produced which can interfere with ground waves at some distance from the transmitting antenna.

Sky Wave Propagation

The distance between a transmitting station and the point at which the first re-directed sky wave signals return to the earth's surface is known as the **skip distance** for that particular signal.

For transmissions on certain frequencies, notably in the upper part of the HF communications band, significant ground waves do not extend to the skip distance, effectively creating a *zone of silence*. This zone, where neither sky wave nor ground wave signals are present, is known as the **skip zone** or **dead zone**.

Radio waves from the upper part of the HF frequency band are refracted to a lesser degree in the ionosphere than those of lower frequencies. As a result of this, a greater proportion of these higher-frequency waves penetrate to the upper levels of the ionosphere, or pass right through into space. Only those waves that 'graze' the ionosphere at a relatively shallow angle of incidence will undergo sufficient refraction to form sky waves. Therefore, the skip distance for the higher frequency HF waves will be greater than for waves in the lower part of the HF band.

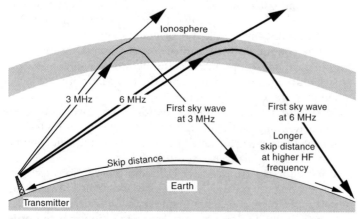

■ Figure 12-15 **As the frequencies of HF waves increase, the skip distance increases**

It is important to be aware that there are many variables affecting the propagation of sky waves in the HF band. This tends to make the range and quality of HF communications considerably more unpredictable and less reliable than is the case for VHF communications, which rely primarily upon direct wave signals, i.e. high-quality signals over a predictable line-of-sight range.

Summary

Despite the uncertainties arising from the constant variation in the ionosphere, voice communications utilising HF sky waves can be achieved with reasonable reliability up to ranges of between 200 nm and 3,000 nm. This depends, however, upon the intelligent selection of suitable frequencies by radio operators.

Some important considerations affecting HF frequency selection are as follows:

1. During daylight hours, optimum HF communications are generally available on frequencies between 5 and 8 MHz and higher, since they will produce the strongest sky wave signals; the lower HF band frequencies (around 3 MHz) are usually unsuitable, owing to severe attenuation within the ionosphere.

2. At night, when the ionosphere is higher and less intense, sky waves are refracted from higher levels in the atmosphere and the skip distance for any given frequency is consequently greater than during the day. The absence of one particular layer in the ionosphere during the hours of darkness also means that the lower HF frequencies, in the region of 3 MHz, can produce strong sky waves. Their skip distances are less than those of higher frequency waves, because as frequency decreases, skip distances are also reduced, owing to increased refraction. In general, then, the lower HF frequencies are more suitable for night-time communications.

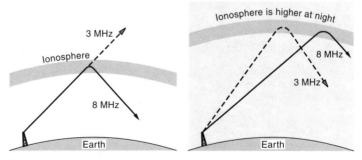

■ *Figure 12-16* **The variable state of the ionosphere is a significant consideration for HF frequency selection**

3. The distance from the station with which communication is desired is also a consideration for HF frequency selection. As a general rule, the closer the station, the lower the most suitable HF frequency will be. For instance, if you are unable to establish communication with a particular station, but you are receiving strong signals from more distant transmitters, then change to a lower frequency because the aircraft is probably within the dead zone for the station on that particular frequency.

Now complete:

Exercises 12 – Radio Wave Propagation & Long-Range Communications.

The Air Pilot's **Manual**

Volume 7

Exercises and Answers

Exercises

Exercises 1

Cockpit Radios

1 High quality short-range voice communications are provided by the (VHF/HF)-COM radio set.

2 Electrical power gets to the radios and other avionics via the electrical ..., and, in some cases, an additional ... . Each radio (has/does not have) an individual ON/OFF switch.

3 A VHF-COM set that functions as both a transmitter and a receiver may be referred to as a t... .

4 The radios normally receive electrical power from the (alternator/battery) when the engine is running.

5 To avoid electrical shocks to the sensitive radio equipment when the alternator comes on-line or drops off-line, the radios should be switched (ON/OFF) when starting and stopping the engine.

6 If you leave the radios on for a long time with the alternator not functioning, you could f... the b... .

7 The VOL control adjusts the volume of (transmission/reception/transmission and reception).

8 The frequency range allotted to aeronautical VHF voice transmissions is between ... and ... MHz.

9 The next higher frequency to 131·5 MHz is ... MHz, because the spacing between adjacent frequencies is ... MHz.

10 Write down all possible frequencies that you can select on a VHF-COM between 121 MHz and 122 MHz inclusive. Alongside each one write down two ways they might appear on different types of VHF-COM sets. (*This may seem repetitious, but it shows you just how many frequencies there are that begin with 121· MHz.*)

11 How many individual frequencies are available in the VHF-COM range with 121 as the first three digits, i.e. from 121·00 MHz up to but not including 122·0 MHz?

12 How many individual frequencies are available in the VHF-COM range, i.e. from 118·00 MHz up to but not including 137·0?

13 Specific radio frequencies for particular Air Traffic Service Units are listed in the ... sections of the A... I... P... .

14 On many VHF-COM radio sets background noise can be minimised using the ... control.

15 The squelch control is used to adjust the sensitivity of the (receiver/transmitter).

16 If you are transmitting on a particular frequency, can other people in the vicinity transmit on that frequency at the same time as you?

17 If your transmit button becomes stuck in the transmit position, or if you forget to release it after completing your transmission, will that affect other transmissions? Will it block out that frequency?

18 A stuck PTT switch causes what is called a s... m... or an o... m... .

19 When speaking on the radio, you should speak at a rate slightly (faster/slower) than in normal face-to-face conversation.

20 You (should/need not) listen out for any radio calls addressed to you.

21 You switch to a new frequency as instructed and make a call. No response is received. After a second attempt is also unsuccessful, your first action should be to ... .

22 If you are unsure of the frequency you were instructed to change to, you could ... .

23 If it appears that the VHF-COM set is not working, what three switches could you check? You could then check that no ... has popped or f... blown, and that the h... and m... are properly plugged in. Throughout this, you (must/need not) control the flightpath and airspeed of the aircraft accurately.

24 VOR frequencies are selected on the (VHF-COM/VHF-NAV/DME/ADF) radio.

25 NDB stands for ..., and its frequency can be selected on the (VHF-COM/VHF-NAV/DME/ADF) radio.

26 The cockpit equipment which enables an air traffic radar controller to identify your aircraft's position and altitude by receiving coded signals is the ... . It is part of the s... s... r... system.

27 The ON position allows the transponder to operate on the four-digit code set in its control panel and provides (position/position and altitude) information to a radar controller. This is known as Mode (A/C), and is pronounced ... .

28 The ALT position allows the transponder to operate on the four-digit code set in its control panel and provides (position/position and altitude) information to a radar controller. This is known as Mode (A/C), and is pronounced ... .

29 When asked to squawk 5413, you should set ... in the code selection panel, and make sure that the transponder is switched to either ... or ... .

30 Whilst squawking a conspicuity code with Mode C, ATC asks you to confirm your altitude or flight level; this is to ...

31 The number of possible codes that can be set in a typical transponder is ... . Where does this number come from?

32 When asked to squawk ident, you should ... .

33 The conspicuity code is ... .

34 The radio failure code is ... .

35 The emergency code is ... .

Exercises 2

What to Say

1 Write out and say the phonetic alphabet that is used to transmit letters.

2 The word *Wilco* means ...

3 The word *over* means ...

4 The word *out* means ...

5 How would you transmit the number 59?

6 How would you transmit the number 8,500 when it refers to altitude?

7 How would you transmit the number 2,400 when it refers to altitude?

8 What word or phrase would you use to express *yes* or *that is correct*?

9 What standard radio word or phrase means *no*?

10 How would you transmit the callsign of an aircraft registered G-ABCD?

11 What initial radio call would you make if you are flying a Cessna registered G-PRKI? How would you transmit this in abbreviated form?

12 Aircraft callsigns may only be abbreviated when …

13 What initial radio call would you make if you are flying a Warrior registered G-QOSW? How would you transmit this in abbreviated form?

14 How would you transmit the callsign of the US-registered Cessna N-4376HU?

15 How would you abbreviate the callsign Monde Air G-ARMP?

16 The time reference for aviation is c… u… t…, which is abbreviated to … . This is sometimes referred to a Z… time, symbolised by the letter … .

17 How would you transmit Runway 36?

18 How would you transmit an altimeter setting of 1013 millibars?

19 How would you transmit an altimeter setting of 996 millibars?

20 How would you transmit Runway 08?

21 How would you transmit frequency 118·725?

22 How would you transmit a cloud coverage of three-eighths of the sky?

23 How would you express a wind of 320/25?

24 How would you transmit the hours and minutes of 0835 UTC?

25 If there is no doubt regarding the hour you are referring to (say the present hour or the one just about to begin in a few minutes), how would you transmit the time 1958 UTC in abbreviated form?

26 How would you transmit the transponder code 1735?

27 How would you transmit the transponder code 1500?

28 How would you transmit the time 1500 UTC?

29 How would you transmit the altitude 1,500 feet?

30 How would you transmit the transponder Mode A?

31 How would you transmit the transponder Mode C?

32 Air traffic control advise you to *standby*. This means that you should …

33 The term *Roger* means: I have received all of your last … .

34 What radio call do you make to the tower at an aerodrome with an air traffic control (ATC) service when all of your pre-take-off checks are complete?

35 Does the instruction "Line up" from the tower permit you to enter the active runway? Does it permit you to take off?

36 You are passed an instruction to which you are unable to conform. Your response should be …

37 You want to establish your bearing by obtaining a QTE (a true bearing of the aircraft from the VDF station which you can plot directly on your chart relative to true North). The correct RT procedure is to request a …

38 What words must you hear, preceded by your callsign, for you to commence take-off at a ATC aerodrome?

39 The term *take-off* may only be used by the pilot when …

40 What words must you hear, preceded by your callsign, for you to land at an ATC aerodrome?

41 How would you respond to a request, "How do you read this transmission?" if it is readable, but with difficulty?

42 Readability scale 5 means:

43 How would you respond to a request, "How do you read this transmission?" if it is totally readable?

44 How would you describe the position of an aircraft straight ahead of you at a higher level?

45 Run through the list of abbreviations beginning on page 207, concentrating on the important ones in grey boxes. See if you can pronounce them correctly, and also recall what terms they are abbreviations for.

Exercises 3

Aerodrome Operations

1 My aerodrome (has/does not have) an active control tower.

2 At an ATC aerodrome, you (require/do not require) an ATC clearance to enter and operate on the runway.

3 At an ATC aerodrome, you (require/do not require) ATC approval to taxi.

4 At an aerodrome with no ATC, you (require/do not require) an ATC clearance to enter and operate on the runway.

5 At an aerodrome with no ATC, you (require/do not require) ATC approval to taxi.

6 At an aerodrome with no ATC, it (is/is not) good airmanship to take advantage of any information services available.

7 At an aerodromes with no ATC, it (is/is not) good airmanship to make advisory radio calls of your intentions.

8 My home aerodrome (has/does not) have an automatic terminal information service. Its frequency is ... .

9 At my home aerodrome, my initial radio call in the parked position is ... .

10 Readability scale:
1 (*wun*) means ...
2 (*too*) means ...
3 (*tree*) means ...
4 (*fower*) means ...

11 5 (fife) means ...

12 At my home aerodrome, my initial radio call prior to entering the runway is ... .

13 Sketch how to depart the circuit pattern for the training area from each of the possible runways. Include radio calls.

14 You are approaching to land at an airfield supplying an Aerodrome Flight Information Service (AFIS), e.g. Leavesden Information, and are advised to "land at your discretion". Your RT response should be ...

15 The correct phrase to ATC when ready to request take-off permission is ...

16 The term 'take-off' maybe used by the pilot only when ...

17 Sketch how to return from the training area and join the circuit pattern for each of the possible runways. Include radio calls.

18 A pilot (is/is not) required to read back weather information following ATC messages.

19 FIS stands for ... . FIS is a (control/information only) service. A FIS (is/is not) authorised to issue clearances to enter and operate on a runway.

20 Who takes the authority for you to enter and operate on a runway at a aerodrome with no ATC service?

21 An Air to Ground unit (A/G) is indicated by its place-name, followed by the word ...

22 Is an Air/Ground radio station authorised to issue take-off and landing clearances?

23 Is a FIS authorised to issue take-off and landing clearances?

24 The phrase *long final* means ...

25 Sketch the dimensions of a typical ATZ.

26 Sketch the dimensions of the ATZ surrounding your home aerodrome.

27 Sketch the dimensions of a typical MATZ.

28 What is the minimum range or time that is required before requesting transit of Military Aerodrome Traffic Zones (MATZ)?

29 Should you book out before a flight? If so, with whom?

Exercises 4

Aerodrome Information

1 You (should/need not) know about the weather conditions at any aerodrome where you are about to operate.

2 You (should/should not) take advantage of any weather information made available by authorised experts such as an A... T... S... U... .

3 The recorded information broadcast for one particular airport is known as the ..., which is usually abbreviated to ..., and pronounced ... .

4 What is the approximate duration of an ATIS broadcast?

5 Which radios can you use to select the ATIS frequencies?

6 Where are the ATIS frequencies for a particular aerodrome published?

7 The ATIS (is/is not) periodically updated.

8 What would the first ATIS of a day be likely to be called? What would the following ATIS be called?

9 When are regular weather observations taken at a busy aerodrome, and how often is the ATIS typically updated?

10 You have one VHF-COM radio and one VHF-NAV radio. The ATIS is available only on frequency 120·575 MHz. Which radio would you use to select this frequency?

11 Should you advise the ATSU you are in contact with that you are leaving the frequency for a brief period to obtain the ATIS?

12 Should you advise the ATSU when you are back on frequency?

13 You are airborne and have one VHF-COM radio and one VHF-NAV radio. The ATIS is available on frequency 121·85 MHz and also on 114·3 MHz. Which radio would you use to listen to the ATIS, and which frequency would you select? Explain.

14 Should you advise an aerodrome ATSU that you have received an ATIS?

15 What words would you use to advise an aerodrome ATSU that you have received an ATIS?

16 See if you can write out some typical ATIS broadcasts. Write them out in full English, and then see if you can write them down in shorthand.

17 VOLMET provides weather information for (one/a number of) aerodromes(s).

18 A VOLMET broadcast will last (longer than/shorter than/the same time as) an ATIS broadcast. Explain.

19 You are cruising along, several hours from your destination, and decide to get the latest weather for your destination and some other aerodromes in its vicinity. You would listen to the (ATIS/VOLMET). Explain. If the time was 1218Z, would it be more logical to listen to the weather immediately or wait for another 10 minutes or so. Explain.

20 With QNH set in the pressure window, the altimeter should indicate (zero/aerodrome elevation) when the aeroplane is on the aerodrome.

21 With QFE set in the pressure window, the altimeter should indicate (zero/aerodrome elevation) when the aeroplane is on the runway.

22 If the aerodrome has an elevation of 300 feet and the QNH is 1008 mb, what would you expect the QFE to be?

23 If the aerodrome has an elevation of 300 feet and the QFE is 1005 mb, what would you expect the QNH to be?

24 There is a greater likelihood of fog forming if the *temperature/dewpoint* relationship is:
A. +6/−5
B. +15/+14
C. +15/+8
D. +2/−7

25 A wind of 080/25 would favour Runway (35/17/07/25).

26 Could the term CAVOK be used if the cloud base was 3,000 feet aal. Explain.

27 Could the term CAVOK be used if there was a cumulonimbus cloud with a base 6,000 feet aal. Explain.

28 Could the term CAVOK be used if the visibility was 8 kilometres. Explain.

29 Could the term CAVOK be used if the cloud base was 6,000 feet aal and the visibility 9 kilometres. Explain.

30 Could the term CAVOK be used if the cloud ceiling and visibility requirements were met, but rain was falling from high level stratus with base 7,000 feet aal? Explain.

31 List the requirements that must be satisfied before the term CAVOK is used

32 In an ATIS, cloud base is described with reference to (mean sea level/aerodrome level).

Exercises 5
Airspace Classification

1 The international airspace classification system starts with Class A and ends with Class … .

2 Controlled airspace comprises Class A to Class …, with ATC clearances being required to operate in controlled airspace from Class A to Class … .

3 Uncontrolled airspace consists of Class … and Class … airspace.

4 There are three main types of aeronautical communications services; they are …

5 Advisory routes are Class … airspace and are (uncontrolled/controlled). You (need/do not need) an ATC clearance to operate along an advisory route.

6 Class G airspace is also known as the … FIR. It is (controlled/uncontrolled) airspace. Do you require a clearance to operate in Class G airspace?

7 As a VFR pilot, you require an ATC route clearance to enter controlled airspace from Class A through to Class (B/C/D/E/F/G) inclusive.

8 Are ATC route clearances required for Classes F and G uncontrolled airspace?

9 Does an ATC *route* clearance authorise you to take off at an ATC aerodrome? Explain.

10 At a FIS or A/G aerodrome in Class G airspace, do you require an ATC clearance to enter and operate on the runways? Do you need an ATC route clearance to operate in the Class G airspace?

11 At an ATC aerodrome in Class G airspace, do you require an ATC clearance to enter and operate on the runways? Do you need an ATC route clearance to operate in the Class G airspace?

12 Do you require an ATC route clearance to operate in Class D airspace?

13 At an ATC aerodrome in Class D airspace, do you require an ATC clearance to enter and operate on the runways? Do you need an ATC route clearance to operate in the Class D airspace?

14 An en route procedural service is a (radar/non-radar) service.

15 The Aeronautical Mobile Services categorise their messages in the following order or priority; they are ...

16 What information is required in a position report and in what order?

Exercises 6

R/T in Uncontrolled Airspace

1 Class G is (controlled/uncontrolled) airspace and is known as the ... FIR.

2 What services can ATC provide in uncontrolled airspace?

3 You understand an airborne flight may be filed with an Air Traffic Service Unit (ASTU). This flight plan would normally be filed with ...

4 On your first transmission to a Air Traffic Service Unit (ATSU) you should pass your ...

5 LARS stands for ... . It (is/is not) available in uncontrolled airspace.

6 The LARS service known as R... A... S... (will/will not) provide you with avoiding action regarding potentially conflicting traffic.

7 As a VFR pilot, should you accept an advised heading change that will take you into cloud?

8 It is your intention to transit (penetrate) a Military Aerodrome Traffic Zone (MATZ). When asked by the controller to "pass your message", what information should you give and in what order should it be passed?

9 The LARS service known as R... I... S... (will/will not) provide you with avoiding action regarding potentially conflicting traffic.

10 It is your intention to request a Radar Information Service (RIS). When asked by the controller to "pass your message" what information should you give and in what order should it be passed?

11 Who is responsible for maintaining terrain clearance when you are using RAS or RIS – you or the radar controller?

12 VDF stands for ... . It makes use of your (VHF-COM/VHF-NAV) radio.

13 Requesting a QDM means ...

14 Requesting a QDR means ...

15 Requesting a QTE means ...

16 To indicate that you wanted a heading to steer to the aerodrome, you would use the word (homer/tracking/heading guidance).

17 To find the magnetic direction to the aerodrome you would request Q... .

18 To track to the aerodrome if the QDM was 145 degrees, what direction would you steer in nil-wind conditions?

19 DACS stands for ... . It may be pronounced as ... .

20 DAAIS stands for … . It may be pronounced as … .

Exercises 7

R/T in Controlled Airspace

1 Controlled airspace surrounding a very busy aerodrome and extending from the surface (i.e. the ground) up to a specified altitude or level is called a (control area/control zone/airway).

2 Controlled airspace that exists between two specified altitudes or levels over an area is called a (control area/control zone/airway).

3 Controlled airspace in the form of a corridor along busy air routes is called a (control area/control zone/airway).

4 An airway is … nm wide, i.e. … nm either side of the centreline joining the two specific ground-based navigation aids.

5 The correct order of information in an aircraft position report is …

6 Do you need an ATC route clearance to enter Class D airspace surrounding a busy aerodrome?

7 Do you need an ATC route clearance to enter Class C airspace surrounding a busy aerodrome elsewhere in Europe (Class C is not allocated in the UK)?

8 Do you need an ATC route clearance to enter Class E airspace on a VFR flight?

9 Do you need an ATC route clearance to enter a Class A control zone surrounding a very busy aerodrome on a VFR flight? If so, what name is given to this clearance.

10 Do you need an ATC route clearance to enter a control zone surrounding an aerodrome on a VFR flight if the weather conditions are below VMC, for instance poor visibility and/or low cloud? Is so, what name is given to this clearance.

11 Special Visual Flight Rule clearances (SVFR) are only issued for …

12 Is ATC obliged to give you an SVFR clearance if you request one?

13 A Special VFR clearance is a (right for a pilot/concession from ATC).

14 Air traffic control must be passed certain items of information when requesting a Special VFR clearance; they are …

15 You have obtained an SVFR clearance to enter a control zone. As you proceed, you discover that the cloud base is so low that you have to descend to a lower altitude to remain beneath it. At this altitude you would be unable to land clear of the housing area beneath you if you lost an engine. Would you proceed?

16 You have obtained an SVFR clearance to enter a control zone. As you proceed, you experience a radio failure which you are unable to remedy. Would you proceed to the busy controlled aerodrome, or would you turn around and depart the control zone? What would you do with your transponder?

17 Airways are Class … (controlled/uncontrolled) airspace. Do you need an ATC clearance to operate in an airway?

18 A Basic PPL pilot (may/may not) cross the base of an airway?

19 What are the provisos a Basic PPL holder must meet in order to cross the base of an airway?

Exercises 8

Emergency Procedures

1 State the three priorities you have as pilot-in-command in order of importance.

2 Name two items of aircraft equipment that you can use to make known an emergency situation.

3 What are the two categories of emergency, and what words do you use to precede the two different types of emergency calls?

4 On which frequency would you first make a distress Mayday call or an urgency Pan-Pan call?

5 If there is no response to your emergency call on the ATSU frequency you are currently using, what would you do with your transponder?

6 If you are unable to get through on the frequency supposedly in use, to which frequency would you transfer in order to transmit your distress Mayday call or urgency Pan-Pan call?

7 121·5 MHz is the international aeronautical emergency frequency. It is also known as the g… frequency.

8 Which is the main ATSU north of latitude N55 that is always listening out on 121·5 MHz?

9 Which is the main ATSU south of latitude N55 that is always listening out on 121·5 MHz?

10 If you are in a radar environment, but unable to make radio contact, which transponder code would you squawk to indicate an emergency?

11 Is fire on board a distress situation or an urgency situation? Which words would you start your radio call with to signify this?

12 Is engine failure a distress situation or an urgency situation? Which words would you start your radio call with to signify this?

13 Is the unexpected onset of darkness a distress situation or an urgency situation if you are inexperienced and unqualified for night flight? Which words would you start your radio call with to signify this?

14 Is it a distress situation or an urgency situation if one of your passengers starts experiencing severe stomach pains? Which words would you start your radio call with to signify this?

15 Is it a distress situation or an urgency situation if you, as pilot, start experiencing severe stomach pains making it difficult for you to fly the aeroplane? Which words would you start your radio call with to signify this?

16 Is it a distress situation or an urgency situation if you observe a sinking yacht with the crewmembers possibly experiencing difficulties? Which words would you start your radio call with to signify this?

17 The word *Tyro* during a radio transmission means …

18 You are a student pilot flying alone in G-BATC, a PA-28, 5 miles south of York at 3,000 feet amsl, heading west, in radio contact with Church Fenton on 126·5 MHz, when you suffer an engine failure. You select a forced landing field which requires you to turn onto a southerly heading, and carry out the engine failure drill. On which frequency would you make a radio call, would you change your transponder squawk, and what would your radio call be – word for word?

19 You are a Basic PPL flying in G-BEEV, a Cessna 152, with two passengers on board, 7 miles south-west of Crewe at 2,000 feet amsl, heading south, in radio contact with Shawbury on 120·77 MHz, when you suffer an engine fire. You elect to shut the engine down, and select a forced landing field which requires you to turn onto a easterly heading, and carry out the engine failure drill. On which frequency would you make a radio call, would you change your transponder squawk, and what would your radio call be – word for word?

20 If you are not in direct contact with an ATSU, would you change your transponder squawk prior to transmitting a message? If so, to which squawk?

21 What would you do if the local ATSU, or another aircraft, did not respond to your emergency call?

22 You (will/will not) be tested on the format and content of the Mayday call during your radio test.

23 Make up your own distress scenario(s) for the area in which you usually fly, and then write down your Mayday call word for word.

24 Is it required, or recommended, that you include your pilot qualifications in a Mayday call?

25 Who should you address an emergency call to on frequency 121·5 MHz?

26 You are a Basic PPL flying in G-BEEV, a Cessna 152, with two passengers on board, 7 miles south-west of Crewe at 2000 feet amsl, heading south, in radio contact with Shawbury on 120·77 MHz, when you experience a rough-running engine that sounds as if it could fail. The oil pressure is normal, but the oil temperature is gradually

rising. You elect to keep the engine running, and to turn onto a north-westerly heading and proceed towards Hawarden which is approximately 20 miles away. On which frequency would you make a radio call, would you change your transponder squawk, and what would your radio call be – word for word?

27 If the oil temperature continues to rise, would you keep the ATSU informed of the worsening situation? Would it be good airmanship to keep an eye out for a suitable forced landing field?

28 If the oil temperature continues to rise towards its published limit, and then the oil pressure starts to fluctuate, what are reasonable actions that you might take.

29 The next sequence following the "Mayday Mayday Mayday" prefix (assuming that it is known) is …

30 You are a Basic PPL flying in G-BMED, a Robin, with two passengers on board, overhead Bettyhill on the north coast of Scotland at 5,000 feet and out of contact on the local frequency. One of your passengers suddenly becomes very ill. You elect to divert to Wick, which is 36 miles to the east. On which frequency would you make a radio call, how would you handle your transponder, and what would your radio call be – word for word?

31 You (may/will not) be tested on the format and content of the Pan-Pan call during your radio test.

32 Make up your own urgency scenario(s) for the area in which you usually fly, and then write down your Pan-Pan call word for word.

33 Are you permitted to make a Practice-Pan call for training purposes?

34 While you may practise using frequency 121.1 to obtain, for instance, simulated uncertain of position information, you (may/may not) simutate a distress situation.

35 Are you permitted to make a Practice-Mayday call for training purposes?

36 Make up your own imaginary urgency scenario(s) for the area in which you usually fly, and then write down your Practice-Pan call word for word.

37 If you are uncertain of your position, but in no danger, you could make a … call to ask for assistance. This is a (distress/urgency) call.

38 If you are uncertain of your position, and extremely bad weather is developing, and you feel that a dangerous situation is developing, you should make a … call to ask for assistance. This is a (distress/urgency) call.

39 If you wish to confirm your position for training purposes, you may request a … on frequency … MHz. You (must/need not) give priority to a distress Mayday call. You (must/need not) give priority to an urgency Pan-Pan call. You (must/need not) give priority to a Practice-Pan call.

40 On which frequency and how would you request a Training-Fix in G-BWDS?

41 List the following calls in order of priority: Practice-Pan, Mayday, Training-Fix, Pan-Pan.

42 What is the morse code for SOS in dits and dahs?

43 In an emergency, should you feel comfortable asking Radar for a heading for you to steer to reach the nearest suitable airport?

44 An aircraft makes a distress Mayday call to Coventry, and during busy exchanges on the radio between the ATSU and the aircraft, several aircraft come on the frequency and start to interrupt. What would Coventry say?

45 G-BRED makes a distress Mayday call to Coventry. G-BATC comes on the frequency with the call "Coventry, this is G-BATC". What is Coventry likely to say if emergency calls are interrupted, or likely to be interrupted?

46 Asking other aircraft to stop transmitting is called … radio silence.

47 If you hear another aircraft making an emergency call, you (should/would not) note the details down. Explain.

48 If you hear another aircraft making an emergency call, you (should/would not) self-impose radio silence.

49 If you hear an emergency radio call from another aircraft that is not acknowledged by an ATSU, perhaps because the aircraft is out of radio range of the ATSU, what could you do?

50 When relaying an emergency message from another aircraft, you should say the callsign of the aircraft in distress (once/twice/not at all). You should pass the message (once/twice).

51 If an emergency situation with your aircraft G-BRAT over which you have made a distress Mayday call is resolved, what radio call would you then make?

52 If an ATSU has imposed radio silence over a distress situation that no longer exists on that frequency, perhaps because the situation has been resolved or because the aircraft in distress has transferred to another frequency or has landed, what words would you expect to hear from the ATSU?

53 Is 121·5 normally a busy frequency? What sorts of message or signal are you likely to hear on 121·5?

Exercises 9

Radio Failure Procedures

1 What are the two main steps to take if radio communication is lost?

2 What takes priority – restoring communications or flying the aeroplane?

3 The most common cause of communications failure is (human error/equipment failure).

4 If a radio circuit breaker has popped, you should attempt to reset it (once/twice/unlimited).

5 Radio failure is always a total failure. True/false? Explain.

6 Intervening high terrain (can/will not) cause a loss of VHF radio communications.

7 Flying some distance away from a ground station (can/will not) cause a loss of VHF radio communications.

8 Other aircraft (may/will never) relay messages if you are out of range of the ATSU.

9 ATSU ground equipment (never/sometimes) fails.

10 The transponder squawk for radio failure is … .

11 Explain how you would check your equipment following radio failure.

12 If your radio was totally unserviceable, what actions would you take in flight?

13 With a transmitter failure, you (may/will not) be able to receive voice messages.

14 With a receiver failure, you (may/will not) be able to receive voice messages. You (may/will not) be able to transmit voice messages.

15 With a failure of the modulator, the carrier wave will not be modulated with the voice message. Communication by carrier wave only using the … code may be possible.

16 The speechless code using carrier wave only is achieved by pressing the … button of your microphone (once/twice) to signify "yes", and (once/twice) to signify "no".

17 If you were forced to use the speechless code and are not sure of your position, how could you request a homing heading to an airfield? What name is given to this heading in the Q-code?

18 Following a radio failure in flight, you overfly an ATC airport and receive a continuous red signal from the tower. This means … .

19 This is then followed by a flashing green signal, which means … .

20 This is then followed by a continuous green signal, which means … .

21 A flashing red signal when you are overhead the aerodrome means … .

22 If you are on the ground, a steady red signal from the tower means … .

23 If you are on the ground, a flashing green signal from the tower means … .

24 If you are on the ground, a steady green signal from the tower means … .

25 If you are on the ground, a flashing white signal from the tower means … .

26 If you have experienced radio failure, you (should/must not) transmit blind.

27 When transmitting blind it is usual to say the message (once only/twice).

28 What general action would you take if you have experienced radio failure in VMC and outside controlled airspace?

29 What general action would you take if you have experienced radio failure in VMC while within controlled airspace, or outside but with a clearance to enter? May you proceed to the airport in controlled airspace?

30 What general action would you take if you have experienced radio failure inside controlled airspace when operating on a Special VFR clearance? May you proceed to the airport in controlled airspace?

31 You are taxiing at an ATC airport and your radio fails. Would you continue with the flight?

Exercises 11

Radio Fundamentals

1 The unit of frequency is called the ..., abbreviated as ... .

2 A frequency of 1,000 hertz can also be described as one (kilohertz/megahertz/microhertz).

3 Sketch a typical wave and label it with wavelength and amplitude.

4 In your own words, define wavelength and amplitude.

5 Radio waves travel at the speed of (light/sound).

6 Light waves travel (slower than/the same speed as/faster than) sound waves.

7 Sound waves, such as a voice, are attenuated, i.e. weakened, as they pass through the air. True/false?

8 Radio signals (remain strong/are greatly attenuated) over long distances.

9 A high frequency radio wave will have a (short/long) wavelength.

10 HF radio is also known as ...-... radio.

11 Audio frequencies are much (lower/higher) than radio frequencies that can be satisfactorily transmitted.

12 Audio signals can be s... onto a radio carrier wave.

13 The process of superimposing a voice message onto a radio carrier wave is called m... .

14 Two different means of modulating a radio carrier wave are to change its amplitude, a process known as ..., abbreviated as ..., or to change its frequency, a process known as ..., abbreviated as ... .

15 The process of sending a radio signal out into the atmosphere from an antenna is known as ... .

16 The process of receiving a radio transmission from the atmosphere with an antenna is called r... .

17 The desired radio signal can be received from the atmosphere by selectively tuning the radio receiver to its particular ... .

18 The process of extracting the voice message from the received radio signal is called ... .

19 Unwanted radio signals, such as background hash, are known as n... .

20 If the desired signal on the selected frequency predominates over unwanted signals, then we have a (good/poor) *signal-to-noise* ratio.

21 The preferred frequency band for aeronautical radio communications is (HF/VHF/MF).

22 The range of VHF transmissions (increases/decreases) with gain of height.

23 When obtaining Very High Frequency Direction Finding (VDF) information you understand that bearing information of Class A, B, C and D refer to an approximate accuracy of ... .

Exercises 12

Radio Wave Propagation and Long-Range Communications

1   List the frequency bands used in aviation, and state what each band is used for.

2   The range over which VHF transmissions can be received is known as the (visible/radio) horizon.

3   What is the expected range of VHF reception for an aeroplane flying at 7,000 ft?

4   Draw a diagram showing reflection and refraction of radio waves.

5   Draw a diagram to show the difference between amplitude and frequency modulation.

6   List five fundamental components of a radio transmitter, and briefly explain their function.

7   If two radio waves arrive simultaneously at a receiver, and are in phase, the resultant signal will be (stronger/weaker) than when they are received out of phase.

8   The layer in the atmosphere which refracts radio waves back to the surface of the earth is called the (troposphere/ionosphere/mesosphere).

9   The radio waves which are refracted back to the earth's surface by a layer in the atmosphere are in the (VHF/HF/UHF) band.

10 When using HF for voice communications at night, the (lower/higher) the frequency, the greater the transmission range.

11 Draw a diagram and show skip distance and skip zone.

12 As a general rule, when using HF communications, the closer you are to a station, the (lower/higher) frequency you should use.

Answers

Answers 1

Cockpit Radios

1 VHF
2 master switch, avionics master switch, has
3 transceiver
4 alternator
5 OFF
6 flatten the battery
7 reception
8 118 and 137 MHz
9 131·525 MHz, 0·025 MHz,
10 121·0;   121·00 or 121·000;
    121·025; 121·02 or 121·025;
    121·05;   121·05 or 121·050;
    121·075; 121·07 or 121·075;
    121·1;   121·10 or 121·100;
    121·125; 121·02 or 121·125;
    121·15;   121·15 or 121·150;
    121·175; 121·17 or 121·175;
    121·2;   121·20 or 121·200;
    121·225; 121·22 or 121·225;
    121·25;   121·25 or 121·250;
    121·275; 121·27 or 121·275;
    121·3;   121·30 or 121·300;
    121·325; 121·32 or 121·325;
    121·35;   121·35 or 121·350;
    121·375; 121·37 or 121·375;
    121·4;   121·40 or 121·400;
    121·425; 121·42 or 121·425; etc. etc. to
    122·0.
11 40
12 720 (40 × 18)
13 AD and ENR, Aeronautical Information
    Publication
14 squelch
15 receiver
16 no
17 yes, yes
18 stuck mike, open mike
19 slower
20 should
21 check the frequency

22 revert to the previous frequency, identify
    yourself and ask, *"Say frequency again."*
23 electrical master switch, avionics switch,
    VHF-COM ON/OFF switch, CB, fuse,
    headset, microphone, must
24 VHF-NAV
25 non-directional beacon, ADF
26 transponder, secondary surveillance radar
27 position, A, Mode Alpha
28 position and altitude, C, Mode Charlie
29 5413, ON or ALT
30 confirm the altitude or flight level as dis-
    played on the air traffic controller's radar
    screen
31 4096, each of the four digits has 8 possibili-
    ties (i.e. from 0 to 7) and 8 × 8 × 8 × 8 =
    4096
32 press the transponder ident button
33 7000
34 7600
35 7700

Answers 2

What to Say

1 (see page 19)
2 your message is understood and will be
   complied with
3 my transmission is ended and I expect a
   response from you
4 this exchange of transmission is ended and
   no response is expected
5 five nine (pronounced *fife nin-er*)
6 eight thousand five hundred (pronounced
   ait tousand fife hun-dred)
7 two thousand four hundred feet
   (pronounced *too tousand fow-er hun-dred*)
8 affirm
9 negative
10 *Golf Al-fah Brah-voh Char-lee Dell-tah*
11 *Cessna Golf Pah-pah Row-me-oh Key-loh In-
   dee-ah; Cessna Golf Key-loh In-dee-ah*

12 when they have first been abbreviated by the station addressed

13 *Warrior Golf Keh-beck Oss-cah See-air-ah Wiss-key; Warrior Golf See-air-ah Wiss-key* or *Golf See-air-ah Wiss-key*

14 *Cessna No-vem-ber fow-er tree sev-en six Hoh-tell You-nee-form*

15 Monde Air Mike Papa

16 coordinated universal time, UTC, Zulu, Z

17 *Runway tree six*

18 *wun ze-ro wun tree*

19 *nin-er nin-er six millibars* (say "millibars" when pressure is below 1000)

20 *Runway ze-ro ait*

21 *wun wun ait day-see-mal sev-en too* (no need to mention the 5)

22 *tree OKTAs*

23 *tree too ze-ro degrees, too fife knots*

24 *ze-ro ait tree fife*

25 *fife ait*

26 *wun sev-en tree fife*

27 *wun fife ze-ro ze-ro*

28 on the hour, or *wun fife ze-ro ze-ro*

29 *wun tousand fife hun-dred*

30 *Mode Al-fah*

31 *Mode Char-lee*

32 remain silent and wait until called

33 transmission

34 ready for departure

35 yes, no

38 cleared for take-off

36 unable to comply

37 true bearing ("G-ABCD request true bearing")

39 specifically cleared by ATC to take off

40 cleared to land

41 *readability tree*

42 perfectly readable

43 *readability fife*

44 twelve o'clock high

45 (refer to table on page 207)

Answers 3

Aerodrome Operations

1 (check your aerodrome)

2 require

3 require

4 do not require

5 do not require

6 is

7 is

8 (check your aerodrome)

9 (check your aerodrome)

10 1 – unreadable
2 – readable now and then
3 – readable with difficulty
4 – readable
5 – perfectly readable

12 (check your aerodrome)

13 (check with your instructor)

14 "G-ABCD" or "landing G-ABCD"

15 "Ready for departure"

16 acknowledging a take-off clearance

17 (check with your instructor)

18 is not

19 Flight Information Service, information only, is not

20 you as pilot-in-command

21 radio

22 no

23 no

24 you are established on the final approach path at a range of between 8 and 4 nautical miles

25 (see Figure 3-17, page 47)

26 (refer to your flight instructor)

27 (see Figure 3-22, page 51)

28 15 nm or 5 minutes, whichever is the sooner

29 yes, with the ATSU or other authority at the aerodrome of departure

Answers 4

Aerodrome Information

1 should
2 should, Air Traffic Service Unit
3 automatic terminal information service, ATIS, *ay-tiss*
4 less than 30 seconds
5 the VHF-COM and/or the VHF-NAV
6 in AIP AD and other publications such as *Pooley's Flight Guide*
7 is
8 Information Alpha, Information Bravo
9 every 30 minutes at 20 minutes past the hour and 50 minutes past the hour; every 30 minutes
10 VHF-COM
11 yes
12 yes
13 VHF-NAV; 114·3 MHz since this is a VOR frequency which can be selected on the VHF-NAV, leaving the VHF-COM selected to the ATSU frequency for normal voice communications
14 yes
15 Information (and phonetic designator)
16 (see Chapter 4)
17 a number of
18 longer than; VOLMET is for a number of aerodromes whereas an ATIS is for just one
19 VOLMET, since you would not be able to pick up the correct ATIS so far from the destination aerodrome, and also it is the VOLMET which contains the weather for a *group* of aerodromes; wait for another 10 minutes until the 1220Z routine weather observation has been recorded on the VOLMET tape
20 aerodrome elevation
21 zero
22 998 mb
23 1015 mb
24 B
25 07
26 no, for CAVOK the cloud base must not be below 5,000 feet aal
27 no, for CAVOK there must be no cumulonimbus clouds

28 no, for CAVOK the visibility must be 10 km or more
29 no, for CAVOK the visibility must be 10 km or more (even if the other requirements for CAVOK are met)
30 no; CAVOK requires no precipitation at ground level
31 (see page 66)
32 aerodrome level

Answers 5

Airspace Classification

1 G
2 E, D
3 F, G
4 air to ground, Air Traffic Control (ATC) and Flight Information Service (FIS)
5 F, uncontrolled, do not need
6 Open, uncontrolled, no
7 D
8 no
9 no, you need a *take-off* clearance from ATC before you may take off
10 no, no
11 yes, no
12 yes
13 yes, yes
14 non-radar
15 (1) distress messages, (2) urgency messages, (3) direction finding, (4) flight safety messages, (5) meteorological messages, (6) flight regularity messages
16 Callsign
    Position and Time over that position
    Level
    Next position and estimate for it

Answers 6

R/T in Uncontrolled Airspace

1 uncontrolled, Open FIR
2 an advisory service, a flight information service, an alerting service, a distress and diversion service
3 a Flight Information Region (FIR)
4 aircraft callsign and the service requested, e.g. "Essex Radar, this G-ABCD, request flight information service"

5   Lower Airspace radar service, is
6   Radar Advisory Service, will
7   no
8   callsign, type of aircraft, position, heading, altitude/flight level, intentions
9   Radar Information Service, will not
10 callsign, aircraft type, point of departure, position, heading, level, intention, flight rules, type of service requested
11 you
12 VHF direction-finding, VHF-COM
13 magnetic heading to be steered by the aircraft to reach the VDF station (assuming no wind)
14 magnetic bearing of the aircraft from the VDF station (assuming no wind)
15 true bearing of the aircraft from the station (assuming no wind)
16 homer
17 QDM
18 145°
19 Danger Area Crossing Service, "dacks"
20 Danger Area Activity Information Service, "day-iss"

Answers 7

R/T in Controlled Airspace

1   control zone
2   control area
3   airway
4   10 nm, 5 nm
5   callsign, position, time, level, next position, ETA
6   yes
7   yes
8   no
9   yes, Special VFR clearance
10 yes, Special VFR clearance
11 flights in Control Zones
12 no
13 concession from ATC
14 callsign, type, intentions and ETA at entry position
15 no
16 turn around and depart the control zone, squawk 7600
17 A, controlled, yes

18 may – but with some provisos
19 the lower limit of the airway must be defined as a flight level, i.e. on standard pressure 1013 mb, and not as an altitude on regional QNH; you must cross at the lower level of the airway at 90 degrees to the airway

Answers 8

Emergency Procedures

1   aviate, navigate, communicate
2   radio, transponder
3   distress; Mayday, Mayday, Mayday urgency: Pan-Pan, Pan-Pan, Pan-Pan
4   the frequency in use
5   squawk 7700
6   121·5 MHz
7   guard
8   Scottish Centre
9   London Centre
10 7700
11 distress; Mayday, Mayday, Mayday
12 distress; Mayday, Mayday, Mayday
13 distress; Mayday, Mayday, Mayday
14 urgency; Pan-Pan, Pan-Pan, Pan-Pan
15 distress; Mayday, Mayday, Mayday
16 urgency; Pan-Pan, Pan-Pan, Pan-Pan
17 I am an inexperienced pilot
18 On the frequency in use 126·5 MHz; not unless requested;
    Mayday, Mayday, Mayday
    Church Fenton
    Golf Bravo Alpha Tango Charlie
    PA-28
    Engine Failure
    Carrying out a forced landing
    Position 5 miles south of York
    Descending through 2,500 feet
    Heading 180
    Student PPL (or TYRO)
    One POB
19 On the frequency in use 120·77 MHz; not unless requested;
    Mayday, Mayday, Mayday
    Shawbury
    Golf Bravo Echo Echo Victor
    Cessna 152
    Engine Fire

Carrying out a forced landing
Position 7 miles south-west of Crewe
Descending through 1,500 feet
Heading east
Basic PPL
Three POB

20 yes, 7700

21 squawk 7700, then transfer to 121·5 and repeat the call

22 will

23 Check all details are included, and in the right order (see page 117)

24 recommended

25 Scottish Centre if you are north of latitude N55; London Centre if you are south of latitude N55

26 On the frequency in use 120·77 MHz; not unless requested;
Pan-Pan, Pan-Pan, Pan-Pan
Shawbury
Golf Bravo Echo Echo Victor
Cessna 152
Rough-running engine
Proceeding to Hawarden
Position 7 miles south-west of Crewe
Maintaining 2,000 feet
Heading north-west
Basic PPL
Three POB

27 yes, yes

28 make a precautionary shutdown of the engine, declare an emergency with a May-day call and squawk 7700 as appropriate, and make a forced landing (preferably on an airfield, otherwise in a suitable field)

29 the callsign of the station addressed

30 On the emergency frequency 121·5 MHz; squawk 7700
Pan-Pan, Pan-Pan, Pan-Pan
Scottish Centre
Golf Bravo Mike Echo Delta
Robin
Sick passenger
Proceeding to Wick
Position overhead Bettyhill
Maintaining 5,000 feet
Heading east
Basic PPL
Three POB

31 may

32 Check all details are included, and in the right order (see page 120)

33 yes

34 may not!

35 no

36 Check all details are included, and in the right order (see pages 120 and 122)

37 Pan-Pan; urgency

38 Mayday; distress

39 Training-Fix; 121·5 MHZ; must; must; need not

40 121·5; Training-Fix, Training-Fix, Training-Fix, G-BWDS

41 Mayday, Pan-Pan, Training-Fix, Practice-Pan

42 dit-dit-dit dah-dah-dah dit-dit-dit

43 yes

44 All stations, stop transmitting, Mayday

45 G-BATC, stop transmitting, Mayday

46 imposing

47 should, the message might not be repeated and you may have to relay it

48 should

49 relay the emergency message to the ATSU

50 twice, once

51 G-BRAT, cancel Mayday

52 Mayday traffic ended

53 no; distress Mayday calls, urgency Pan-Pan calls, Training-Fix calls, Practice-Pan calls, Emergency Locator Transmitter signals, ATC trying to contact an out-of-contact aircraft

Answers 9

Radio Failure Procedures

1 try to restore communications; if not successful, follow standard radio failure procedures

2 flying the aeroplane

3 human error

4 once

5 false, sometimes only the transmitter or only the receiver fails

6 can

7 can

8 may

9 sometimes
10 7600
11 (see page 132)
12 (see page 133)
13 may
14 will not, may
15 speechless
16 PTT *(press-to-transmit)* button or *transmit* button, once, twice
17 give the transmit button four short presses, QDM
18 give way to other aircraft and continue circling
19 return to this aerodrome for a landing
20 authorised to land if you are satisfied no collision risk exists
21 aerodrome unsafe, do not land, i.e. go somewhere else
22 stop
23 authorised to taxi if you are satisfied no collision risk exists
24 authorised to take off if you are satisfied no collision risk exists
25 return to starting point on aerodrome
26 should
27 twice
28 squawk 7600, stay in VMC, stay outside controlled airspace, transmit blind, and land at the nearest suitable airport
29 squawk 7600, stay in VMC, transmit blind, and land at the nearest suitable airport; yes
30 squawk 7600, proceed outside controlled airspace (if you consider it safe to do so), stay in VMC, transmit blind, and land at the nearest suitable airport; no
31 no

Answers 11

Radio Fundamentals

1 hertz, Hz
2 kilohertz
3 (see Figure 11-4, page 159)
4 (see page 159)
5 light
6 faster than
7 true

8 remain strong
9 short
10 short-wave
11 lower
12 superimposed
13 modulation
14 amplitude modulation, AM; frequency modulation, FM
15 transmission
16 reception
17 frequency
18 demodulation
19 noise
20 good
21 VHF
22 increases
23 Class A = accurate to within ± 2°
   Class B = accurate to within ± 5°
   Class C = accurate to within ± 10°
   Class D = accuracy less than Class C

Answers 12

Radio Wave Propagation and Long-Range Communications

1 • low frequency (LF) and medium frequency (MF) – non-directional beacons (NDB);
   • high frequency (HF) – long-range voice communications;
   • very high frequency (VHF) – normal, everyday voice communications, VOR and ILS localizer directional signals (radio navigation aids);
   • ultra high frequency (UHF) – military voice communications, ILS glideslope, secondary surveillance radar (SSR);
   • very low frequency (VLF) – global navigation systems such as Omega
2 radio horizon
3 *Working:*

   VHF range in nm $= \sqrt{(1.5 \times 7,000)}$

   $ = \sqrt{10,000}$

   $ = 102 \text{ nm}$
4 (see page 170)
5 (see Figure 12-5, page 172)

6 • a power supply to provide direct current;
 • an oscillator to generate a radio frequency
 (carrier wave) and a device for controlling
 the frequency of the generated signal;
 • an amplifier to increase the output of the
 oscillator;
 • a modulator to add the audio signals
 (from the microphone) to the carrier wave;
 • an antenna to transmit the signals

7 stronger

8 ionosphere

9 HF (high frequency) band

10 lower

11 (see page 180)

12 lower

Radiotelephony
Abbreviations

Aviation has a jargon of its own, and many common terms are simply convenient abbreviations. It is a lot easier to say *"vee oh ar"* than "very high frequency omnidirectional radio range". The following list contains common abbreviations, with the more important ones for beginning pilots highlighted by shading.

When terms are either pronounced as words rather than abbreviations (*"ar-nav"* for RNAV), or spoken in full (*"kilometre"* for km), the pronunciation is printed in **bold**. You should gradually learn the shaded items.

ABBREVIATION	PRONUNCIATION	TERM
aal	ay ay ell	above aerodrome level
a/c	aircraft	aircraft
ACAS	**ay-kass**	airborne collision-avoidance system
ACC	ay see see	Area Control Centre
ADF	ay dee eff	automatic direction-finding equipment
ADR	ay dee ar	Advisory Route
ADT	ay dee tee	approved departure time
AFIS	**ay-fiss**	Aerodrome Flight Information Service – term now replaced by **FIS**
AFISO	**ay-fy-zoh**	Aerodrome Flight Information Service Officer – term now replaced by **FISO**
AFTN	ay eff tee enn	Aeronautical Fixed Telecommunication Network
A/G	ay gee	Air/Ground radio
agl	ay gee ell	above ground level
AIC	ay eye see	Aeronautical Information Circular
AIP	ay eye pee	Aeronautical Information Publication
AIS	ay eye ess	Aeronautical Information Services
amsl	ay emm ess ell	above mean sea level
ANO	ay enn oh	Air Navigation Order
ATA	ay tee ay	actual time of arrival
ATC	ay tee see	Air Traffic Control
ATD	ay tee dee	actual time of departure
ATIS	**ay-tiss**	automatic terminal information service

ABBREVIATION	PRONUNCIATION	TERM
ATS	ay tee ess	Air Traffic Service
ATSU	ay tee ess you	Air Traffic Services Unit
ATPL	ay tee pee ell	airline transport pilot licence
ATZ	ay tee zed	Aerodrome Traffic Zone
CAA	see ay ay	Civil Aviation Authority
CAVOK	**kav-okay**	Visibility, cloud and present weather better than prescribed values or conditions
CB	see bee; or Charlie Bravo	cumulonimbus cloud
CPL	see pee ell	commercial pilot licence
c/s	callsign	callsign
CTA	see tee ay	Control Area
CTR	see tee ar	Control Zone
CW	**carrier wave**	carrier wave
D&D	dee and dee	Distress and Diversion
DAAIS	**day-ess**	Danger Area Activity Information Service
DACS	**dacks**	Danger Area Crossing Service
DF	dee eff	direction finding
DME	dee emm ee	distance measuring equipment
EAT	ee ay tee	expected approach time
ETA	ee tee ay	estimated time of arrival
ETD	ee tee dee	estimated time of departure
FIR	eff eye ar	Flight Information Region
FIS	eff eye ess	Flight Information Service
FISO	**fy-zoh**	Flight Information Service Officer
FL	**flight level**	flight level
ft	**feet**	feet
GAT	gee ay tee	general air traffic
GMC	gee emm see	Ground Movement Control
GMT (now UTC)	gee emm tee	Greenwich Mean Time
GPS	gee pee ess	global positioning system
H24	aitch **too fow**-er	continuous day and night service
HF	aitch eff	high frequency
HJ	aitch jay	sunrise to sunset
HN	aitch enn	sunset to sunrise
hPa	**hecto-pascals**	hectoPascals (equivalent to millibars)

ABBREVIATION	PRONUNCIATION	TERM
I/C	*intercom*	intercom
ICAO	*eye-kay-oh*	International Civil Aviation Organization
IFR	*eye eff ar*	Instrument Flight Rules
ILS	*eye ell ess*	instrument landing system
IMC	*eye emm see or India Mike Charlie*	Instrument Meteorological Conditions
in	*inches*	inches of mercury (unit of pressure)
kHz	*kilo-hertz*	unit of frequency
km	*kilo-metre*	unit of distance
kt	*nots*	knots
LARS	*lars*	Lower Airspace Radar Service
LF	*ell eff*	low frequency
MATZ	*matz*	Military Air Traffic Zone
mb	*millibars*	unit of pressure, equivalent to hectopascals
MET	*met*	meteorology or meteorological
METAR	*met-ar*	routine aviation aerodrome weather report
MF	*emm eff*	medium frequency
MHz	*mega-hertz*	unit of frequency
NATS	*nats*	National Air Traffic Services
NDB	*enn dee bee*	non-directional beacon
nm	*nautical mile(s)*	unit of distance
NOTAM	*no-tam*	notice(s) to airmen
OAC	*oh ay see*	Oceanic Area Control Unit
OCA	*oh see ay*	Oceanic Control Area
PAPIS	*pah-pee*	precision approach path indicating system
PIC	*pee eye see*	pilot-in-command
POB	*pee oh bee*	persons on board
PPL	*pee pee ell*	private pilot licence
QDM	*kew dee emm*	magnetic heading from aircraft to ground station (zero wind) (Sometimes used to indicate magnetic heading of a runway)
QDR	*kew dee ar*	magnetic bearing from a ground station to an aircraft

ABBREVIATION	PRONUNCIATION	TERM
QFE	kew eff ee	observed pressure at a specified datum (usually aerodrome or runway threshold elevation) corrected for temperature
QGH	kew gee aitch	ground interpreted let-down procedure using direction-finding equipment
QNH	kew enn aitch	altimeter subscale setting to obtain elevation when on the ground and indications of altitude when airborne
QTE	kew tee ee	true bearing
RAS	radar advisory	Radar Advisory Service
RIS	radar information	Radar Information Service
RNAV	ar-nav	area navigation
R/T or RTF	ar tee or ar tee eff	radiotelephone/radiotelephony
RVR	ar vee ar	runway visual range
Rx	receive	receive
SAR	ess ay ar	search and rescue
SID	sid	standard instrument departure
SIGMET	sig-met	significant information concerning en route weather phenomena which may affect the safety of aircraft operations
SRA	ess ar ay	surveillance radar approach
SSR	ess ess ar	secondary surveillance radar
STAR	star	standard instrument arrival route
TACAN	tak-an	tactical air navigation – UHF navaid giving bearing/distance of aircraft from ground station
TAF	taff	terminal area forecast
TCAS	tee-kass	traffic alert and collision avoidance system
TMA	tee emm ay	Terminal Control Area (terminal manoeuvring area)
Tx	transmit	Transmit
UHF	you aitch eff	ultra high frequency (military only)
UIR	you eye ar	Upper Flight Information Region
UTC	you tee see	coordinated universal time
VASI(S)	vah-zi	visual approach slope indicator system
VDF	vee dee eff	very high frequency direction-finding station
VFR	vee eff ar	Visual Flight Rules

ABBREVIATION	PRONUNCIATION	TERM
VHF	*vee aitch eff*	*very high frequency*
VHF-COM	*vee aitch eff com*	*VHF communications radio*
VHF-NAV	*vee aitch eff nav*	*VHF navigation radio for VOR and ILS*
VIP	*vee eye pee*	*very important person*
VLF	*vee ell eff*	*very low frequency, e.g. Omega*
VMC	*vee emm see or Victor Mike Charlie*	*Visual Meteorological Conditions*
VOLMET	**voll-met**	*meteorological information for aircraft in flight*
VOR	*vee oh ar*	*very high frequency omni-directional radio range*
VORTAC	**vor-tack**	*VOR and TACAN combination*
WAC	**wack**	*World Aeronautical Chart (a series)*
Z	**zoo-loo**	*same as UTC*

Index